EXES

EXES

Dan Greenburg

A Marc Jaffe Book

HOUGHTON MIFFLIN COMPANY · BOSTON

1990

This novel is a work of fiction. Names, characters, places,
and incidents either are the product of the author's
imagination or are used fictitiously, and any resemblance
to actual persons living or dead, events, or locales
is entirely coincidental.

For information about permission to reproduce selections from
this book, write to Permissions, Houghton Mifflin Company,
2 Park Street, Boston, Massachusetts 02108.

Library of Congress Cataloging-in-Publication Data
Greenburg, Dan.
Exes / Dan Greenburg.
p.   cm.
"A Marc Jaffe book."
ISBN 0-395-51423-1
I. Title.
PS3557.R379E9   1990   89-20041
813'.54—dc20   CIP

Printed in the United States of America

M 10 9 8 7 6 5 4 3 2 1

For
Mildred, Bernie,
Stan, Gerri,
Carole, Kathleen,
Bob, and Joe

For technical assistance I'm indebted to:

Lieutenant John J. Doyle, Commanding Officer, Manhattan North
    Homicide Squad, NYPD
Detective John L. Hartigan, Manhattan North Homicide Squad, NYPD
Detective Scott E. Jaffer, Manhattan North Homicide Squad, NYPD
Detective Gerard F. O'Rourke, Crime Scene Unit, NYPD
Captain Edward Mamet, former Commanding Officer, Manhattan Sex
    Crimes Squad, NYPD

Roger L. Depue, Unit Chief of the National Center for the Analysis of
    Violent Crime, Behavioral Science Instruction/Research Unit, FBI
Ronald P. Walker, Special Agent, Behavioral Science Instruction Unit,
    FBI
William E. Trible, Special Agent, Office of Congressional and Public
    Affairs, FBI

Dr. Lawrence Kobilinsky, Associate Professor of Biology and
    Immunology, John Jay College of Criminal Justice, City University
    of New York
Dr. Michael M. Baden, Director of Forensic Sciences, New York State
    Police; former Chief Medical Examiner, City of N.Y.
Candice A. Skrapec, criminological psychologist, John Jay College of
    Criminal Justice, City University of New York

Stephen G. Michaud, co-author, *The Only Living Witness*
Alan B. Osofsky, member, New York Futures Exchange
Howard Z. Rosenman, Sandollar Productions

EXES

1

"Maggots are my friends," said Dr. Chernin, the medical examiner, gazing amiably at the naked corpse on the bed.

The short, pudgy body was alive with maggots. A large "ninety-five" i.d. tag was tied to its ankle and made out to the morgue. The deceased was Irving Smiley, thirty-three, an executive at Manhattan Cable TV. Someone had severed the carotid artery in Smiley's neck, then bashed his face in.

Three days in the warm room had caused the body to emit the characteristically strong rotten-egg smell of hydrogen sulfide. Between the maggots and the smell, the less experienced men in the room were teetering between total macho laid-back coolness and the unthinkable faux pas of either retching or fainting. The more experienced men in the room relished the others' discomfort.

"Do you know why maggots are my friends?" Chernin asked the two young plainclothes detectives from the Seventeenth Precinct Detective Unit (PDU).

"No, sir," said O'Rourke aloud, but under his breath, just loud enough for his partner, Moreno, to hear, he muttered, "Because you're a fucking *ghoul,* sir."

Moreno compressed his lips and suppressed the laugh. Both O'Rourke and Moreno had short, powerful builds and somewhat stylish sportcoats. O'Rourke had reddish blond hair, Moreno's was black. Both were twenty-eight, looked twenty-one, and wore full moustaches, hoping this would make them look older. It didn't.

"Flies lay eggs on the mucous membranes of dead bodies," said Chernin. "Eyes, mouth, nostrils, and, of course, wounds. In twenty-four hours the eggs become motile larvae. In seven days they're three

quarters of an inch in length. In their pupa stage they turn from white
to brown to black so predictably you can use it as a timing device.
On the twenty-first day they emerge from their pupa cases as mature
flies and the cycle is complete. If you find the body anytime during
that twenty-one day cycle the maggots will tell you exactly how long
it's been dead. These maggots tell me Mr. Smiley has been dead for
three days."

"How *about* that," said Moreno. He was not unimpressed with the
information, he was just camping for his partner. He also didn't want
to hear about maggots, which sickened him even more than the smell
that pervaded the apartment.

"During the Civil War," said Chernin, warming to Moreno, misread-
ing his sly disrespect as a thirst for forensic knowledge, "they used
maggots to treat soldiers with infected wounds. Did you know that?"

"No, sir, I sure didn't," said Moreno.

"Antibiotics hadn't been invented yet, of course," said Chernin, "so
doctors put maggots on the infections, which is really not a bad idea,
even now — maggots eat only dead tissues. They're programmed to
increase their body weight a thousandfold in only a few days, so they
eat fast. And, unlike surgeons, maggots know exactly where to stop."

"And unlike *you,* sir," said O'Rourke sotto voce.

Moreno squelched a guffaw, in the process emitting a sound that he
had to mask with a fit of coughing. Chernin always told you a little
more about things than you wanted to know. Moreno figured this was
due to the fact that most of the people the M.E. hung out with were
poor conversationalists, on account of being dead.

Chernin had a salt-and-pepper crewcut, a gray military moustache,
and tinted Porsche aviator glasses. He was six feet tall, and although
he was fifty-six he had a lean build and a flat belly from thrice-weekly
workouts at the Vertical Club. Despite Smiley's state of decomposi-
tion, Chernin was able to note with some satisfaction that the much
younger man hadn't been in nearly as good shape as was the M.E.
himself.

The two plainclothes cops from CSU, the Crime Scene Unit, had
arrived at five P.M., about the same time as Chernin, and were busy
in the bedroom of the small, upscale East Fifty-ninth Street apartment.
One of them had already shot stills of the body from all angles with a
Nikon and a strobe and was now dusting for latent prints. The other
was taking measurements with a retractable steel tape of the body's

distance to adjoining walls and nearby pieces of furniture, noting them on a sketch he'd made of the crime scene. The closest of the walls was spattered with dried blood. The bed was encrusted with it.

"What is this," asked the CSU man with the Nikon, "a revenge thing?"

"Looks that way to me," said O'Rourke. "Smiley coulda been humping some guy's old lady."

"Right, it *coulda* been revenge," said the uniformed patrolman who'd been first officer on the scene, now trying to participate in the senior men's speculation. They cut him with an icy stare for presuming to join their conversation and he clammed right up, his cheeks and forehead flushing.

The door opened and two homicide detectives in sportcoats and ties swaggered into the apartment. Their attitude said, O.K., you can relax now, the pros are here. Homicide detectives were at the top of the status ladder in the NYPD, and as such were often envied and resented by their inferiors. Everybody at the crime scene exchanged guarded greetings.

The two gold shields were Segal and Caruso from Manhattan North Homicide. The uptown task force was based in Harlem and dispatched seasoned homicide detectives to assist PDUs on all murders as far south as Fifty-ninth Street.

Max Segal was thirty-two, blond, slim, and Jewish. Only a set of somewhat crooked teeth stood between him and serious handsomeness. Salvatore Caruso was forty-six, dark, heavy-set, and Italian. He had a thick neck, a pock-marked but pleasantly rugged face, a heavy frame, and a massive beer belly that would have been appropriate in the third trimester of pregnancy.

Max and Caruso glanced at the body on the unmade queen-sized bed.

"Jesus Christ," said Max softly. He had never gotten used to decomposed bodies and was secure enough by now to express his revulsion.

"As you can see from the mere trickle of blood from the facial area," stated the M.E., "the mutilation of the face occurred after the heart stopped — postmortem wounds, as you know, don't bleed."

"The neck wound looks like a surprise attack," said Max. "The attacker was probably someone the victim knew and trusted. Smiley was naked when he died, right?"

3

"Right," said Chernin.

"So probably it was his girlfriend," said O'Rourke.

"More likely his *boy*friend," said Max.

Everyone turned to look at him.

"Stab wounds to the neck," said Max. "Very common in gay homicides. Also, facial mutilation."

"Right," said Caruso. "You find a nude male D.O.A., it's a pretty good shot it's a fag homicide. This isn't no female's m.o."

The CSU man who'd been dusting for prints with the white powder unique to the NYPD now pressed cellophane tape to the ones he liked, lifted them, and transferred them to dark-colored backing paper. The other CSU man pulled on thin, off-white surgical gloves and rolled the body over on its side, looking for further wounds.

"That's all you're going to find," said Chernin. "The incision to the lateral aspect of the neck is the cause of death."

"Projectile bleeding," said the CSU man with the surgical gloves, glancing at the dumbbell splatter pattern on the wall, so named for the shape of the droplets.

The M.E. nodded.

"The killer severs Smiley's carotid," said Chernin. "Smiley's heart is pushing out two ounces of blood with every pulsebeat. Smiley is hysterical. He grabs the end of the sheet here and presses it to his neck to stop exsanguinating. It doesn't work. He grows weak, he sinks back down on the bed, he goes to sleep. The killer watches him die. When Smiley's dead, the killer decides killing him isn't enough and goes to work on his face."

Chernin turned toward the senior detectives for corroboration.

"Sounds good to me, Doc," said Max.

"*Christ,* it stinks in here!" said Caruso, finally opting to mention it. "Didn't anybody open the windows?"

"I already opened the windows and sprinkled ammonia," said the uniform, hoping to redeem himself, but nobody acknowledged him.

"Anybody check the traps in the sink and the tub?" asked Max.

"Not yet," said O'Rourke. "You want me to do it?"

"I'll do it," said Max.

"*I'll* do it," said O'Rourke, "it's my case."

O'Rourke took a clear plastic evidence bag from the CSU kit and went into the bathroom to remove the traps from the drains and collect any hairs or other material that might give them a lead on the killer.

4

"You want me to bag his hands, Doc?" said the CSU man with the surgical gloves.

"Sure, why not?" said Chernin.

The CSU man took two small brown paper bags out of his kit and fitted one over each of Smiley's hands. The bags would preserve whatever hairs, fibers, blood, or skin the victim might have lodged under his fingernails from clawing at the killer before he died—the procedure was routine for rape-murders of females, though not for males. Paper bags were better than plastic ones, which tended to putrefy blood, semen, or mucus. Brown paper bags in which liquor stores wrapped wine bottles were the best of all.

Three uniforms were out in the hall trying to control the growing knot of curious tenants and to keep out anybody whose presence at the crime scene wasn't vital so as to protect it from contamination—destruction of evidence. A young female assistant district attorney named Rona Marshad, reporters from the *Post,* the *News,* and *New York* magazine, three freelance photographers, a camera crew from Channel 5, and eight more detectives arrived at the apartment. The reporters, photographers, and camera crews were forced to wait outside, which made them grumpy.

Two of the newly arrived detectives were from the Seventeenth PDU, six from Manhattan North Homicide. They'd come to help canvass the neighborhood for witnesses. There was an axiom among detectives that if you couldn't solve a homicide in seventy-two hours you'd probably *never* solve it. After seventy-two hours witnesses forgot what they'd seen and began making it up. Since the M.E. estimated this homicide had taken place three days earlier, some haste was clearly in order here.

They broke up into two-man teams. Starting with the tenants outside in the hall and proceeding through the building from top to bottom, the detectives tried to find anyone who'd heard or seen anything worth noting on the night of the murder or anyone who was familiar with the deceased.

Max and Caruso interviewed the doorman downstairs in the lobby, a stocky Irishman about sixty years old, named Grogan.

"Mr. Grogan," said Caruso, taking out a little spiral-bound steno notebook and a Bic ballpoint pen, "I understand you were working the four-to-midnight shift Friday night when Mr. Smiley was killed. That correct?"

Grogan nodded.

Caruso, with the frowning concentration of one who wrote things with difficulty, gripped the Bic tightly as if it might try to get away from him and wrote "Grgn. on dty. 1600–2400 hrs."

"And did you see the deceased on the night in question?"

Grogan nodded again.

"About seven or eight o'clock," said Grogan. "On his way out. And then a few hours later, coming back. I think—"

"Just a minute," said Caruso, writing slowly and painfully in his spiral-bound notebook: "Dcsd. lft. bldg. 1900–2000 hrs., ret. fw. hrs. ltr."

"Was Mr. Smiley alone on the two occasions you saw him," asked Max, "or was he with somebody?"

"Alone the first time. And when he come back . . . when he come back he was with somebody, I think. I'm not sure, though."

"Aln. 1st tme., wth. smbdy. 2nd tme.," wrote Caruso.

"Why can't you be sure?" said Max.

The doorman gave him a patronizing smile.

"Hey, gimme a break, wouldja, sarge? How many tenants you think I got here? How many entrances and exits you think I get on a eight-hour shift, huh? On *three* eight-hour shifts?"

"Was the individual you think he was with on the return a male or a female?" asked Max.

Grogan thought about this.

"I honestly couldn' say, pal. Being as how it was a Friday night, it was probably a female."

"Thnks. prbly. a fmle.," wrote Caruso.

"I could be wrong, though," said Grogan. "It coulda been a male."

"What kind of a guy was this Smiley?" asked Max.

"Whattaya mean?"

"I mean," said Max, "was he a good guy? Was he a good tipper? Was he polite when he saw you or did he have an attitude? You know, stuff like that."

Grogan pursed his lips and peered at the ceiling, as if the answers to Max's questions might be up there on crib sheets.

"He was O.K. Not a great tipper, but O.K."

"Was he straight or a fag?" said Caruso.

6

Max glared at Caruso for being so direct, and Caruso raised his eyebrows, pleading ingenuousness.

"I dunno," said Grogan. "He was short is all I know."

"So?" said Max.

"So I dunno nothin' about was he straight or a fag. I'm the guy's *doorman,* not his fuckin' priest."

"But Mr. Grogan," said Caruso, using the "mister" partly as a shuck and partly as a deference meant to elicit added cooperation, "you see people go in and outta this building all the time. Do you ever recall his being in the company of individuals who you would describe as . . ." He looked briefly at his partner. "Screamers?"

Max winced.

"Yeah, sometimes," said Grogan.

Max and Caruso exchanged significant glances.

"But that don't necessarily mean nothing," said Grogan. "Being as how the guy was in show business, I mean."

Max and Caruso knocked on three dozen doors. Of the tenants who were home most didn't even know who Smiley was. Of those who did, only a few recalled what he looked like. On Smiley's own floor they had better luck.

His next-door neighbor was a woman of at least eighty named Mae Wilhelm, who wore steel-rimmed spectacles and had thinning curls of white hair and, Max thought, unexpectedly good legs. She invited the two detectives into her apartment and had them sit on the overstuffed couch.

The apartment was extremely tidy, though it smelled of old people. The modern architectural lines of the apartment had been camouflaged — no, obliterated — by someone whose sense of well-being obviously derived from homey touches of the past — ruffles, fringes, flounces, tassels, laces, doilies, antimacassars, anything to soften the hard edges.

A small color television was playing softly in the background, too low at present volume to be anything but a companion to the elderly woman.

"May I offer you gentlemen some coffee or tea?" said Mrs. Wilhelm.

"Oh, no thanks, ma'am," said Max.

"No thanks," said Caruso.

"Perhaps something harder?" she said with a twinkle.

7

"Ma'am?"

"A little apricot brandy or some schnapps?"

"Oh, no, no thanks, ma'am, we're not supposed to drink on the job," said Caruso, getting out his little notebook.

"What a dreadful thing to happen to poor Mr. Smiley," said Mrs. Wilhelm. "Who on earth would have done such a thing?"

"Well, that's what we're trying to find out," said Max.

"In my day such things were not done," she said. "People did not kill and mutilate their friends. Nowadays it's commonplace, though, isn't it? These are violent, shocking times. There is no regard for the sanctity of human life, no regard whatever."

"No, ma'am," said Max, deciding against mentioning folks like Lizzie Borden and Jack the Ripper because he did agree with her in spirit.

"Did you know Mr. Smiley well?" asked Caruso.

Mrs. Wilhelm frowned and stuck out her lower lip in thought.

"No," she said, "I would not say well. I would not characterize our relationship that way at all. I did encounter him frequently in the hallway, however — coming in, or going out, or on the way to the incinerator. This type of thing."

"Knw. hm. frm. incnrtr.," wrote Caruso, clutching the Bic.

"What sort of man was he?" asked Max.

"Well, he was very short, but quite courteous," she replied.

"You related before that in your day people did not kill or mutilate their friends," said Caruso. "Do you have reason to believe Mr. Smiley was killed by one of his friends?"

The woman's eyebrows climbed her forehead.

"Why, no," she said, "but I do think that is something you ought to look into."

"Oh, we will, ma'am, don't you worry," said Caruso.

"Mrs. Wilhelm," said Max, "the medical examiner feels that Mr. Smiley was killed three nights ago, which was Friday, April eighth. Would you happen to remember whether you saw Mr. Smiley or anybody else entering or leaving his apartment on Friday evening?"

Mrs. Wilhelm once more furrowed her brow and pushed out her lower lip. The expression appeared to be necessary for her to do any heavy-duty thinking.

"Well," she said, "I can't say as how I did. Although . . ."

"Yes?"

8

"Now that I think of it, I did go to the incinerator chute sometime around midnight, and I thought I saw somebody come out of Mr. Smiley's apartment."

Caruso had stopped writing in midsentence.

"Could you describe this individual, ma'am?" said Max.

"I'm afraid not," she said. "Seeing as how he was already walking down the hall, his back was toward me."

"You say *he*," said Caruso. "That would indicate this individual was a male?"

"Well, yes," said Mrs. Wilhelm. "He was dressed in slacks and a man's jacket and he was wearing a fedora, but I do think he was, uh . . ."

"Yes, ma'am?"

"What is the word I'm looking for?"

"What word, ma'am?"

"I did think at the time he walked a bit like a . . . a fruit — is that the term you use?"

"I get your meaning, ma'am," said Max, smiling.

With the evidence of the neck wounds and the facial disfigurement, Max and Caruso were now certain that they were dealing with a sado-masochist homosexual slaying.

Max Segal met his wife, Babette, in the waiting room of the family therapist's office.

The waiting room had an odd assortment of furniture that looked as if it had been purchased at garage sales. Two chairs that might have come from somebody's kitchen in the 1950s — chrome tubing with back and seat cushions upholstered in turquoise vinyl. Two long couches, benches really, on which were placed square polyurethane foam cushions upholstered in a worn plaid material. A boomerang-shaped coffee table with three wooden legs capped with brass feet, and a chipped Formica top upon which sat a sheaf of dog-eared magazines as varied as *Modern Screen, Popular Mechanics, Scientific American, People,* and *Wood Finishing Annual,* none of which was fewer than ten months old.

Three young pregnant Black girls with prominent bellies sat on the benches, reading magazines. The family therapist had many welfare clients.

Babette looked strained and nervous, older than her twenty-seven years. She'd pinned up her long, honey-colored hair, and though she hadn't cut it she hardly ever wore it down anymore. She'd regained her slim, dancer's body shortly after their son Sam's birth, but her muscles seemed constricted by stress. The lines of her otherwise attractive face had hardened from too little smiling and too much crying.

Max kissed Babette perfunctorily and sat down. He hated the idea of coming here. He hated the idea of acknowledging to anyone that his marriage wasn't working. He didn't know if he was going to be able to talk to the therapist. More cop than Jew, he had never been in therapy and he distrusted the process, considering it somehow unmanly.

He looked at Babette and managed a weak smile. Unable to think of anything to say to her, he asked if Sam was at Mrs. Rensvold's apartment. Of *course* Sam was at Mrs. Rensvold's apartment, said Babette, how could she even *be* here if Sam weren't at Mrs. Rensvold's apartment?

Max nodded his head. So kill me for fucking asking, he thought to himself. Babette was sure under a lot of strain these days.

After a fifteen-minute wait, the therapist beckoned them into her sunny office.

The therapist's name was Joan Jarvis. A pudgy woman in her probably late forties. Frizzy blond hair, a cupid's bow mouth, bags under her eyes radiating lines like crooked rays of light. A dewlap under her chin. Fat, saggy breasts. Max checked her fourth finger and found a wedding ring. And how is *your* marriage going, Dr. Jarvis? How does your husband like that dewlap under your chin and those fat saggy breasts?

The therapist plumped herself down on a broken swivel chair and turned to face Max and Babette.

"So," said Jarvis with a reassuring smile. "How's it going, guys?"

"O.K.," said Max.

"O.K.," said Babette.

"If it's going O.K.," said Jarvis, "then why are you here?"

They looked at her and then at each other. There was an uncomfortable pause. A thick fog of self-consciousness and apprehension hung in the small office.

"It's *not* going so O.K.," said Babette.

"Tell me about it," said Jarvis.

Another uncomfortable pause.

"Dr. Jarvis . . ." Babette began.

"Please," said Jarvis. "I'm not a doctor. Call me Joanie."

Babette smiled self-consciously, uncomfortable with the first-name invitation but no longer able to address her as Doctor. She compromised by not addressing her at all.

"Well, it's just that . . . it used to be fun," said Babette, "and it isn't anymore."

"What isn't fun anymore," said Jarvis, "living together? Sex? What?"

Anything, thought Max.

"Anything," said Max, surprising himself.

"Why not?"

His face grew hot, but he'd already taken the first step.

"I come home after a hard day's work," said Max, "I'm tired and bummed out from working in Harlem with crack dealers and killers and other human garbage, hoping for some compassion, some warmth, you know what I get? News briefs on what major appliances broke during the day."

"If something breaks," said Babette, "what am I supposed to do, not tell you?"

"Sure, tell me," said Max. "But every once in a while tell me something *nice*. All you tell me now is what broke. I feel more like a handyman than a husband, for Christ's sake."

"If anything nice happened while you're gone, I'd tell you," said Babette. "Nothing ever does."

Max raised his eyebrows, cocked his head, and looked at Jarvis, as if she now had no choice but to side with him.

"You feel Babette complains a lot?" asked Jarvis.

"She doesn't complain," said Max. "She walks around the house *not* complaining. Suffering silently. Sighing. Living with her is like living with my mother, you know what I mean? I always feel it's my fault somehow, her walking around suffering like that, but I never know what it is I've done."

"You feel guilty all the time?" asked Jarvis.

"*All* the time," replied Max. "And don't tell me it's because I'm Jewish either. Catholics understand guilt as well as Jews. Better."

"You're Jewish and Babette is Catholic."

"Yes," said Babette.

"Is religion an issue in your marriage?"

Max and Babette looked at each other, then looked away. There was a long pause.

"I take it from your silence that it is," said Jarvis.

"Babette would like to raise our son as a Catholic," said Max, as if that were self-explanatory.

"And?" said Jarvis.

"And I would not," said Max.

"Why not?" asked Jarvis.

Max looked startled, as if Jarvis were going to insist the boy be raised Catholic after all. Babette was a regular churchgoer and although Max hadn't stepped inside a synagogue since he started college, Judaism was an emotional issue for him. And not only because of his grandparents —his father's parents had lived in Germany and been killed in a concentration camp.

At his parents' insistence Max had gone to Hebrew school every afternoon after grammar school and to a Hebrew-speaking camp every summer. He loved the Jewish holidays, the songs and ceremonies of Passover, Hanukah, Purim, Rosh Hashanah, and Yom Kippur, although he was too restless in formal services to attend them as an adult.

It hadn't occurred to Max to suggest that Sam be raised as a Jew because it didn't seem fair; but that hadn't stopped Babette from lobbying for him to be raised as a Catholic. Max felt he could never let that happen. To do so would be selling out himself, his parents, his grandparents who'd died in Dachau, and the entire Jewish people.

"It's a long story," said Max.

"Why don't you tell me about it?"

"Some other time," said Max.

"Guys, guys," said Jarvis reproachfully. Then she shrugged and smiled.

"Do you still have sex together?"

Max and Babette looked at each other.

"Not much," said Max.

"Hardly at all," said Babette.

"Never," said Max.

"Why not?" asked Jarvis.

Why not? thought Max. Because sex had become a duty, an obligation, something to be gotten through for the sake of your health, like a grueling aerobic workout or like having your teeth scraped at the dentist. Because when they first knew each other Babette had been so responsive in bed and now she just lay there, daring him to arouse her, daring him to make her come, and if he couldn't she added that to her collection of grievances against him. Because sex had become one more source of things to be resentful about. Because she didn't seem to want him anymore. Because she didn't seem to care about him anymore, to delight in him, to treasure him, to touch him and fondle him and nuzzle him and caress him like she did when they first met and fell in love. Because he was no longer her hero. And what was worse, because he was no longer his own.

"I don't know," said Max.

13

"Your son is — what? — three years old now?" asked Jarvis.

They both nodded.

"Has having a child changed your sex life?"

Both Max and Babette erupted in spontaneous, hysterical, and joyless laughter. After a moment Jarvis laughed too. The laughter seemed to dissipate the fog a little.

"How has it changed it?" said Jarvis.

"It's just . . . very different now," said Babette. "It's not what I thought it would be like at all, having a child."

"What did you think it would be like?"

"I don't know. Happy times. Sharing the joys of caring for a child." Babette shook her head. "I don't know."

"And you don't share the joys of caring for a child?"

"First, there aren't that many joys," said Babette, "and second we don't share them."

"Oh, for Christ's sake!" said Max.

"I don't mean that there aren't that many joys — there are," said Babette. "But there is also a lot more grief than I thought there'd be. And I don't mean that Max doesn't share the responsibilities of childcare when he's home. It's just that he's never home."

"Jesus, give me a break, would you?"

"As I think I told you," said Babette, continuing as though Max weren't present, "Max is a cop, and cops work long, strange hours — two day-tours from eight A.M. to four P.M., followed by two night-tours from four P.M. to one A.M. I realize that isn't Max's fault but . . . I don't know, it just seems that whenever I've needed him to help with the baby or to help with *me*, he hasn't been there. I feel completely alone."

Max sighed audibly.

"Do you have any help with the child?" Jarvis inquired.

"No."

"Why not?"

"Well, we've all heard the horror stories about day-care centers," said Babette, "and we just didn't want to risk putting him in one."

"What about hiring someone to take care of him in your home?" asked Jarvis.

"Max says we can't afford it," said Babette.

"*Max* says we can't afford it, right?" said Max. "Jesus. You know, I make thirty-six thousand dollars a year, Dr. Jarvis—"

"Joanie."

"Joanie. I make thirty-six thousand dollars a year as a detective third grade, Joanie. Do you know how far thirty-six thousand dollars a year goes in this city? Not too fucking far—excuse me."

"That's O.K.," said Jarvis, smiling, "you can say 'fucking.'"

"Thank you. I borrow money for us to live on, Joanie. I fucking borrow money to pay the *interest* on the money I borrow for us to live on. You know that song: 'You load sixteen tons and what do you get, you get another day older and deeper in debt'? That's my song. Some day I'm going to be promoted to second grade, which pays forty-two thousand, but by then it'll be worth about twelve and I'll be even deeper in the fucking hole than I am already."

"I see money is a fairly hot issue with you guys," said Jarvis.

Max shrugged.

"I just resent having to be the person who says we can't afford things," said Max. "I mean, I just resent always being put in that role."

"And what would happen if you didn't *take* that role?" said Jarvis.

"If I didn't take it?" said Max. "Then nobody would. *She* wouldn't, that's for sure."

Babette rolled her eyes, sighed heavily, and looked away.

"Does that mean you feel Babette spends money on non-essentials?"

"Yeah, that's what I feel," said Max.

Another sigh from Babette.

"And you don't?" said Jarvis.

"I . . . restrict myself to things I absolutely need," said Max defensively.

"So you get to play the role of cheapskate and she gets to play the role of spendthrift," said Jarvis. "Is that it?"

"I guess," said Max.

"Uh-huh. Well, that's interesting," said Jarvis, "and not at all uncommon. *He* makes the money, *she* spends it. Except in a lot of marriages these days where *she* makes the money and *he* spends it. So. That's the game you're playing in the area of money. What about the area of sex? What game are you guys playing there?"

"What do you mean?"

"What are the roles? Whose *fault* is it you don't have a better sex life?"

Max and Babette exchanged covert looks.

"It's nobody's *fault*," said Babette.

"Sure it is," said Jarvis cheerily. "Each one of you knows whose fault it is — the other's, right?"

Babette caught herself smiling but turned it off.

"Come on, you guys," said Jarvis. "O.K. Let's play a completion game. Babette, finish this sentence: 'Sex might work with us if only he . . .' If only he *what?*"

"Acted like he wanted to be there," said Babette without looking in Max's direction.

Max uttered a disbelieving sound halfway between a laugh and a sigh.

"Good," said Jarvis. "O.K. Max, finish this one: 'Sex might work with us if only she . . .' If only she *what?*"

"What is this," said Max, "the fucking Newlywed Game?"

"Come on, Max, indulge me," said Jarvis. "'Sex might work with us if only she . . .'"

"Was in the room," said Max.

Babette wheeled on him, glaring.

"Great," said Jarvis. "I'm starting to get the picture. Max is the guy who doesn't want to be there, and Babette is the guy who *isn't* there, right?"

Neither of them reacted.

"Neither of you feels loved or appreciated. Each of you is so hurt that the other guy doesn't act interested. You punish each other by withdrawing further and further," said Jarvis. "Is that it?"

"Can I ask you something?" said Max.

"Sure," said Jarvis.

"How is this helping us?" said Max.

"Helping comes later," said Jarvis. "First we have to find out what the hell you guys are *doing*."

3

A favorite joke in the squad was the term "misdemeanor homicide."
Whenever a really repulsive drug dealer killed another really repulsive
drug dealer, the detectives designated it a misdemeanor homicide.

At the time of the Smiley killing, over ninety percent of the homicides being investigated by Manhattan North were drug related. The
most popular drug in Harlem was crack. The most popular means
of protecting your stash of crack was pit bulls. The most popular
weapons were Uzis, Mac-10s, and Intratechs — all nine-millimeter
submachine guns. The most popular automobiles for crack dealers to
drive were BMWs. Most of the killers and most of their victims were
between the ages of fourteen and nineteen.

If you killed somebody and were sixteen or older, you were considered an adult by the law, which meant you could go to prison for life. If
you killed somebody and were under sixteen, no matter how premedi-
tated and ghastly your crime, you were considered a juvenile and could
receive nothing more severe than three years in a state reception center
or a stint in a training school from which you could be paroled at any
point by school officials.

Detectives at Manhattan North worked an average of five cases at a
time. Because the Smiley homicide occurred in Midtown on the East
Side and the victim was white, the case was sure to get a lot of attention
in the media, which meant City Hall was going to put a lot of pressure
on the Detective Bureau to solve it quickly. When the Smiley case
broke, five other cases being worked by Max and Caruso and the squad
at Manhattan North were temporarily set aside:

Two Colombian brothers named Garcia, who were transporting coke
for a dealer, decided to have themselves robbed by a cousin named

Vargas and divide the spoils. "Just shoot us in the arm to make the rip-off look believable," said the Garcias. Vargas, who was not bright, used a shotgun instead of a pistol and blew both Garcias away. The dealer repaid the surviving Vargas with a "Colombian necktie," which was what dealers did to couriers or "mules" who tried to rip them off. It involved slitting the throat, reaching up inside the neck, and pulling out the tongue by the windpipe.

A crew of four Black boys, aged thirteen to fifteen, had followed a series of elderly women into their apartments, robbed them, then brutally slashed them to death just for the fun of it. The identities of the boys were known by people in the neighborhood, but they were too frightened to identify them.

A Hispanic teenager named Jesus Torres, stoned on crack, held up six bodegas with an Uzi. Although every bodega owner immediately complied with the boy's request for cash, he shot each one of them and fled. All of his victims died. Torres was known but had not yet been collared.

Not far from St. Luke's Hospital, at 113th and Amsterdam, a Black teenager named Coco McGovern was shot in the arm and two vital organs. As Coco was being rushed into surgery at St. Luke's, doctors found a thirty-eight caliber Charter Arms Special in his waistband. "Coco came in second," said Caruso. "He got the silver medal. Now we're lookin' for the guy that got the gold."

One fifteen-year-old boy shot another for throwing an egg at him. The identity of the shooter was known and he was being sought. "Hey, there was justification," said Max wryly. "It was a hard-boiled egg."

Manhattan North Homicide had its headquarters on the second floor of the Twenty-fifth Precinct in Harlem — "the Two-Five," in cop jargon — on 119th Street between Park and Lexington. The neighborhood was a depressing mix of tenements, bodegas, burned-out buildings, empty lots strewn with garbage, and burned-out skeletons of automobiles.

West of the precinct the neighborhood was ninety percent Black, east it was ninety percent Hispanic and was referred to as Spanish Harlem or El Barrio. If you were white it wasn't safe to walk in this neighborhood, either east or west of the precinct, especially after dark, unless you were a police officer carrying a loaded revolver.

The building that housed the Two-Five Precinct, like most police stations in New York, had a grimy, institutional appearance. On the second floor of the building was the Two-Five PDU and the offices of Manhattan North Homicide. The offices had tan cinderblock walls, a floor made of whitish-gray linoleum squares, and a white composition ceiling with fluorescent lights. The hallways had light-green ceramic tiles and, unaccountably, doors of bright blue which were the only appealing color in the entire building and which looked as if they'd been done by a cheerful upscale painter from downtown who went to the wrong job by mistake.

Although all precincts had plainclothes cops in their PDUs, these were usually young, relatively inexperienced men and women who covered a variety of crimes, including homicide. Like Caruso, the seasoned specialists from the homicide task forces who assisted them had ten to twenty years on the job and considered themselves superstars.

By the end of the night tour on April 11, the canvass of Smiley's building had produced seven tenants who said that Smiley was often seen going into his apartment with attractive young women, two tenants and a doorman who said he was occasionally seen with gay men, and a neighbor who'd seen an effeminate man leaving Smiley's apartment on the night of the murder. Max, Caruso, and the rest of the task force felt that Smiley was bisexual and that homicide resulting from contact with a gay lover was the most likely scenario.

Since a search of Smiley's apartment revealed no missing valuables, robbery was ruled out as a primary motive. Ritual murder and revenge homicide were felt to be possibilities.

Several latent prints had been lifted from the crime scene, but these proved to have come from the deceased, from Assistant D.A. Marshad, and from Detectives O'Rourke, Segal, and Caruso.

Smiley's parents had been informed of their son's death and his father was taken to the morgue to identify the body. An autopsy was scheduled by the M.E. for the following day. Following the autopsy the body would be released to the Smileys' funeral director, and Smiley's funeral would take place at the end of the week. At least four detectives from Manhattan North Homicide planned to attend and take photographs of the guests. It was astonishing how many killers attended their victims' funerals.

Max and Caruso went to Manhattan Cable TV to interview Smiley's co-workers. Smiley's address book had been photocopied and copies given to all the detectives in the task force and the PDU. Every person listed who could be tracked down was interviewed about his or her relationship to the deceased. Nobody they had talked to thus far seemed either helpful enough or suspicious enough for further questioning.

Max and Caruso went to two gay bars in the West Village to develop leads, but Caruso had such an obvious attitude about "nellies" he couldn't disguise it, and the bartenders and patrons they talked to gave them nothing. Max realized he was better off doing that sort of research by himself.

"There's no fist-fucking anymore, even at the Meat Rack in L.A.," said Brady, a gay patrolman Max knew in the Two-Five. "Just a hundred guys sucking and fucking in the dark."

Brady was a member of GOLD, the Gay Officers something or other. Gay officers — Jesus, how the job had changed!

"Aren't they afraid of AIDS?" asked Max.

"Not really," said Brady. "Most gay people are in denial about AIDS anyway, although it's harder to get it than people think."

"How's that?" said Max dubiously.

"Well, first you have to be genetically predisposed to the HIV virus. Then you have to be inoculated with the virus by a needle or by anal penetration, and you have to be exposed to enough of the virus, too. Then you have to have either herpes or Epstein-Barr or hepatitis or CMV. The HIV virus piggybacks onto those or genetically mixes with them in the DNA. Also, your immune system has to have been exposed to many diseases over the years and be very fragile and worn thin, like the fabric of an old shirt. No, people who get AIDS are real players."

If anyone was in denial it was Brady himself, but Max felt it was useless to point that out to him.

"So tell me some gay clubs in Manhattan," said Max instead.

"Gay clubs in Manhattan," said Brady. "Well, there's Jay's on Ninth Avenue and Fourteenth Street. That's a heavy motorcycle crowd. Older, tougher guys. It used to be the Hellfire Club — you remember that?"

"Oh, yeah, sure," said Max. He'd heard of the Hellfire Club, where you could either watch people being whipped and pissed on in a bathtub or else you could participate. Max had most certainly never been there. Probably Brady had, though.

"Then there's the Locker Room," said Brady, "right near Jay's — it's about the same as Jay's, only slightly less so. There's Private

Eyes at Twenty-first and Fifth—very preppy, very collegiate—a gay dance and video bar owned by a Sephardic Jew. There's the Tunnel, on Twenty-eighth and Twelfth Avenue—"

"The *Tunnel?* The Tunnel isn't gay—I've *been* there," said Max, as if his presence ensured heterosexuality.

"On Sunday nights it is," said Brady. "It's Black and Puerto Rican, a Fire Island crowd—drag queens. Then there's the Pyramid Club on the Lower East Side and the Boy Bar on St. Mark's Place, both of which are very arty and postmodern. And Rounds, on Fifty-third and Second, which is hustlers. The Spike and the Eagle, both on the waterfront between Twentieth and Twenty-first—they're leather, motorcycle, construction workers."

"That sounds more like what I'm looking for," said Max, wondering whether he had to explain again that this was for the Smiley case.

"The roughest one of all, of course," said Brady, "is the Mindshaft. Cowboys, construction workers, teamsters, things like that. The butcher they dress, the heavier their sex scene. Wearing leather, for example, means a heavier S and M trip than wearing jeans."

"I think I'll go to the Mindshaft first," said Max. "Want to come along?"

"No thanks," said Brady. "It's not exactly my bag."

"Then I guess I'll just have to go alone," said Max.

"Lotsa luck, Mary," said Brady.

4

"Caruso, Segal, come into my office a minute."

"What's up, boss?" asked Caruso.

Grateful for any excuse to stop typing up forms, Caruso and Max stood up and walked into Lieutenant McIlheny's office.

McIlheny was huge. Six-foot-six and maybe two hundred eighty pounds. From a distance his face looked ruddy and healthy, but up close you could see that the ruddiness of his skin was merely the hundreds of burst capillaries of a heavy drinker. McIlheny was fifty-seven and had been in the job thirty-six years. Though only a lieutenant, as commander of the Manhattan North Homicide squad he was drawing captain's pay.

Seated primly on the green leather psychiatrist's couch next to McIlheny's desk — the NYPD had picked up a storeful of the things at an enormous discount — was a stunningly attractive woman. High cheekbones, brown eyes, long black hair that flipped up at the ends, and a slim body in a perfectly tailored gray suit.

"This is Miss Simon," said the lieutenant. "These are two of my men, Miss Simon, Detective Segal and Detective Caruso."

Max and Caruso mumbled greetings that Miss Simon acknowledged with a diffident nod of her head.

"Miss Simon is a reporter from *New York* magazine," said McIlheny. "She's doing an article on the Smiley case and needs to talk to some-body from the squad to hear what we're doin'. I told her you guys were as good as I got."

Caruso flashed McIlheny a sour look. The transparent compliment from the boss did not dissipate his displeasure at having to deal with the visitor. The last thing they needed was some broad from the press hanging around and asking them to *explain* everything.

22

"How long you think you'll need with us, Miss Simon?" said Caruso.

"Oh, golly, I don't know," she said. "Not too long. I know how busy you must be."

"You go with them, Miss Simon," said the lieutenant. "They'll tell you whatever you need to know."

Miss Simon got up and went back into the squad room with Max and Caruso.

"So," said Max, unable to think of how to get the conversational ball rolling, "how'd you get up here?"

"By subway," she said. "I took the Lexington Avenue train up to 116th and then walked."

Max rolled his eyes.

"What's wrong?" she said. "Was that dangerous?"

"Not really," said Max. "Not if you're armed. Are you armed, Miss Simon?"

She giggled.

"No," she said. "And please, it's Susan."

"O.K., Susan," said Max, permitting himself a swift canvass of her body. It was a very nice body, with a small, perfectly shaped tush and long, dynamite legs, but she caught him at it and he had to look away.

"How much time you think you're gonna need with us, honey?" said Caruso in a neutral tone.

She stiffened almost imperceptibly at the "honey," but Caruso caught it.

"Oh, I don't know," she said. "Not too long. Not more than a few sessions, I guess."

A few *sessions?* Caruso made his eyes bug out and shot a glance at Max, who pretended to ignore him.

"Tell you what," said Max. "Next time you want to come up here, give us a call and we'll meet you at the subway."

Caruso closed his eyes.

"Better yet," said Max, irked at Caruso's mugging, handing her one of his business cards, "next time you want to come up here, call us at this number and we'll come down and get you."

Caruso audibly exhaled his breath.

"Oh, I couldn't ask you to do *that*," she said. "I mean, wouldn't I be terribly out of your way?"

"Where you located?" asked Max.

"I live at Fifty-second between First and Beekman," she said, blushing faintly.

Max caught the blush. She's blushing because she just told me where she lives, he thought. What could that mean?

"Hey, we're at 119th between Park and Lex," said Caruso sarcastically. "We're practically neighbors."

Max and Susan both looked at him.

"Anytime you want us to pick you up," said Max, "just give us a call at the number on the card."

Max began to fill Susan in on almost everything they knew about the Smiley case. Caruso noticed that she took notes with her left hand in a steno notebook much like his own.

"The way we figure it happened," said Max, "the killer, who was known to Smiley, had some kind of S and M sex with him, then severed his carotid artery. Smiley got hysterical. He grabbed the end of a sheet and pressed it to his neck to stop the bleeding, but it didn't work. He sank down on the bed and lost consciousness. The killer watched him die."

At ten-thirty A.M. Caruso said they'd have to stop because he and Max were due at the morgue at eleven for Smiley's autopsy. Max said that, since the morgue was at Thirtieth Street and First Avenue, they could drop Susan off at her place on the way. Susan was uncomfortable with Caruso's attitude and said she'd take the subway. They compromised by dropping her at the corner of Fifty-second and Second.

When she got out of the car, Caruso shook his head.

"That broad you're so hot to get in her pants is one of the worst fuckin' phonies I've met yet," said Caruso by way of opening up a discourse on her.

"I'm not hot to get into her pants," said Max, easing the Plymouth Fury down Second Avenue. "I'm a married man."

"Bull*shit* you don't wanna get in her pants," said Caruso.

"And I suppose you don't?" said Max.

"No way, José," said Caruso. "She's a fucking phony if I ever seen one."

"And you'd tear off your fucking right arm for a chance to fuck her," said Max.

"No *way* I'd fuck that phony broad," said Caruso, as if being caught having sex with a phony was the depth of indignity. "I wouldn't fuck that broad with *your* cock."

The first thing to hit Max upon entering the autopsy room, as always, was the stench. Rotting meat and cat litter full of old feces was how it smelled to him.

The second thing, far worse than the first, was the sight of eight cadavers lying on the eight stainless steel autopsy tables, heads nearest the door — most of them with chest cavities gaping and skin peeled back to reveal their multicolored internal organs, heads flung back, skulls with their tops sawed off, rubber-mask faces contorted into hideous open-eyed grimaces.

All suspicious or unattended deaths required autopsies. In New York, where there were an average of five homicides a day, all eight tables in the autopsy room were generally taken. Today the eight tables were occupied by a middle-aged Black woman and a middle-aged Black man, both dead of drug overdoses; two young Black men, both dead of multiple gunshot wounds; a young Hispanic woman, dead of forty-two stab wounds from a jealous lover; two Black babies, dead of unknown but suspicious causes; and Irv Smiley.

The room was packed. In addition to the eight dead people, there were eight medical examiners, six morgue workers dignified by the title Mortuary Technician, a morgue photographer, seven visiting medical students, Max, Caruso, O'Rourke, and Moreno. Everyone but the cops and the dead wore scrub suits.

"How many autopsies you been to?" Max asked the younger PDU men, recalling a time seven years before when senior men had hazed him unmercifully.

"Not that many," said O'Rourke. He was still taking in the sight and the smell of the eight cadavers.

"More than one?" asked Caruso.

"Uh . . . no," said O'Rourke. "Less."

On Max's first autopsy they'd set him up. He would never forget it. Caruso, two homicide detectives named Mahoney and Cassidy, and then-deputy M.E. Rizzo told Max to come at three P.M., which was after all the other autopsies were finished for the day. When Max arrived, Rizzo was eating spaghetti out of the cadaver's open chest cavity. Max began to back out of the room, but his legs telescoped inward and he passed out on the floor. Rizzo laughed so hard he choked on his spaghetti.

It was eleven A.M. and Chernin had just begun to work on Smiley. The stainless steel autopsy table upon which he lay was twin-bed width and about ten feet long. The table surface was steel mesh, a glorified hurricane fence. Underneath the mesh was a sloped drain pan to catch bodily fluids. A hose in the pan provided a continuous cascade of water on the inclined surface, like a waterfall in the atrium of a Hyatt Hotel. Another hose ran continuously in a perforated steel tub at the end of the table. Overhead hung a scale with a steel pan for weighing removed organs.

Smiley's neck, like those of all the adult cadavers, was supported on a hunk of wet and weathered wood about four inches square and a foot and a half long, which looked like a miniature railroad tie.

"Morning, Doc," said Max. "As you can see, O'Rourke and Moreno couldn't stay away."

"Hope you gentlemen had a hearty breakfast," said Chernin, winking at Max and Caruso.

"If not," said Caruso, "grab a bite here."

"I just might do that," said O'Rourke, checking to see if his partner was any steadier than he.

"You will note the deterioration in Mr. Smiley's appearance since last we saw him," said Chernin. "The more pronounced odor of hydrogen sulfide. The greenish cast to the skin and the marbling effect — the greater prominence of the veins. The little blebs or blisters forming on his sides and back. The bloating of the cheeks and abdomen. Our maggot friends are a quarter of an inch in length today and beginning to warm up and move about freely after an overnight stay in their refrigerated locker. Some of them will undoubtedly fall to the floor as we work. I suggest you look down at your shoes from time to time and make sure they don't crawl up your pantleg. They don't make good house pets."

26

Chernin chuckled to himself, switched on his grimy Thoughtmaster tape recorder, and began speaking into a microphone wrapped in a Baggie.

"All right, this is Dr. Horace Chernin, forensic pathologist for the City of New York, office of the Medical Examiner. We are about to conduct a postmortem examination on the body of a male Caucasian, one Irving I. Smiley, thirty-three years of age, height five feet three inches, weight one hundred fifty-eight pounds. . . ."

Chernin examined and described to the microphone the wounds to Smiley's neck and face. Narrow white adhesive strips, with calibrations in centimeters, had been affixed to Smiley's skin alongside his wounds. The morgue photographer took several shots with his strobe.

"Doc, I'd like combings of the pubic hair," said Max. "Also oral and anal swabs for semen."

"You've got it," said Chernin, reaching for his scalpel. "An autopsy, gentlemen, is surgery without anesthesia, and the patient never recovers."

With a glance at Max and Caruso, then at the two young PDU men, Chernin made a coronal mastoid incision in Smiley's scalp, slicing a deep cut from a spot above and behind Smiley's left ear, across the top of his head to a corresponding spot above and behind his right ear.

He then pulled the portion of the scalp in front of the incision away from the pinkish white bone of the skull and down over the forehead, down over Smiley's face, as if he were peeling the skin of an orange or a latex Halloween mask. The inside of the scalp was smooth, yellowish-whitish-pink and rubbery. Attached to it was the grotesquely wiglike hairy part of the scalp.

O'Rourke inhaled audibly and everyone turned to look at him.

"Howya doin', Timmy?" said Max not unkindly.

"Great," said O'Rourke. "I'm loving this."

O'Rourke and Moreno both looked like they were about to faint. The senior men exchanged superior smirks.

"Go ahead, maestro," said Caruso.

Chernin peeled the portion of the scalp to the rear of the incision down in back till it folded over Smiley's ears. The top of the skull was now fully exposed. Chernin picked up a small electrical autopsy saw and switched it on. He inserted the vibrating blade into Smiley's skull and moved it in a slow arc from the right temple to the left in the front, then from left to right in the rear. The saw produced a horrid grinding noise and spewed forth a rain of bone and hair sawdust.

Moreno coughed and tried mightily to keep the cough from escalating into a vomit.

"Still having fun, guys?" said Caruso.

"Time of my life," said O'Rourke.

Moreno was too sick to speak.

Chernin pried the sawed section of bone away from the skull. It came off with a sickening, sucking sound that almost caused Max to lose it. Chernin put the sawed skullcap down on the table. It looked to Max like the rind of a honeydew melon. The morgue photographer moved in close on the opened skull and fired off several shots.

With his scalpel Chernin freed the brain, removed it from the skull cavity, and held it aloft. It was convoluted, tannish pinkish gray, and spiderwebbed with delicate red lines.

"Behold, gentlemen, the repository of human intelligence," said Chernin. "'The brain may devise laws for the blood, but a hot temper leaps o'er a cold decree' — William Shakespeare."

"So that's the brain of a TV executive," said Max. "Funny, I expected it to be about the size of a walnut."

"I'll be right back," said O'Rourke over his shoulder, beating a swift retreat to the door.

"I better make sure the poor fucker's all right," said Moreno, racing after him.

Caruso, Max, Chernin, and two mortuary technicians roared with laughter. Then Chernin proceeded with the autopsy. Without O'Rourke and Moreno to play off, it was less fun for everybody.

Chernin took his scalpel and began a thoraco-abdominal incision. With his left hand in the middle of Smiley's chest, he began his incision at the left shoulder. He brought the blade around in a shallow curve, slicing deeply and quickly through fatty tissue and pectoral muscle, passing low over the breastbone, swinging up and finishing the cut at Smiley's right shoulder. Starting at the breastbone incision, he made another cut, slicing all the way down to the pubic bone. The Y-shaped cut yawned open, and a stronger odor of hydrogen sulfide permeated the room.

Max breathed through his mouth and looked down at the floor, checking for maggots. His ankles itched and he wondered if any had managed to crawl up his leg.

Chernin peeled the flesh away from the ribcage and the underlying cartilage, revealing the abdominal and thoracic region from breastbone to bladder. Using a pair of cutters, he crunched through the breastbone till he could pry the breastplate free. Then he peeled it back over Smiley's shoulder, revealing the internal organs.

To steady himself Max pretended he was in a butcher shop, staring at spare ribs, sides of beef, chicken gizzards. The stomach was an inflated pink balloon, the intestines links of pinkish-yellow sausage. The lungs and kidneys were blackish purple. The fatty tissue under the skin was bright yellow, the muscles a deep purplish pink. The bright colors had a certain ghastly beauty.

Max looked away then, at the pale yellow ceramic tiles on the walls, at the rolling steel gurney that shuttled bodies between autopsy tables and lockers in the morgue, at the other M.E.s.

The seven other M.E.s were a diverse lot — three elderly Russian men, a stocky Russian woman with bright red hair, an anorexically skinny Asian man, a middle-aged Hispanic woman, a pudgy Black woman. The Black and Hispanic women were working on the babies. They had taken the tops off the babies' heads and were now removing their exquisitely tiny internal organs. Everything was in perfect, terrifying miniature, like the HO gauge electric trains at FAO Schwarz. It looked like a doll repair shop, except that these dolls were real and unrepairable.

One of the babies reminded Max of his son. A wave of profound sadness and loss washed over him and he had a sudden horrid premonition that he might one day see his own baby on an autopsy table. He decided that Chernin and Smiley were the more comfortable direction after all.

With his scalpel and a large carving knife Chernin removed Smiley's lungs, heart, liver, kidneys, and other organs. He weighed them in the overhead scale, dissected them, and withdrew sections from each organ. The sections he placed in labeled bottles and Mason jars for toxicology. With a syringe Chernin extracted urine from Smiley's bladder. Then he dipped a steel soup ladle and a series of small plastic bottles into the now-hollow body cavity and collected other fluids to be sent to toxicology.

Watching Chernin was difficult. No matter how many autopsies he attended Max couldn't get used to either the sight or the smell. He let his thoughts stray to Susan. She seemed so wholesome, so innocent. Such a contrast to a place of death like this. He wondered what kind of men she went out with. He wondered if she had a steady boyfriend. He wondered if she'd go out with a cop.

At the table on the other side, the M.E. had finished the postmortem of his female junkie. A young Black man in a green scrub suit and a white baseball cap with the bill off to the side hosed the woman down and began sewing up her chest cavity. The needle was the heavy curved variety used for sewing canvas sails of boats. It was threaded double with heavy off-white twine. As the technician sewed the corpse's breast with large overhand stitches, he joked with a female colleague. Max wondered why people took jobs like this.

"What kind of training did you get to work here?" said Max suddenly.

The technician gave Max a wry laugh.

"Pumpin' gas in a Sunoco station and bein' box boy at the A&P," he said.

"And what made you choose *this* line of work?"

"I needed a job," said the young man. "I put my name on a lotta lists for jobs. This one come up first."

Max nodded.

"How can you stand it?" Max said.

The technician took out a roll of oakum, a grayish-yellow fiber obtained by untwisting old ropes. He stuffed it into the woman's empty skull cavity and began sewing up her head.

"You get used to it," he said. "First you get used to the smell, and you go from there. Least here you don't got to take no abuse from the customers. Here the customers be *dead*."

"Yeah, they be dead," said his companion gleefully. "You kill 'em, we chill 'em. You stab 'em, we slab 'em. You slice 'em, we ice 'em. You cain't beat us for the fetus."

They both whooped with laughter. Max chuckled politely and turned back to Chernin and Smiley.

Max had heard bad stories about morgue workers. How they took gold out of cadavers' teeth. How they loved when decomposed bodies came in, because homicide cops were too squeamish to search them well and morgue workers got to keep the valuables. How they sometimes deliberately substituted the wrong decomposed body in the viewing room for relatives as a goof. How they sometimes did sexual things with corpses that were attractive and in good condition.

Chernin was still dissecting and putting things into labeled bottles. The average autopsy of an adult took about an hour and a half. Stabbing homicides took two to four hours. Gunshot homicides could take up to several days, because you had to recover all the bullet fragments

30

and trace their paths with a steel tracking probe. Babies took about thirty minutes.

"We're not going to find any surprises here," said Chernin. "As I told you at the crime scene, cause of death was the incision to the lateral aspect of the neck, severance of the carotid artery, exsanguination, consequent shock to the central nervous system, and heart failure due to blood pressure loss."

Chernin dropped some of Smiley's dissected organs into a garbage can labeled *Caution: Biological Hazard.*

"Here, Doc," said Caruso. "Lemme save the City a lotta trouble —I'll just take that stuff directly to a beach on Long Island and dump it for ya."

6

Freddy Petlin was thirty-five, had sandy hair thinning at the crown, an infectious wheezing laugh, and what his parents had always called the gift of gab. He was a commodities broker who'd been shrewd enough to finesse the crash of October '87 by buying out-of-the-money S&P puts on October 14 and selling them a week later. For the first time in his life he'd started really pulling money out of the pit and had emerged as a player.

The gimmicky three-button phone with the three lines on the desk in his apartment made its distinctive non-ringing sound. He put the call on the speaker.

"Yeah?" he said.

There was no reply.

"Hel*lo*," he said a bit impatiently.

No reply. There was definitely someone on the line, but for some reason they were choosing not to speak.

"Ira, you dorkhead, that you?" said Petlin, chuckling.

Silence. Petlin had thought at first it might be a gag call, the old "breather" routine, which Ira Feldman at the Exchange loved to pull on people. But if it had been Ira he would've made a sound by now. Heavy breathing, the exaggerated sounds of a guy masturbating to climax. There was no sound, not even breathing, but Petlin knew the caller was still there. It was creepy.

"Who the fuck is this?" said Petlin.

The line went dead.

Petlin hung up. He laughed and shook his head, but he was unsettled. He turned on the TV.

7

Irving Smiley had been dead three days by the time a worried neighbor's call brought police to his fashionable East Fifty-ninth Street bachelor apartment, and the smell was so strong when the cops entered that they had to sprinkle ammonia before they even dared to breathe

No.

Irving Smiley had been dead three days by the time the cops discovered him. In three days terrible things happen to a body. There is bloating, there are maggots, and worst of all there is the smell. The smell hung in the hallway outside the sealed apartment on East Fifty-ninth Street, where the feeding frenzy of the reporters and the paparazzi and the TV camera crews mirrored that of the maggots on Smiley's decomposing

No.

Irv Smiley, thirty-three, a minor executive at Manhattan Cable TV, was found dead in his apartment on East Fifty-ninth Street late in the afternoon of Monday, April 11. Smiley's carotid artery had been severed, his face bludgeoned beyond recognition. Police seemed reasonably certain the perpetrator was a member of the gay community on Manhattan's Lower West Side, but on the day following the discovery of the body they were not optimistic about their chances of apprehending him.

"The way we figure it happened," said Detective Max Segal, thirty-two, a plainclothes detective based at Manhattan North Homicide in Harlem, "the killer, who was known to Smiley, had some kind of S and M sex with him, then severed his carotid artery. The killer watched him die, then bludgeoned his face beyond recognition."

Maybe.

"Mama, do you have a penis or a vagina?"

"A vagina."

"Can I see it?"

"No."

"Why can't I?"

"Because."

"Why?"

"Because I said so."

"But I *want* to."

"Come on, Sam," said Babette. "Dada is waiting to get you ready to go night-night."

"I don't *want* to go night-night."

It was eight P.M., Sam's bedtime. Max stood in the tiny living room of the tiny three-room apartment located on two floors of a brownstone on East Nineteenth Street, surveying what had once been an area where adults sat and drank and socialized and occasionally even made love and was now primarily a playroom scattered with an awesome assortment of plastic trains, trucks, cars, planes, boats, and submarines, all in various stages of disassembly.

Max was poised to begin Sam's going-to-bed rituals, which could take anywhere from twenty minutes to two hours, depending upon Sam's mood. Sam was never eager to get into the going-to-bed countdown, and tonight he seemed less so than usual, trying to stick his head up under his mother's dress and behaving so sexually it would have astounded anyone but the parent of a toddler.

"Max?" said Babette entreatingly, an accusation more than a request.

"Come on, buddy," said Max. "Tell Mama you'll see her in a little while."

"Mama, do you want to come to bed with me and sleep in my crib?"

"No, sweetie," said Babette.

"Why not?"

"Because I have my *own* bed," said Babette. "I sleep with Dada."

"Why do you sleep with Dada?"

The question was one that she herself had pondered on many occasions.

"Because Dada is my husband," she said.

"Do I have a husband?"

"No," said Babette.

"Then who will sleep with *me?*"

"Your teddy and your bunny and your raccoon and all of the rest of your animal friends," said Babette.

"If you don't sleep with me, Mama, I will be *lonely,*" said Sam.

"Sam, how could you be lonely?" said Max. "You have so many animals in your bed with you now it looks like a tenement in El Barrio."

"What's a barrio?"

"C'mon, buddy, let's go," said Max.

He picked Sam up to drag him off to the bathroom and the boy began to cry. Max unexpectedly hoisted him high in the air and Sam's crying turned to squeals of joy.

"Again!" said Sam.

Max swung him down and then high up in the air again. Shrieks of laughter. The crying was entirely forgotten. It had happened last year.

"Again!" said Sam.

Max continued to swing Sam into the air over and over until his arms and shoulders and back ached and he had to put the boy back down on the floor.

"Again!" said Sam.

"Maybe tomorrow," said Max. He dragged the boy off to the bathroom adjoining the living room and filled up the bathtub and undressed him. Although Max had never admitted it to anyone but Babette, certainly not to his fellow cops, he never ceased to marvel at his son's perf t little body or the miracle — that corny, uncoplike word — of its creation.

Before Sam was born Max hadn't liked children at all. He'd thought them not cute but irritating and had been extremely uncomfortable in their presence. He'd only agreed to have a child to humor Babette. But when Sam was born Max fell hopelessly in love with him, and the older Sam got the more in love with him Max grew. Max liked nothing more than holding Sam on his lap, reading him stories and burying his nose in the boy's fragrant hair.

That Max was second to Babette in his son's affections was a source of continuous pain. That his son appeared to be constantly hitting on his wife sexually was the final indignity. It upset him in a way that he couldn't fathom. Could it be that he felt sexually competitive with a three-year-old? That was utter nonsense, and yet the emotions that Sam's flirting evoked in Max were disturbingly similar to those he'd experienced in the past toward male romantic rivals.

"Dada, do you want to count my toes?" said Sam, as if he'd suddenly been inspired to grant an exotic privilege.

"I do," said Max, for whom it was.

She gets invited to sleep with him, thought Max, *I* get invited to count his toes. Well, take what you can get.

Max counted Sam's toes and kissed them. He put a laundry basket full of floating toys into the filling bath, then carefully inserted the boy himself into the tub. Sam was only able to appreciate toys in quantity — hordes of stuffed animals crowding him to the corner of his crib, flotillas of bath toys floating and bobbing in the tub, gridlock traffic jams of Matchbox and Hot Wheel cars on the living room floor. Max worried that this hunger to be engulfed by crowds of toys came from the boy's loneliness, and felt guilty that his detective job's insane hours didn't allow him to spend more time with his son.

As usual, Sam cried when Max rinsed his hair, and as usual Sam demanded that Max not let the water out till he'd rescued all his toys from the tub, convinced beyond reasoning that the toys would otherwise slide down the drain and disappear.

When Max was finished drying Sam and lubricating him with Baby Magic and dressing him in his Spider Man pajamas and brushing his teeth and helping him to make a weewee, he put him in bed with all his animals and went through the boy's obsessive bedtime rituals: the story, the songs, winding up the musical mobile above his bed, winding up the bear with the music box in its back, turning his pillow over, covering him with his blankie, and on and on into infinity.

Then came the best part, the exchanging of hugs and kisses and squeezes. Kisses were on the mouth, and there was no discernible difference between hugs and squeezes, but Max was grateful for any excuse to get affection from the boy and didn't argue.

When Sam was finally in bed, Babette came in for hugs and kisses and squeezes, and then they both exited the room, leaving the door ajar the precise number of millimeters that Sam demanded. Sam called Max back into his room seven times to turn his pillow over, wind up his bear, and cover him up again with his blankie before he finally surrendered to sleep.

Max walked wearily into the living room where Babette was reading a magazine. It was still early. Jarvis had given them an assignment — three sessions of romantic love before their next therapy appointment.

"O.K.," said Max, "let's do the assignment."

"*That* sure sounds romantic," said Babette without enthusiasm.

Max went into the bathroom, moved Sam's bath paraphernalia out of the way, and began filling the tub with warm water and bubble bath. Then he went to the kitchen cupboard, got out a dozen votive candles, lined them up around the edge of the tub and lit them. Then he took a bottle of white wine out of the cupboard, opened it, and inserted it into a bucket of ice by the side of the tub.

With an ambivalent show-me expression on her face, Babette allowed herself to be coaxed into the candlelit bathroom and out of her clothes and into the tub. Max poured wine, clinked glasses, and sponged her breasts with bubblebath. It was strange taking a militantly romantic bath with his wife in the very tub where he had just bathed his three-year-old son. He drank two glasses of wine but the strangeness didn't go away. Neither did his awareness that his well-intentioned efforts at romance had gone wholly unacknowledged.

"So, how do you like it so far?" said Max.

"Meaning what?" said Babette, instantly on guard.

"Meaning how do you like it so far?"

"Meaning why don't I say how wonderful you are to have put this all together?"

A sigh.

"I dunno. Yeah, I suppose."

"Max, it's sweet, but you spent six minutes setting this up. It's not like you've built me the Taj Mahal or anything, you know?"

Another sigh.

"O.K., forget it," said Max.

He opened the drain and stood up.

"Max?"

"Yeah?"

"Where are you going?" she said.

"I dunno."

"I'm sorry," she said.

"I know," he said.

He stepped out of the tub, inadvertently knocking three votive candles onto the tiled floor. They shattered on impact.

"Fuck!"

He began cleaning up the glass. She remained in the rapidly emptying tub, watching him, immobilized, trapped in her own ambivalence. He finished cleaning up the fragments of glass, wiped down the whole floor with moist toilet paper lest Sam step on a shard and bleed to death, then towelled himself dry and pulled on his jeans.

"Are you going out?" she asked.

"Yeah."

Silence.

The last of the water gurgled out of the drain. Babette didn't move. Max walked out of the bathroom. So much for romance by decree.

9

Freddy Petlin's phone made its distinctive non-ringing sound. He scooped up the receiver and clamped it to his ear.

"Petlin," he said.

There was no reply, and suddenly he knew it was the person who had called before. The non-breather.

"Who is this?" he said, controlling his voice, his pulse beginning to race.

There was no reply. He wondered if he should call the police. But what could he tell them?

"Listen," he said, "I got enough grief in my life without this, O.K.? You got something to say to me, say it. Otherwise get the fuck out of my face."

There was a click and the line went dead.

He put the receiver back in its cradle and remained staring at it for several minutes, wondering what to do if it rang again, knowing that it would ring again, and knowing that he would still pick it up. He had never been able to resist picking up a ringing telephone. He loved to talk. That was both his blessing and his curse.

10

The Mindshaft was a private club on the Lower West Side, near the Hudson River in the belly of the wholesale meat packing district. It catered to sadomasochistic gay men. The neighborhood was bleak and terrifying, loading docks steel-shuttered against whatever roamed the streets at night, parked meat trucks in whose bowels desperate gay men had found anonymous sex in a tangle of bodies until AIDS made them microscopically less self-destructive and drove them into less accessible places.

Max walked nervously down the deserted street, looking for some sign that he was in the right place — not that the Mindshaft could ever be considered the right place.

He had a bad feeling about the abortive romantic bath. He shouldn't have asked for acknowledgment. *How do you like it so far?* What a pathetic, needy thing to ask. As if he required her approval to exist. He should have known she'd answer the way she had. *It's not like you've built me the Taj Mahal or anything, you know?* Perhaps that was why he'd asked her. Because he *had* known. Because he knew he could count on her to ruin it.

Still, she'd said "I'm sorry." Why hadn't he accepted the apology and gone on from there? Why did he have to take that as the signal to end the experience? Because he was already too damned mad at her to do otherwise, that's why. Because he knew that was how it was going to end, sooner or later, and he had just gotten it over with sooner. The hell with her anyway.

In the shadows of a seemingly deserted building, Max found the number. No sign saying *Mindshaft,* no other evidence that this was indeed the place. But it *was* the right number. Max felt for the thirty-eight caliber Smith & Wesson in the shoulder holster under his leather jacket, opened the exterior door, and stepped inside.

At the entrance to the dimly lit bar was a muscular-looking bouncer with a flashlight examining potential guests for proper attire. The man ahead of Max wore ballooning slacks, a broadly striped shirt, an expensive-looking jacket with lapels notched fashionably low, tennis shoes, and a loosely tied silk scarf, the ends flung over his shoulders with studied carelessness.

"No striped shirts," said the bouncer. "No tennis shoes. No jackets with lapels like that. No fucking silk scarves. This ain't no fucking tea party."

The man was banished from the club. Max took his place under the bouncer's scrutiny. The bouncer flashed his light briefly on Max's genuinely-old-and-not-distressed leather jacket, his genuinely-faded-and-not-stone-washed jeans, his scuffed hightop work boots.

"You're O.K.," said the bouncer and ushered Max inside.

Max was both relieved and chagrined. He wasn't glad he'd gotten in so easily. He knew it was because of the clothes. For years he'd compensated for his slight frame and unathletic build by dressing somewhat more macho than the dictates of fashion. Now the very symbols by which he'd signaled his masculinity had been co-opted right out from under him by the group with which he least wished to be identified.

Max looked around. The room he'd entered was big and dark and had a high ceiling and a bar at one end. Forty or fifty men stood around, drinking and talking. Some of them were dressed like cowboys. Some looked like construction workers. No one was under six feet tall. Most of them looked like they lifted weights. There was the sound of low voices and raucous male laughter.

It occurred to Max that he had entered the wrong place, maybe a private club for horse wranglers or longshoremen or movie stuntmen or drivers of sixteen-wheeler tractor-trailers. These men were clearly not homosexuals. These men were more masculine than Max himself. Then why were there no women present? Why indeed? Perhaps because these men were so masculine they didn't even *need* women.

Max walked to the bar. He drank two beers and got into a conversation with a guy who looked like a construction worker. Torn and faded jeans, heavy work shoes, a yellow hardhat, and a sweatshirt with the arms ripped out. Tattoos of eagles gripping writhing snakes in their beaks and talons adorned the man's well-developed deltoids.

Max steered the conversation around to the Smiley case. The guy had heard of it and thought Smiley deserved what he got for taking tricks back to his apartment. The guy said that a man named Albert Prince, a carpenter at a jobsite on Fifty-seventh between Park and Lex, had been heard bragging that he knew Smiley. The guy thought there was a fifty-fifty chance Prince was telling the truth.

Max thanked him and then the guy asked if Max wanted to have sex. Max shook his head and backed swiftly away, wondering why he was surprised. Somebody grabbed Max's buns. Max spun around to find a gargantuan trucker grinning at him.

"Hi, honey, can I buy you a drink?" asked the trucker.

Max shook his head and moved laterally through the thickening crowd at the bar. Somebody else grabbed his ass. Max didn't even look around, but just kept moving. He was beginning to feel pawed and angry. He realized women got this kind of treatment all their lives.

Max got back to his apartment about three A.M. He was exhausted and wanted only to sleep, but when he crept into the bedroom, slipped off his clothes, and quietly slid under the covers in the dark, Babette announced she was awake.

"I want to talk about our relationship," she said.

"O.K.," said Max, but his eyes slid closed and he was snoring softly three minutes into the discussion.

11

When his phone flashed in the bank of eye-high cubicles that bordered the CRB pit on the floor of the Commodities Exchange, he wasn't looking at it. When Ira Feldman picked it up for him, said hello, and yelled "Petlin!" they were screaming so loud in the pit he didn't hear it.

"Petlin, you dickhead, there's a call for you!" shouted Ira Feldman.

"I'll call back!" shouted Petlin.

"It's a chick!" shouted Feldman.

Petlin bounded up the two maroon-carpeted steps from the pit and grabbed the receiver out of Feldman's hand.

"Petlin," said Petlin.

"Hi," said the caller, "it's Judy Wells."

Judy Wells, Judy Wells, Judy Wells. The name didn't mean dick to him.

"We met a couple of summers ago at the beach," said the woman helpfully. "In Bridgehampton."

"I got to be honest with ya, sweetheart," said Petlin, "I can't truthfully say I remember you. Are you sure you're not confusing me with somebody else?"

"Sold four at forty!" shouted someone from the pit in Petlin's direction.

"You can't trade forty, I'm forty-five bid for five!" shouted Petlin, then uncovered the receiver and said, "Sorry."

"You had a share in a house in Bridgehampton," said Judy Wells. "We had dinner at Bobby Van's. You were drinking margaritas."

Petlin *had* bought a share in a house in Bridgehampton a few years ago, before he'd started pulling in the bigger bucks, and he'd been into margaritas around that period too, but he couldn't for the life of him remember anyone named Judy Wells.

"How's the front spread?" yelled someone else from the pit in Petlin's direction.

"Forty bid at sixty!" shouted Petlin, then uncovered the receiver again.

"I'm sorry, hon," he said. "I wish to Christ I *did* remember you."

Silence at the other end.

"Hey," he said, chuckling, "at least we didn't sleep together, right?"

"Oh, but we did," said Judy Wells.

Petlin laughed sheepishly.

"Shit," said Petlin, "now my face *is* red."

"How's the two-forty straddle offered?" shouted someone from the pit.

"The two-forty straddle's at seven dollars!" shouted Petlin without covering the receiver. "Tellya what, hon," he said in a normal voice. He opened his datebook and saw that tonight was completely free. "How's about I shift a couple things around and we get together tonight for drinks?"

"What time?" said Judy Wells.

Judy Wells had suggested the bar of the Four Seasons restaurant on Fifty-second and Park at six o'clock. Petlin had been there a couple of times, though never to eat. Not his style, and for that kind of bread he preferred to take people to places where he was known.

When Petlin got to the Four Seasons his customary twenty minutes late, he strolled upstairs to the bar area and looked around expectantly. He remembered the enormous ficus trees, the huge cylindrical planters filled with seasonal flowers, the French walnut paneling, the nearly thirty-foot floor-to-ceiling windows curtained with thousands of tiny brass chains, the sculpture composed of hundreds of delicate vertical brass rods hanging over the four-sided oak bar. He was intimidated by all that costly elegance.

Long blond hair, she had said, and a beige silk blouse. After no more than forty seconds Petlin spotted her standing at the bar, sipping a drink.

Judy Wells was a looker. Long blond hair for sure, deep blue eyes, very attractive face, very good body — skirt just tight enough across

44

her buns to get you hot, hem just high enough to make you think you might see something. Stylishly dressed, beautifully made up. About thirty-five was his guess.

Petlin vaguely remembered having spent the night with her now and tried to conjure a vision of her unclothed body, but failed. Hot-looking chick. Though he'd promised to call her again, he never had. He didn't recall why. Not that it mattered.

Petlin asked the maître d' at the desk for a banquette in the grill area, then joined Judy at the crowded bar. At first he was going to drink what she was, Absolut on ice, but then he had a better idea.

"Dos margaritas," he said to the clearly non-Hispanic bartender, adding to Judy, "for old times' sake."

They had several. Petlin regaled Judy with anecdotes about the commodities business in which he always came out shrewder than everybody else. He told her how he'd anticipated the drought of '88 and the effect it would have on grain markets and commodities as a whole. He'd got long soybeans and CRBs and was rewarded when panic in the pits forced grains limit-up for several days. He sold the contracts and made a fucking fortune.

She either understood commodities or was a good listener, probably the latter. He told her how he never stopped working, how he sometimes called Hong Kong at three-thirty in the morning to find out where gold was at, to trade that market. He told her that most of the people he worked with trusted him but feared him, and that they did business with him as much for the fear as for the trust.

"The essence of trading is fear," he said. "Only people with a high threshold for pain can manipulate the market."

"Where does the fear come in?" she said.

"Mainly in long-term positions. In my business, thirty minutes is a long-term position. People in overnight positions wake up in a cold sweat." He chuckled. "That may be one reason traders can't commit to long-term relationships."

She looked at him intently for a moment.

"Are *you* ever afraid?" she asked.

"All the time," he said. "If I'm long, I sometimes wake up in the middle of the night screaming 'Sold!' If I'm short, I wake up yelling 'Buy 'em!'"

She smiled with her mouth, though not, he noticed, with her eyes. The woman was not as young as Petlin liked them, now that he was thirty-five himself, but she was certainly no slouch in the looks department. If he leaned over far enough he could look down her loose silk blouse and make out nice-sized breasts in a low-cut bra. Petlin considered sleeping with her again chiefly because he couldn't recall what she'd been like in bed the other time.

They were never able to get a banquette in the grill area, and after several more rounds of margaritas Petlin suggested they move on to dinner at the Palm Too on Second Avenue where he pretended to know the owner. They had to wait an hour at the bar for a table, and it was so noisy they could barely hear each other, but finally they were seated. Petlin called the waitress "sweetheart" and ordered a white wine with dinner which he told Judy was his personal favorite but which was too sweet by half.

During dinner Judy casually dropped her hand onto Petlin's knee. At first he thought it was a mistake, but she never moved it. Marveling at his good fortune, Petlin invited her back to his place for a nightcap.

Petlin's apartment was a one-bedroom condo in a pretentious but cheaply built luxury building on Second Avenue at Eighty-second Street. The building had both a doorman and a concierge, lots of marble, brass, and polished granite in the lobby.

The apartment itself had a smallish living room that featured a champagne-colored crushed-velvet seating arrangement, color prints of sporting events by Leroy Neiman, and a microscopic terrace with high-floor views of ugly rooftops.

Petlin made Irish coffee for them in his walk-in kitchen, and after slurping down half of his he gave Judy a big open-mouthed kiss and led her toward the bedroom. Stepping carefully out of her caramel leather Bennis and Edwards shoes, she picked up her bulky leather purse and allowed herself to be led.

Keeping his mouth fastened to hers, as if he feared a broken connection would cut off whatever voltage was passing between them, Petlin unbuttoned her blouse and let it fall to the floor. He unzipped her skirt and pulled it down, then reached behind her back with one hand and unhooked her bra with three fingers, a trick he always thought identified him as a swordsman.

Petlin slid her half-slip down over her hips, then her pantyhose and panties, then undressed himself, only breaking the mouth-to-mouth connection when they were both naked.

46

He regarded her naked body and winked. She was even better without clothes. Judy smiled at him, reached into her purse, and produced a rolled condom. Petlin raised his eyebrows, shrugged, then laughed.

"Why not?" he said.

He rolled the thing on. Then he pushed her down on his king-sized bed and climbed on top of her.

At the conclusion of their brief but breathless love-making Petlin sighed deeply, sank back into his pillow, shut his eyes, and composed himself for sleep.

With her heart beating in her ears, Judy again reached into her purse, withdrew a small, flat, plastic object the size of a pack of matches on which was printed in embossed letters *Kwik-Kut Touch-Knife,* and slid out a retractable razor blade. With mounting excitement of a decidedly sexual nature she caressed the dozing Petlin's neck. Then, with one swift motion, she plunged the blade deeply into the flesh and severed his carotid artery.

Bright red arterial blood began spurting out of Petlin's neck, two ounces per pulsebeat. It hit her in the face and the eyes, spattering all over her upper body. Petlin, incredulous, popped his eyes open and couldn't believe what was happening.

"What the *fuck!* Oh my *God!* What the *fuck!*" he said, continuing to pulse out two ounces of blood with every heartbeat.

"Jesus fucking Christ, what did you *do* to me! Are you *crazy?* Oh, Jesus, look at that fucking *blood!* Help me! Call an ambulance! Call the *cops!* Help me!"

He grabbed for a pillow and tried to press it against his wound, but the pressure barely slowed the bleeding. He was already weak from sex and drinking, and the sudden loss of blood was making him so dizzy he couldn't think straight. He looked wildly around for help, for a phone, for anything, but there was nothing within reach.

"What the fuck *is* this? What did you do to me? Oh my God, I'm going to *die!*"

Judy Wells studied Petlin's dying throes with great interest, her eyes bright, her pulse pounding.

"*Help* me, for God's sake, *help* me!"

He lunged at her. She backed away just beyond his reach and continued to watch him intently.

Petlin's eyes glazed over. He sank slowly down on the bed, staring up at the naked blond woman splattered with his blood, streaming with his blood.

"Why?" he asked, as gray cotton wool descended over his vision. "*Why?*"

"Because I don't want you to live anymore," she said simply, and her mind drifted back to the summer in Bridgehampton.

What Judy thinks she'll do this August is spend some weekends in the Hamptons, cool out a little from the stress of the city, take long, leisurely walks on the beach, do some body surfing, get a tan, maybe do a bit of writing. And, O.K., who's she kidding, maybe meet a nice guy and have a summer romance or even something that goes on into the cold weather.

What a lot of the girls she knows are doing is taking shares in houses on or near the beach. Not that she needs to do that financially, what with her trust fund and all, but hanging out with a bunch of girls might be a way to get into the social whirl — get blitzed with fellow group-ers at Melon's or Bobby Van's and if a cute guy happened along it would take a bit of the awkwardness out of a first meeting.

The only problem is, she doesn't know anybody well enough to ask if she can go in on a group house with them. So what she does instead is rent a room for four weekends in August at the Green Acres motel, just outside of Bridgehampton on Route 27, which turns out to be a bargain in neither cost nor charm. For the same money she's spending in a depressing little shoebox of a room with traffic whooshing by six feet from her window at all hours of the day and night she could probably have rented a whole house, albeit a modest one, and really enjoyed herself.

The first Saturday morning of her month in Bridgehampton she stands in front of the cracked full-length mirror on the motel bathroom door and checks out her new bathing suit, the one Rose Brill insisted she buy even though it's cut so high on the thighs she's had to wax off prac-tically all her pubic hair except for a little thatch right in the middle.

It's not a bad effect, not bad at all. With the weight she's taken off and the way the new bathing suit fits, she looks pretty damned sexy, despite her slug-white skin. She packs her beach bag, gets into her rented Mustang convertible, and drives to the beach.

The weather is perfect, the sun baking into her SPF 25–coated skin, the breeze off the Atlantic just cool enough to check the sweat and prevent her from feeling like she's working on a melanoma. She unrolls a straw beach mat and sits down to read the *New York Times Book*

Review until somebody nice walks by. There are plenty of nice-looking somebodies on the beach, but they all seem to be in clusters, and she knows there isn't much chance a cluster of guys is simply going to cruise over to her mat and start shooting the shit.

The clear sky is as littered with commercial messages as prime-time TV. Two biplanes trail dangerously heavy signs in opposite directions along the beach between West Hampton and Montauk, urging sunbathers to buy Reebok running shoes and to attend a disco in Wainscott called the Slime Pit. Higher up five planes flying in tight formation release simultaneous puffs of smoke, trying to spell out something in the turbulent upper air that spreads into indecipherable balls of cotton before anyone can read what it is.

Judy doesn't meet anybody on that first weekend at the beach or on the second one either, and by weekend number three she realizes that she's doomed to spend the entire month alone and that the investment in the Green Acres motel has been a colossal fiasco.

Coming out of the surf on the fourth and final Saturday of the month, pulling at her wet suit that has ridden up into her crotch, she is struck hard in the right temple by the edge of a fluorescent pink Frisbee. The guy who threw the Frisbee is all over her with apologies. He's reasonably cute looking, so even though he's nearly taken out her eye she pretends it was nothing. The guy has thinning blondish hair and not a bad build. He tells her his name is Freddy Petlin. He is, he says, a trader.

She knows nothing about the commodities market and cares less, but by appearing to be interested in it she manages an invitation to dinner. He suggests they meet at Bobby Van's. She doesn't want him to see her depressing room at the motel but thinks it would've been nice if he'd at least made the gesture of offering to pick her up.

"Dos margaritas, por favor, señor," says Petlin to the bartender at Bobby Van's when he sees Judy come in the door. The bartender chuckles as if he knows Petlin. Petlin seems to know a lot of people at Bobby Van's.

"I got to be honest with ya, sweetheart," Petlin tells Judy just loudly enough to be overheard when she joins him at the bar, "I almost didn't recognize you with your clothes on."

The bartender guffaws and Petlin throws him a huge wink, as though he's already scored with her. She considers leaving, then stays because she is, A, hungry and, B, cannot bear the thought of even one more dinner by herself in her motel room or in a restaurant where everybody

49

else has somebody to eat with and is staring at her with pity.

Instead of leaving she chugalugs her margarita, which prompts Petlin and several people at the bar to shout *"Olé!"* She congratulates herself on having made a healthy decision.

By the time they finish dinner neither of them is feeling any pain, and when Petlin suggests she come back to his place for a drink she is both too drunk and too horny to be coy.

Petlin's room in the weathered white clapboard house in the dunes is not much larger than hers in the motel, lending scant support to his claims of being a hot trader. Their love-making doesn't make the earth move, hardly makes the innerspring move, but it's her first intimate contact with the opposite sex in a very long time and this inflates its importance disproportionately.

When Petlin drops her back at the Bobby Van's parking lot he pulls out a worn black leather phone book and makes a big display of entering both her city phone number and the one in the motel, even though tomorrow is her last day there.

"Talk to ya tomorrow, sweetheart," he says, giving her a smooch and a squeeze, gallantly opening the door of her convertible. "We'll spend the day together, maybe stop by Loaves and Fishes first and pick up something to eat at the beach. That sound good?"

"Perfect."

She drives back to the motel glowing, reviewing the day like a video, rewriting Petlin's dialogue at the beach and in the restaurant, revising his love-making, making him presentable to her internal review board.

She smiles. So he's a little coarse. Given some time, she'll sand down his rough edges and teach him some class. She'll use what Rose Brill taught her and enjoy reversing the roles.

The next day, Sunday, she gets up early, walks into the motel office, and sits down in the rickety wicker rocker opposite the check-in desk, awaiting Petlin's call.

A teenaged girl with a modified blond crewcut and three pimples on her face chews bubble gum and listens to Steve Winwood through headphones. Judy can hear the tinny beat, though not the melody.

An old electric fan on the counter alternately blows on the desk clerk and on Judy. The room is warm. Judy gazes outside at the bright sunshine she is missing on her last day of the summer, then watches the hands click slowly around the office clock.

She grows increasingly self-conscious and apologetic in front of the desk clerk. Petlin will call any minute now, she thinks. Maybe he's hungover and slept late. After all those margaritas that's probably it. She doesn't want to call him. Anyway, she doesn't have his number.

Shortly after one she figures the hell with him, hungover or not, this is ridiculous. What the fuck is she waiting around for, she'll go to the goddam beach alone — but she doesn't. The teenaged girl shares a club sandwich with her and she drinks a Diet Pepsi from the machine.

When Petlin hasn't called by four o'clock Judy swallows her humiliation, bids farewell to the girl, packs up all her things, and drives back to the city.

She doesn't know what to think. To think she has been just a one night stand is too painful. She decides that some emergency has come up — Petlin cut himself savagely while shaving and was rushed to Southampton Hospital to be stitched up, or his mother went into cardiac arrest and he had to race back to the city, something like that. He'd call her later that night or the following morning in the city for sure and apologize, and she'd be sympathetic and not even mention that he'd totally ruined her last day in the Hamptons.

She turns in her rented Mustang at Hertz and takes a cab back to her apartment. Unlocking her door, she hears the phone ring and bursts in, tripping on the throw rug, managing to spear the phone on the ninth ring, only to find it's Rose Brill, wanting to know what time Judy is planning to pick up the cat.

She persuades Rose to deliver the cat, a shameless imposition, and for the rest of the night she is never more than a foot from the phone. When she finally climbs into bed that night she installs the phone on the pillow beside hers, a sad substitute for a lover.

The next morning, Monday, before taking a shower she puts a message on her answering machine meant only for Petlin, then erases it, not wanting to look that anxious. She turns off the shower three times and bolts from the stall, certain she's heard the phone ring.

He never calls. He *never* calls. For the longest time she's simply not able to understand how he can make love to her and promise to call her the next day and then totally forget her. And then, finally, she is able.

When Petlin was quite dead she approached him closely and studied his face. Its expression of utter amazement was one he would now wear until it rotted. Gazing at him and recalling the incident in Bridgehampton, she was suddenly overcome by a wave of fury, and pummeled his nose and mouth repeatedly with both fists. The fury ebbed and she regained control of herself.

Her flesh was as red with Petlin's blood as were the bed and the adjoining walls. She strolled into Petlin's bathroom and ran a hot tub. She carefully wiped all the blood off her body with a warm, wet washcloth, then removed all her makeup. Then she got into the tub and soaked languorously for fully twenty minutes. She was exhausted and the hot water felt delicious.

When she'd toweled herself dry, she reached a final time into her bulky purse and withdrew some recent purchases from the Pleasure Chest. Carefully wiping them clean of her own fingerprints, she held them in a towel and took them over to where Petlin lay. She wrapped his limp fingers around each of the items in turn, making sure to get some clear impressions on the chrome surfaces.

Then she opened the top drawer of his bureau, pushed aside his rolled socks and undershorts and T-shirts, and buried the objects beneath them.

She rummaged around in Petlin's bedroom closet, selected a pair of pleated tan wool slacks and a bulky white fisherman's sweater, and put them on. In the closet adjoining the entry door she found a long tan topcoat and a mouse-colored felt hat with a fairly wide brim. She piled her long blond hair up on top of her head and pushed it under the hat.

Then she rolled up her own clothes, stuffed them into a plastic shopping bag from the Food Emporium, and left the apartment. Descending in the elevator, she looked at her watch. It was almost one A.M. The whole thing had taken only forty minutes longer than she'd planned.

12

Judy Wells lives with her mom and dad in Lake Forest, Illinois, an affluent suburb north of Chicago. The neo-Elizabethan house sits at the edge of five wooded acres on the shore of Lake Michigan. Its fourteen rooms are nine more than the family uses and have been decorated without the usual tiresome limitations of either budget or good taste. The improbable mix of furniture and artifacts has come from garage sales, pretentious antique shops, and furniture stores that advertise on TV after the late-late show.

Judy's dad, Todd Wells, is the brains behind the Todd'ler Town baby furniture dynasty. People love Todd Wells. Todd Wells is the ultimate salesman. Saw the need for a line of products, went right out and sold them before they even existed. Small matter of putting together the right designer and manufacturer once he'd sold the line. If the line hadn't been produced he'd have given back all the money. Well, anyway, that's what he's always maintained. Never had to find out, because the line was so successful that in five years Todd was able to buy out the manufacturer.

Todd is a social drinker. Drinks with the clients, drinks with the suppliers, drinks with the sales reps, drinks with the distributors, then comes home and drinks with the family. Sometimes when he drinks with the family it makes him jolly. Sometimes it doesn't.

"So the fella says to me, Todd, he says, I got to be honest with you. I got to be honest. The only way a clamp-on baby seat coulda collapsed under the weight of an eighteen-month-old baby is if that baby was a goddam baby *walrus*. I says to him, I says, Wesley, I says. . . . Judy, honey, didn't I tell you that the one napoleon was all you were going to have tonight?"

"Mommy said I could have two."

"Mommy said you could have two? *Mommy* said? Well, *I* said you could have fucking *one!*"

"Todd, for pity *sakes*," says her mother, covering her own mouth instead of her husband's.

The chubby child, ignoring her father's coarse admonition, tries to stuff the entire pastry into her cheeks. The slap, although not unexpected, catches her off balance and sends her and her Hepplewhite chair crashing to the floor.

She explodes in tears, more from the indignity than from the sting of the slap.

"You want something to *cry* about, I'll fucking *give* you something to cry about," says Todd, breathing hard. "Now get the fuck out of here and into your room!"

With deep choking sobs, Judy picks herself up from the thick carpet, scuttles crablike from the dining room into the sanctuary of her bedroom, and flings herself upon her bed. She lies there in humiliation and misery, her body convulsed in irregularly spaced sobs, and imagines what her father's face might look like if one of the family Cadillacs ran over it. She can clearly picture the crushed, melonlike skull, the gooey brains, the blood spurting out of the eye sockets. Eventually the sobs subside completely and she drifts into an unrefreshing sleep.

Later. Much later.

A soft tap at her door. The room is still dark. It is well past midnight. A clumsy figure shuffles into the room and sinks heavily down beside her on the too-soft innerspring Beautyrest.

Her dream slowly disintegrates; shards of an incomprehensible scene between her and somebody she doesn't recognize are still very real yet already forgotten. She stirs, senses the presence beside her on the bed, realizes who it is, and feigns sleep. The figure beside her places a bearlike paw on her shoulder and pats it for several minutes, then lays his heavy head on the small of her back and, still patting, begins to weep.

It is not the first time this has happened. It will not be the last. Virginia Wells does not approve of her husband's behavior, but neither does she intercede on her daughter's behalf. Virginia has her own difficulties with Todd but decided some time back never to leave him. "We deserve whatever Daddy does to us," she tells her daughter on more than one occasion. She never explains what she means by this

54

ominous declaration, and the little girl is afraid to ask, fearing she already knows.

Late at night Judy frequently hears shouting from her parents' suite. The shouting is usually about women. Todd Wells is, for reasons not apparent to his male colleagues, irresistible to women. When Todd is out of town on business Virginia telephones his motels to make sure he is registered alone. He is always registered alone, but this proves nothing to Virginia because, as she explains to her daughter, "When you sleep with hookers you don't sign their names on the motel register."

Judy is not sure what hookers are or why anybody would want to sleep with them. She imagines them to be women who, like the pirate captains in her storybooks, have hooks instead of hands. The image of her father asleep in beds with women who have hooks instead of hands is a recurrent theme in her nightmares.

Judy finds her anger toward her father too threatening to bear and begins to deny his abusive behavior. He *can't* be that bad, she decides, she must have caused him to act that way. He is right to abuse her. She's the bad one, he's above reproach.

Judy is painfully shy and secretive. Although she lacks a sense of how human relationships work, she begins to construct a believable public image, a mask of deferential politeness and normality. She learns when and in what tone of voice and in what posture to say "oh, please" and "thank you so much" and "I'm so terribly sorry." Although she lacks normal emotions, she becomes adept at simulating them. Like an alien form of life, she learns appropriate human behavior through mimicry. She secretly fears that she is evil.

At age nine she discovers Robert Louis Stevenson's *Dr. Jekyll and Mr. Hyde* and is mesmerized by it. She fantasizes nocturnal forays out of her Lake Forest home in which she meets solitary men on the road and caves their skulls in with a fire tool. She comes across the movie *The Three Faces of Eve* and feels she's begun to understand herself. She isn't a multiple personality like Eve, unaware of her other selves: she is Hyde, masquerading as Jekyll.

Todd buys his daughter extravagant presents. An IBM Selectric typewriter. A Funk & Wagnalls dictionary so fat and heavy it requires its own wooden stand. Books of poetry. Keats. Shelley. Swinburne. Poetry too succulent for delicate girls. Todd encourages Judy to write her own poems and praises even her clumsiest efforts.

"This is *dynamite,* puss," he says. "Just look at this stuff, Virginia —our daughter is a *poet,* a goddam natural born *poet!*"

At age ten Judy sends off a turgid poem she's written to *Onyx,* a small literary quarterly published in Lake Forest. It's a passable poem for an adult; for a ten-year-old it's outstanding. Judy hovers near the mailbox at the end of the wooded driveway for five weeks, waiting for a response. She is certain her gift is about to be recognized. She can practically see her byline in the table of contents.

On the thirty-sixth day an envelope arrives from *Onyx.* Judy excitedly rips it open and reads the letter:

> Dear contributor:
> Thank you for the enclosed submission. We regret it does not seem suitable for *Onyx* at the present time and are returning it herewith.

The girl is devastated, the dream of seeing her name in the table of contents smashed. Todd finds her sobbing in her room, tears soaking her robin's egg blue chenille bedspread. Todd reads the printed rejection slip. Then he reads the poem. Then he tries to comfort her. She is inconsolable.

"I'm sure it was an error, puss," he says, holding her in his arms and caressing her back. "I'm sure they sent you the wrong letter. This poem is dynamite."

The following morning Todd goes without an appointment to the offices of *Onyx* magazine and asks to see the editor. The editor, Edward Montrose, is a young man with a wispy moustache and round, wire-rimmed glasses. Montrose has heard Todd's name in the community and welcomes him into his office.

"What can I do for you, Mr. Wells?" asks Montrose, with a slightly perplexed smile.

"You can correct a clerical error that's causing my daughter a good deal of needless pain," says Todd pleasantly.

"What clerical error is that?" says Montrose, frowning.

"The one that caused this poem to be rejected by your publication," says Todd, extending the rejected manuscript.

Montrose scans the poem briefly, then hands it back to Todd.

"There hasn't been any error," says Montrose. "I sent that one back myself."

"In my opinion," says Todd carefully, "this poem is exceptionally well written and deserves to be published in *Onyx.*

"In *my* opinion," says Montrose, "this poem is, at best, the mediocre work of someone who will probably improve with experience. How old is your daughter, Mr. Wells?"

"Ten," says Todd.

"Ten," says Montrose. "Well then, she will most certainly improve with experience. Thank you for coming to see me, Mr. Wells."

Montrose rises, indicating the meeting is over, but Todd makes no move to go.

"Just as a matter of curiosity," says Todd, "if you *had* accepted my daughter's poem for publication, what would you be paying her?"

"I don't know," says Montrose. "Twenty-five dollars, most likely. Our editorial budget here is quite modest, I'm afraid."

"Twenty-five dollars," says Todd.

"Yes," says Montrose.

Todd takes a fat roll of hundred-dollar bills out of his pants, counts out ten of them, and places them carefully on the corner of the editor's desk.

"Publish this poem," says Todd pleasantly, "and you can use this to make your editorial budget less modest."

Montrose stares at the money for a moment without any expression. He has never seen a thousand dollars in cash.

"Is this a bribe, Mr. Wells?" says Montrose.

"If you like," says Todd.

"I see. If you're not out of my office within sixty seconds," says the editor in a tight, controlled voice, "I will summon the police and have you forcibly ejected."

Todd shrugs, slowly picks up his money, puts it back into his pants, and leaves.

By offering its surprised stockholders precisely twice its book value Todd succeeds in buying *Onyx* from them by the close of business that day. The following morning he returns to the publication and strides directly into Montrose's office.

"Now it's *my* turn," says Todd. "If you're not out of my office within sixty seconds, I will summon the police and have you forcibly ejected."

When the shaken Montrose has emptied his desk drawers into a plastic garbage bag and departed, Todd promotes the editor's secretary to her former boss's job, then dictates a letter to Judy explaining that an unfortunate clerical error has caused her to receive a rejection slip instead of an enthusiastic letter of acceptance.

The letter is delivered to Judy by messenger that afternoon. When the girl reads it she is at first incredulous, then ecstatic. When Todd comes home that night Judy shows him the letter.

"I *told* you that rejection was a mistake, puss," he says.

Todd takes out a bottle of Dom Perignon and they toast Judy's new career as a poet. Everyone gets a little tipsy.

When Judy's poem appears in the next issue of *Onyx* Todd quietly sells the publication back to its former stockholders for half of what he'd paid.

One night when Judy is twelve years old, Todd invites several employees of Todd'ler Town and their spouses to dinner. The family cook has prepared coq au vin, and although it's not a good coq au vin, the employees are innocent of this fact.

Todd is drinking heavily. Despite her mother's protests, Judy is now permitted to drink wine at dinner, and she asks for a third glass. When Todd refuses, she becomes disrespectful.

"I'd like you to apologize to me and to our guests," says Todd in a voice that causes crosstalk to cease.

"Oh, shove it up your ass," says Judy.

In front of eight virtual strangers, Todd seizes his daughter roughly by the shoulders and turns her over his knee. She writhes and shrieks, vainly trying to escape. The guests can't believe what they are witnessing.

"Todd," says Virginia in warning.

Todd immobilizes the girl, lifts her skirt above her waist, yanks down her underpants, and spanks her so hard he leaves imprints of his splayed fingers on her plump gluteal cheeks. She flees the room, mortally degraded.

Very late that night Todd once again shambles into her darkened room, sinks heavily to his knees, puts his head on her mattress, and weeps.

"I'm sorry, puss," he whispers. "My God, I'm so dreadfully sorry. I don't deserve to be your father, I really don't deserve it."

He tries to take her in his arms but she resists him.

"Let me make it up to you," he whispers. "I'll do anything. How can I make it up to you?"

She wrenches herself violently out of his grasp.

"Please don't turn away from me, puss," he says. "You don't know how much that hurts me."

58

She will not permit his touch.

"You're my best girl," he says. "Do you know that? I love you more than anybody in the whole entire world, do you know that? I even love you more than Mommy. *Much* more than Mommy.''

Judy doesn't know what to make of this declaration or of anything else about her father's behavior, for that matter. She tells herself over and over that he's not to blame, that she deserves whatever he does to her. She never knows when he's going to be verbally or physically abusive and when he's going to be weepy and affectionate. When he's in his weepy and affectionate moods, he always calls her his best girl. Her mother doesn't like that. Judy doesn't like it herself.

Her mother is not much comfort to the girl emotionally, preferring to concentrate on matters of personal hygiene instead. In years to come Judy will look back on her childhood and decide that the only things her mother ever taught her were to tear off three sheets of toilet paper and fold them neatly in thirds in order to wipe herself, and to spit on both ends of a length of toilet paper before putting it down on the seat in a public restroom so it didn't slide off when you sat down.

Her mother often lectures Judy about the evils of the flesh. Almost every night her mother tucks Judy into bed. She tucks the blankets around her so tightly that Judy can scarcely move, and she always makes sure to put Judy's arms outside the blankets. Her mother never explains why she does this, but in years to come Judy realizes this practice was designed to discourage her from masturbating.

Judy is not at all interested in masturbating. Perhaps her mother is. In fact, Judy has gotten the message that bodies are embarrassing and private parts ugly. Judy doesn't understand why some people enjoy looking at other people without clothes on.

By the time she's fourteen, a woman's breasts and buttocks have erupted through Judy's plump girlish body. She has a pretty face, but is still fat. She has grown to find her father's touch physically repellent. She goes out of her way to avoid physical contact with him and will not even let him kiss her. He acts like a jilted suitor, which confuses and embarrasses her.

Judy goes to her mother for commiseration.

"Don't talk to me about that," says her mother.

"Why not?" says Judy.

Her mother shakes her head.

"Why not?" says Judy.

"Because I can't help you there," says her mother.

"Just tell me why Daddy acts so strangely towards me. At times he acts like I'm not his daughter but his *girlfriend* or something."

"I'm sure you'd know more about that than I," says her mother tersely and turns away.

"What do you mean?"

"Where there's smoke there's fire," says her mother, lips so tight no pink shows, and leaves the room.

Judy can't understand it. Her mom acts as if she thinks Judy's having an affair with her father. Which is ridiculous. At least she *thinks* it's ridiculous.

Both her parents continue to behave as though Judy is her father's lover. Sometimes Judy finds herself feeling as apprehensive and guilty as if this were true. Many years later a psychotherapist would ask if she ever recalled her father touching her in places where he shouldn't have. She would say no, but she'd honestly not be able to remember.

13

"Since when do they got fags working on construction crews?" asked Caruso bemusedly, climbing out of the Plymouth Fury at the Fifty-seventh Street jobsite.

"Yeah," said Max, eagerly anticipating Caruso's reaction when he first saw Albert Prince, assuming Prince looked anything like his buddies at the Mindshaft, "you wonder how they could even swing a hammer with those limp wrists."

But before they could ask for Prince, Max's Motorola handset crackled and they were told to haul ass over to Eighty-second and Second. A man named Frederick Petlin was D.O.A. in his apartment with the same m.o. as the Smiley case. Max slapped the revolving red light on the roof of the car, hit the siren, and began broken-field driving toward Eighty-second Street.

By the time they reached Petlin's building, the street was choked with vehicles: radio cars, a CSU van, unmarked detective Plymouth Furys — the NYPD had gotten a good buy on Furys — and assorted vans from TV stations. Max hit the yelp under the dash to move the civilians out of the way.

A uniform on the sidewalk told them what apartment number. They flashed their shields at the doorman and the concierge and went up in the elevator.

The crime scene was loaded. Because there had been another homicide in Midtown so recently with the same m.o., the chief of detectives had pulled two dozen men "off the chart" — that is, he'd taken them off the day and night tour system — to canvass for witnesses. Two uniforms let them into the apartment.

Max recognized Brannigan, an overweight detective from the Nineteenth PDU who had nicotine-stained teeth and prematurely gray hair.

"Yo, Brannigan," said Caruso.

"Whattaya say, guys?" said Brannigan.

"This your case?" said Max.

"Yeah," said Brannigan. "Chernin just left. He estimates time of death was somewhere around midnight last night."

"Same perp?" said Caruso.

"Looks that way," said Brannigan. "Same m.o. anyways."

"You really think it's the same guy," said Max, "or is it a copycat?"

Brannigan shrugged.

"My money, it's the same guy," said Brannigan. "Also we found something."

"What?" said Max.

Brannigan led Max and Caruso into the bedroom. Petlin's body lay on the bed in about the same position as had Smiley's. There was the wound to the carotid, the bashed face, the blood all over the sheets and on the walls.

"So what did you find?" asked Max.

"This," said Brannigan. Using his handkerchief on the rectangular brass pulls, he carefully slid open the top drawer of the dresser at the foot of the bed and pushed aside piles of rolled socks and undershorts. Under the clothing lay a pair of handcuffs, a couple of alligator clips, a butt plug, an enormous dildo, a cock ring, and a complicated affair composed of chains, buckles, and leather straps.

"S and M stuff," said Max, turning to Caruso. "Fag stuff. Were we right about this guy or what?"

Caruso nodded.

"This the kinda stuff they use on you at the Mindshaft, Max?" said Caruso. "Max here is one of their charter members."

Max flashed Brannigan an uncertain look to see if there was any chance he might be taking Caruso's hazing seriously. He couldn't tell, and didn't want to risk acting as if he was worried about it by explaining what he'd been doing at the Mindshaft, even though it was legitimate police business.

"You better make sure the crime scene guys dust that stuff good," said Max, hoping to ease away from Mindshaft talk.

"Yeah," said Brannigan, "I'll tell 'em. You guys wanna put a few latents on it first?"

Max and Caruso laughed self-consciously, their cheeks and foreheads reddening.

62

"Good news travels fast, I see," said Max.

"It's not like we was the only *ones*," said Caruso defensively. "O'Rourke and Marshad had their mitts all over everything too."

"Whyn't you jokers just wear gloves?" asked Brannigan, carefully putting the stuff back into the drawer.

"Hey, give us a break," said Max.

A uniform walked into the bedroom.

"Detective Segal, there's a female outside wants to come in and look around. I told her this was a sealed crime scene, but she says she's a friend of yours."

"A friend of *mine?*" said Max. "Is she a reporter?"

"Uh, yeah. From a magazine. The *New Yorker*, I think."

"Oh, shit," said Caruso.

"She's O.K.," said Max. "Let her in."

Caruso heaved a huge sigh.

"What do *you* care?" said Max.

"I don't," said Caruso.

"Then shut the fuck up," said Max.

Susan came into the bedroom. She looked sensational. Her cheeks were flushed. Max was surprised how glad he was to see her.

"Hi, Max," she said shyly, glancing at the body on the bed, then looking quickly away.

"Hi, Susan," he said.

"I figured you'd be here," she said. "I hope you don't mind my using your name, but I thought it would be valuable research for my story."

"It *will* be valuable," said Max. "This isn't for publication, but it seems to be the same killer."

"That's what they're saying out in the hall," said Susan.

"Well," said Caruso, "if that's what they're saying out in the *hall*, they must be right."

Susan and Max looked at Caruso.

"Sal and I were just about to start canvassing the building," said Max, holding his gaze on his partner. "Would you like to tag along?"

"Oh, I'd *love* to," said Susan. "But wouldn't I be in the way?"

"Not at all," said Max.

"Max, could I talk to you a minute?" said Caruso.

"Sure, Sal," said Max.

They walked into Petlin's bathroom and closed the door.

"The fuck are you doing?" said Caruso.

"Just humor me, Sal, will you?" said Max.

"I don't *want* to humor you. Why the fuck should I humor you? She has as much place in this investigation as tits on a boar."

"Just do this for me," said Max. "As a personal favor. I'll owe you."

"You owe me already," said Caruso.

"As a personal favor, Sal," said Max. "Please."

"Fuck!" said Caruso.

He opened the door and walked into the bedroom.

"Miss Simon," said Caruso with a trace of sarcasm, "Detective Segal and I would be *honored* if you'd join us on our canvass."

"I hope to hell you guys didn't contaminate that bathroom," said Brannigan.

"We didn't contaminate the fucking bathroom," said Max.

"No?" said Brannigan. "Did you handle the doorknob with a hand-kerchief?"

Max closed his eyes.

On the canvass Max and Caruso interviewed the concierge, who seemed to recall Petlin entering about ten-thirty the previous night with a blond woman, and saw them leave after an hour or so. The doorman recalled Petlin entering alone. A neighbor named George Hutchins, who lived three doors down on Petlin's floor, said he saw a man leaving Petlin's apartment about one A.M. with two shopping bags. The man, he said, looked kind of swishy.

With Susan accompanying them, Max and Caruso spent the entire tour canvassing Petlin's building and local merchants. Petlin's neighbors weren't any more helpful than Smiley's. Unlike Smiley's, Petlin's neighbors were certain he wasn't homosexual. Far from deterring them, this fact only served to convince Max and Caruso that Petlin was gay, but deeply in the closet.

With the discovery of the S and M equipment in Petlin's bureau drawer, alternate theories of ritual murder and revenge had fallen by the wayside. To a man, the entire task force was now convinced they were dealing with a sadistic homosexual murderer.

At about eleven P.M. Max bought slices of pizza and cans of Coke Classic for himself, his partner, and Susan. They were on their way to interview a woman on Central Park South named Jennifer Riker whom they'd gotten from Petlin's address book, when they were redirected by radio back up to Harlem.

It was a "fresh kill" — a Black youth found dead of gunshot wounds at 110th Street and Seventh Avenue, the northernmost boundary of Central Park. Three suspects had been apprehended at the scene and were already in custody.

The case appeared to be a "grounder" — detectives' baseball-oriented term for an easily solved case — but all of Manhattan North's detectives were in Midtown working the Smiley and Petlin cases. The lieutenant urgently needed somebody back uptown. Susan asked if she could come with them. Max looked at Caruso and said it wasn't really kosher, and if she came she had to promise not to write about it.

Susan said she promised.

14

They could see the crowd from a block away: the Crime Scene Unit van, the EMS bus, and four sector cars. Max double-parked the Fury on Central Park North just west of Seventh and locked the doors — more because they kept their twelve-hundred-dollar portable radios under the seat than because they feared the vehicle itself would be stolen.

Caruso, Max, and Susan walked swiftly across the street and shouldered their way through the crowd of Black men, women, and children who were being held behind a fluorescent orange plastic ribbon by half a dozen uniformed patrolmen. The ribbon had been stretched around the perimeter of the outdoor crime scene from tree to tree, with signs hanging from it proclaiming *Crime Scene, Do Not Pass*.

"What've we got?" said Max to one of the uniforms.

"D.O.A.'s named Billy Monroe," said the uniform. "A crack dealer. Had several people working for him. He's sixteen. Victim's family is over on the benches."

Max, Caruso, and Susan glanced where the patrolman was pointing. Off to the left of the body there were three park benches full of weeping relatives. A large Black woman had fainted and lay on one of the benches. On an adjoining bench a white-coated blond EMS man in his early twenties with a stethoscope draped casually around his neck was giving oxygen to a light-skinned Black girl who appeared to be about twelve years old. The woman who'd fainted was identified as the boy's mother, the twelve-year-old girl was his sister.

"I hear they already collared the perps," said Caruso.

The uniform nodded, delighted at the chance to brief gold shields on what had happened.

"Three suspects, Black males," said the uniform. "They were spotted fleeing the scene by a gypsy cab driver. He alerted an anti-crime unit that happened to be nearby and they made the collar."

"Where they holding them?" asked Max.

"At the Two-Eight," said the uniform, indicating the Twenty-eighth Precinct at St. Nicholas and 122nd.

With Susan following, Max and Caruso walked up and inspected the dead boy. He was lying parallel to the Central Park retaining wall, his face mashed down into the dirt, blood seeping from his nose and mouth, one arm outflung as if hailing a cab. The boy's eyes and mouth were open. He was quite tall for sixteen. He was dressed in blue jeans, a white T-shirt, a hooded blue sweatshirt, brand new hightop Reebok basketball shoes, and a blue Yankee baseball cap.

Susan looked at the large wet urine stain at his crotch.

"When people die, their sphincters relax," Max told her.

Two CSU men arrived in a radio car. They were running later than usual. CSU response times to crime scenes had been significantly worsened since the unit moved to the Bronx. The old location at Broadway and Chambers, though rat infested, was at least centrally located and was about a block away from the Latent Fingerprint Unit at One Police Plaza. When the city squeezed the CSU into a woefully inadequate space in one of the most dangerous sections of the Bronx, the official reason was increased efficiency. That was a joke, of course. The space was much too small and the location much too far away from most potential crime scenes. The real reason for the move was that it had been the city's payoff to giant real estate developers in the Bronx who'd been promised a unit of cops who worked twenty-four hours a day in marked cars.

It was an unseasonably warm April night. The CSU men, wearing slacks, short-sleeved white shirts, large revolvers in holsters, and handcuffs in handcuff cases on their belts, went to work. One took photographs, then held a portable searchlight on the body as the other, wearing white surgical gloves, unceremoniously yanked the body this way and that, looking for bullet wounds.

The CSU man with the rubber gloves pulled down the collar of the boy's sweatshirt and T-shirt, revealing a small entry wound in the back of his neck. There was a stippling effect on the boy's skin from powder burns, indicating that the gun had been fired at very close range. The CSU man squeezed the wound to see if the bullet would come out.

67

It didn't. Then he rolled the boy over and pulled his sweatshirt and T-shirt up to his face. There was a much larger wound under the boy's right arm, oozing blood. Again the CSU man squeezed the wound and probed it, hoping to recover the bullet, and again he was unsuccessful.

The CSU man with the gloves searched in the boy's scalp and then in his mouth for more wounds but found none. The CSU man holding the searchlight made marks showing the location of the bullet holes on a physiological diagram of the body clamped to a metal clipboard.

One live nine millimeter round was found alongside the body and one spent shell casing. The two CSU men took the searchlight around the retaining wall and foraged in the tall grass of the park for the murder weapon. A moment later they had it, a new nine millimeter Beretta automatic worth six hundred dollars.

They noted the serial number of the gun on the clipboard and dusted it for latent prints with white powder. Then the man with the searchlight took out a retractable steel rule and began measuring the distance from the body to the retaining wall, from the body to the trees, and from the retaining wall to the spot where they had recovered the weapon.

While the CSU man measured and sketched, two uniformed patrolmen walked up to the body. One patrolman put on rubber gloves and began going through the boy's pockets for money and other valuables, which he handed to the other patrolman, who put them in a brown paper bag to be vouchered back at the precinct. When they were through they walked away, leaving the boy lying face down in the dirt.

"Cain't you cover him?" said a female voice from behind the ribbon.

Max and Caruso spun around and tried to see who had spoken.

"Please," said a young Black woman. "Cain't you cover him up?"

Max and Caruso walked up to the young woman. She was very dark skinned and petite. Her hair was braided in corn-rows, and sections of it had been bleached blond. She had a gold tooth, a small gold nose jewel above her left nostril, and enormous square gold earrings, two in each ear, which clanged together when she talked.

"Of *course* we can cover him up," said Max. "Who are you?"

"His girlfriend," said the young woman.

Max got a sheet from the EMS bus and carefully covered the dead boy, then rejoined Caruso and Susan with the girl behind the tape.

68

"Would you mind talking to us for a couple of minutes?" said Max pleasantly.

The young woman shrugged.

"Can my cousin come?" she said, indicating a young woman about the same age standing next to her.

"Sure," said Max. "What are your names?"

"I'm Asa, she Moriah."

"C'mon," said Caruso.

Max led Susan and the others back to the car.

On the ride over to the Two-Eight they learned that Asa was twenty-two and the mother of a seventeen-month-old boy. The boy's father had, she said, "cracked up" — overdosed on crack. She'd only known the dead boy, Billy, for two months and believed him when he'd told her he was twenty. She was shocked to learn he was only sixteen.

"He jus' a *baby*," she said in wonderment. "He not too long out of *Pampers*."

"Do you know what Billy did for a living?" asked Caruso. "Did he tell you he sold crack?"

"I didn' ax him 'bout his business," said Asa. "Sometime it be better if you don' ax, you know what I'm sayin'?"

"Did you see Billy get shot tonight?" said Max.

"No, he say he got business in the park. He s'pose to meet me after and intraduce me to his folks. I seen him walk into the park with these three boys, and then later, when I fixin' to meet him, I hear he be shot." Asa sighed a deep sigh. "This gone be on my mind now."

"If not, somethin' be wrong with you," said Moriah.

"For real," said Asa.

"Later it gone bug you out," said Moriah.

"For real," said Asa.

"We have three boys at the police station," said Max. "Would you take a look at them and tell us if they're the same boys you saw take Billy into the park tonight?"

Asa nodded.

Max pulled the Fury into a parking place in front of the Two-Eight Precinct. Unlike most other police stations in New York, the Two-Eight looked like it had been designed by a real architect rather than a depressed civil servant. The Two-Eight was an elegant poured-concrete building, at least on the outside. Once you got inside, it looked as grimy and depressing as all the others.

Max and Caruso ushered Asa, Moriah, and Susan into the building and upstairs to the Two-Eight PDU. They asked the women to wait in the hallway while they went inside.

Inside the squad the PDU detectives had separated the three perps. They'd put one in a small interrogation room, a second in the barred holding pen, and the third, a large boy in a yellow tank top and yellow shorts, they'd simply cuffed and sat in a chair against the wall.

Max and Caruso went in to talk to the boy in the interrogation room. He looked to be about seventeen. He was wearing a Lakers shirt, baggy shorts, and a baseball cap.

"How ya doin', bro?" said Caruso unconvincingly.

The kid in the Lakers shirt looked up at them slack-faced, with no expression at all.

"What you want with me?" he said. "Why you be bringin' me here?"

"Listen, bro," said Caruso, "you know why you're here and I know why you're here. Because you and your friends killed that boy in the park."

"*What* boy in the park?" said the kid in the Lakers shirt, convincingly. "I don't know nothin' 'bout no boy in the park. Me and my friends we jus' be walkin' 'long 110th street and the cops be pullin' us in."

"Listen," said Max, "we know one of you shot that boy. We just need you to tell us which. If it wasn't you, you haven't got any problem with us. In fact you can go right home."

"I don' know nothin' 'bout no shootin'," said the boy, frowning, oozing sincerity.

"Now listen, son," said Caruso, his voice getting steely, "you wanna tell me what happened now or you wanna play with my dick? *Now* is the time to make a deal, you unnerstand what I'm saying to you? *Now* is the time to help yourself by telling us who did it. Don't try to protect your buddies, because they ain't gonna do the same for you. Nobody gives a *fuck* about you but *you* — you unnerstand what I'm saying to you?"

"I wanna talk to my lawyer," said the kid in the Lakers shirt.

Max and Caruso exchanged glances. Technically, the instant a suspect said he wanted to talk to a lawyer, the instant he even mentioned the word "lawyer" or "attorney" or "abogado," which was lawyer in Spanish, you could no longer question him or you were in violation of his rights and the case could be thrown the hell out of court. It was the same as failing to read a suspect his Miranda warnings.

Practically speaking, however, defense attorneys proceeded on the assumption that all cops violated all defendants' rights anyway, so the detectives gained nothing by *not* violating them. Even if the kid in the Lakers shirt had given them a voluntary written confession, his defense attorney would claim his client had been coerced and the confession would be worthless.

"Look," said Max, "you're going to be charged with murder in the second degree, which is twenty-five-to-life. Now there's no reason you have to go upstate, man, if you were not the shooter."

Silence from the kid in the Lakers shirt.

"*Were* you the shooter?" asked Max quietly.

"No," said the kid in the Lakers shirt.

"Who was?" asked Max.

The kid just stared at them with dead eyes. They looked at him a moment, then Caruso turned to Max.

"The reason he ain't tellin' us who did it," said Caruso, "is *he's* the shooter. I really think this fuck was the shooter."

The kid said nothing.

"I think you're the shooter, man," said Caruso. "I really think you fucking did it."

The kid said nothing.

"I don't think he did it," said Max, playing the good cop. "I think he's just covering for his friends. But the irony is I don't think they'd do the same for *him.*"

Max realized the *real* irony was the kid didn't know the word "irony." The kid said nothing.

"What are you, scared?" said Caruso. "Or you just don't give a fuck?"

The kid said nothing.

"Use your fucking *head,* man!" said Caruso. "The jig is up! You're here! This is it! You got caught! You either make a deal with us now or you go upstate!"

The kid said nothing.

"Let's go," said Max. "This kid is fucking hopeless."

"Are you a *man?*" said Caruso, "or are you a fucking faggot?"

Max wasn't sure what Caruso's point was. Did ratting on your friends make you a man and trying to protect them make you a faggot?

"I wanna see my lawyer," said the kid.

"Don't worry," said Max, "we'll get you your lawyer."

They walked out of the interrogation room.

"Let's put one suspect at a time in the room and have Asa look at them through the one-way mirror," said Max.

Caruso nodded and went to have the sergeant set it up. Max took Susan aside and tried to explain what was going on.

"If any of these guys is willing to implicate one of his buddies," said Max, "we phone the assistant D.A. for permission to make a formal arrest."

"You need *permission?*" asked Susan.

"Well, we've got an unwritten agreement we won't arrest anybody without checking with the D.A. first," said Max. "Of course, the D.A. doesn't give permission unless he thinks he has enough for an indictment. D.A.s try cases in the precinct instead of in the courtroom."

"Why is that?"

"Because they're in a numbers game, same as we are," said Max. "They've got to maintain a high degree of convictions. The game is about numbers — batting averages — not about justice."

"That's . . . not surprising, I guess," said Susan.

"It's not the D.A.s' preference to have it that way, nor ours," said Max. "It's just the way the system works. Murder is the easiest crime to get away with because it's so hard legally to make a homicide arrest that'll stand up in court."

"What happens if you can't get a statement from one of the three boys soon?" said Susan.

"Then we'll have to cut them loose."

"Even knowing they're guilty?"

"Even knowing they're guilty," said Max. "What we're doing now is playing poker."

Caruso rejoined them in the hallway.

"O.K., they're setting it up," he told Max, then he turned to Asa. "So, Asa, I can't believe you didn't know Billy was sixteen. You were robbing the cradle, Asa."

Asa giggled.

"Did you *rock* the cradle too?" said Caruso. "Was Billy good in bed?"

Max looked at Caruso, then at Susan. He was astounded at Caruso's breach of taste, quizzing the bereaved girlfriend about her sex life with the deceased, but if Asa was offended she didn't show it.

"We didn' rock the cradle yet," said Asa. "We was gone be doin' that the first time Saturday."

72

Now it was Caruso's turn to look astounded.

"What're you saying," said Caruso. "You didn't rock with Billy?"

"No *way* I rock with Billy," said Asa. "I only knowed Billy two *months*. Nobody rocks with me *that* easy."

Caruso glanced at Max and raised his eyebrows. He was clearly impressed.

The sergeant came out and told them the interrogation room was ready. Asa went into the little viewing area adjoining the room and took a look at each of the suspects in turn. She wasn't positive, but they did look to her like the three boys she'd seen go into the park with Billy. It didn't matter whether she could i.d. them or not, of course, since she wasn't a witness to the shooting, but Max and Caruso just wanted to be sure they had the right guys. Caruso took a statement from Asa, then he and Max drove her and Moriah home.

Then they drove Susan all the way down to Fifty-second Street.

"Thank you for showing me all of this," she said. "It was really an education."

"No problem," said Caruso.

"See you soon," said Max and squeezed her hand.

15

English is Judy's best subject in grade school. In high school she becomes interested in journalism, which legitimizes her as outsider, note-taker, voyeur. She goes to college at the University of Illinois in downstate Champaign-Urbana and majors in English with a minor in psych.

In her sophomore year at the U. of I. she comes across a copy of Neil Simon's early plays and is impressed by what he's written in his introduction:

> Like the werewolf . . . I am a creature controlled by some cruel fate that had twisted and warped my personality so that at the first sign of personal involvement, I became transformed from human being into the most feared and dangerous beast on the earth, the observer writer. Like Lon Chaney's portrayal of Lawrence Talbot, the monster-turned-back-into-man, the writer-once-more-human suffers great pangs of guilt the mornings after his transformations, but he is powerless to do anything about it. He is cursed.

She isn't familiar with his plays, but after reading that introduction she thinks she might be cursed like Neil Simon.

Shortly afterwards she comes across an anthology of Joan Didion's articles, *Slouching Towards Bethlehem,* and is even more impressed by what Didion has written in *her* introduction:

> I am bad at interviewing people. . . . I do not like to make telephone calls, and would not like to count the mornings I have sat on some Best Western motel bed somewhere and tried to force myself to put through the call to the assistant district attorney. My only advantage as a reporter

is that I am so physically small, so temperamentally unobtrusive, and so neurotically inarticulate that people tend to forget that my presence runs counter to their best interests. And it always does. That is one last thing to remember: *writers are always selling somebody out.*

She feels kinship with Didion and all writers who are outsiders and observers and voyeurs and who are always selling somebody out. Journalism seems to be an ideal area for her.

Her sophomore year is also the year she loses her virginity. An English instructor of hers named Austin Richards seems able to see past her prudish demeanor and pudginess and finds her attractive. He treats her as a smart person, a good writer, and, what is even more surprising, a desirable woman.

Richards is quite a romantic figure to the naive girl, with his ever-present pipe and his tweedy jackets with their suede elbow patches. It is rumored he's been published in small literary quarterlies like the *Kenyon Review.*

One Saturday Richards invites Judy to his office to discuss a paper of hers. It's a relaxed, informal discussion. He offers her Chianti from a straw-covered bottle. Amazing as it seems, he appears at times to be flirting with her. Is it possible he wants to go out with her? No, that's absurd. Instructors don't date students.

He asks her back for several Saturday sessions in his office. Always they drink Chianti. A lot of Chianti. And then one Saturday he makes a pass at her. Seated beside her on the visitor's side of the desk, he puts his hand on her knee and keeps it there while he holds forth on J.D. Salinger, of all people, pretending the hand isn't where it is.

She's so dumbfounded and so, to be honest, smashed on Chianti, she decides that if *he* isn't going to mention it, neither will she.

"The thing about Salinger," says Richards, inching his hand up under hems of skirt and half-slip, "is that he gives you *The Catcher in the Rye,* which is, in its way, a small masterpiece, of course, and the nine short stories, which are, arguably, as fine as any written in this country in the twentieth century, and then what does he do?"

She shakes her head almost imperceptibly, thinking more about the hand than about Salinger. Richards's hand advances another two inches.

"He begins to get self-conscious and mannered—*Franny and Zooey* and *Raise High the Roofbeam, Carpenters* are extremely self-conscious and mannered, wouldn't you agree?"

She nods slightly, more a two-degree downward tilt of her chin than a nod, actually, because the hand under the skirt has now crept all the way up her thigh and onto the soft white cotton of her underpants.

"And then, by the time he gets to *Seymour: An Introduction*," says Richards, "well, the man has become nothing so much as a parody of himself. I mean, the self-indulgence there, the . . . the narcissism, the unalloyed fascination with his own verbosity. . . ."

The palm of his hand slides smoothly onto the double-ply crotch of her underwear and rests there a moment.

It has occurred to her to call attention to what he's doing, but to mention it at this late stage seems inappropriate, if not rude. If she were going to do it at all, the time to do so would have been when his hand first came to light upon her knee. It is now too late to do anything but wait and see what he might do next.

The funny thing is, she doesn't really mind what he's doing because it seems to have so little to do with her. In fact, she's so detached from what's happening she feels almost voyeuristic. If she's aroused at all, it's less from his touch than from the voyeuristic rush of observing a man with his hand under a girl's skirt. If, before starting, he'd announced, "I am now going to put my hand underneath your skirt," or if, having started, he'd declared, "I am now running my hand up your thigh," then she would probably have said, "Well, Mr. Richards, that doesn't seem like such a good idea to me." But he had said neither of those things, and so she opts not to interfere.

"You could almost compare Salinger's development as a writer to the stages of the Italian Renaissance," Richards continues. His palm on her pudendum now begins exerting subtle but increasing downward pressure, squeezing her labia together under the crotch of her underwear. The effect is curious and not altogether unpleasant.

"His early short stories," says Richards, gently decreasing the pressure on her groin and then gradually increasing it, "and I refer here to the ones *before* he wrote 'A Perfect Day for Bananafish' and 'Uncle Wiggily in Connecticut' and 'Just Before the War with the Eskimos' and 'For Esme—with Love and Squalor' and what have you, are his Early Renaissance period, where he's just learning his craft. Then come *Catcher* and the nine short stories—which, by the way, most people incorrectly assume were the only ones he wrote—and those would comprise his High Renaissance period, the full flower of his genius."

76

With an absence of self-consciousness she finds astonishing, Richards now slides his second hand under her skirt and slip as well, grabs the waistband of her underpants, and pulls them gently off her hips and down her thighs and down her legs and off the ends of her black-and-white saddle shoes, ending up squatting in front of her like a shoe salesman.

"Then, of course, along come *Franny and Zooey* and *Raise High the Roofbeam, Carpenters,* which are his Late Renaissance and Mannerist periods, and finally comes *Seymour: An Introduction,* which initiates his Baroque period and the end of his significance to his epoch as a major producer of contemporary American fiction."

It is, she thinks, about as impersonal as being examined by her gynecologist, and when, squatting there on the floor in front of her, he finally raises her skirt and slip to inspect her naked thighs and pubis, she half expects him to place her feet in stirrups.

Rising to a standing position, he swivels and sweeps a pile of student compositions matter-of-factly off his desk. Then he lifts her out of her chair and deposits her, still seated, atop his desk. Continuing to hold forth on Salinger, he unbuckles his belt, unzips his fly, drops his trousers, and pushes down his boxer shorts.

She hadn't remembered how ugly the male genitalia were. Turkey neck and turkey gizzards was, she recalls, how Sylvia Plath described them in *The Bell Jar.* She squeezes her eyes shut. With her eyes shut and with all that Chianti in her head to numb the revulsion, she doesn't really mind when, still holding forth pedantically on Salinger, he parts her thighs, leans forward, and inserts his turkey neck. The strange thing is that, after the initial pain, she finds the sensation not disagreeable.

Judy and Austin Richards have intercourse in precisely this manner twice more in his office. The only variations are that on the second occasion he holds forth not on Salinger but on Hemingway and undresses her completely, and on the third occasion the author under discussion is F. Scott Fitzgerald and his tortured relationship with his wife, Zelda.

On none of the three occasions does Richards so much as allude to what they're doing. There's something so impersonal about the way he handles their sex that she doesn't find it threatening, although pretending they're having literary discourse rather than sexual intercourse is beginning to play havoc with her sense of reality.

At the conclusion of their third session she decides to speak.

"Austin . . ." she says, "I'm sorry, may I call you Austin?"

"Of course," he says in a way that suggests addressing him by his Christian name might be just a tad inappropriate.

"Austin, I just wanted to say that I . . . love coming here and . . ." she swallows, reddening, "I also love . . . what you do to me."

Richards looks stricken. It is the only verbal reference there has thus far been to their sex. If someone had been bugging his office and transcribing the tapes, this would be the first incriminating remark.

Oh, no, she thinks, noting the change in his facial expression, I've blown it. I have broken some unspoken mutual vow of silence and now he's mad at me.

"I'm sorry," she says. "I guess maybe I shouldn't have said that."

"No, no, no," says Richards. "I'm very glad that you did."

The hell you are, she thinks, watching him apprehensively. Richards spends a moment organizing his thoughts, then clears his throat.

"Judith," he says, "I, too, have enjoyed our time together here, but, well, I feel it might be best at this point if we were to put our Saturday sessions on hold for a while, you know?"

Our Saturday *sessions?* On *hold?* Is he her lover, her shrink, or a goddam telephone operator?

"Why?" is all that she can think of to ask in response to his announcement.

"Well, for a number of reasons," he says, swiftly hoisting his trousers, zipping up, buckling up, and arranging his clothing, "not the least of which is the distinct possibility that my wife might learn of our, uh, activities."

She is utterly speechless. She hadn't known about any wife. If she had even *suspected* a wife she wouldn't have allowed him to do what he'd been doing. She feels suddenly so bereft, so humiliated, so demeaned, so . . . mortified. Tears begin sliding soundlessly out of her eyes and running down her face, dripping off the end of her jaw onto her blouse, forming wet spots on each breast.

She doesn't move. She doesn't make a sound. She merely continues to sit atop his desk, wearing only a blouse, white bobby socks and saddle shoes, her legs dangling over the edge, the tears continuing to spill silently down her cheeks.

Richards looks at her nervously, trying to gauge her next move.

"Well," he says, "I expect you'll want to be getting back to your dorm now."

78

His words strike her face like a handful of stones. Wincing, she climbs off the desk and begins walking, zombiclike, toward the door. He realizes she's not pausing to put on her clothes and hurries after her, catching her just as she opens the office door.

"Here," he says, holding her by the arm with one hand and with the other hastily scooping up her skirt, slip, and underpants, "don't you want to put these on?"

She doesn't acknowledge his words or the proffered articles of clothing. She is like a toy locomotive, wheels turning, pistons pumping, that has encountered an obstruction on the track. It's clear that if he lets go of her arm she will continue right out the door and out of the building and onto the quadrangle with nothing on below the waist but saddle shoes and bobby socks. Just his luck to have chosen to boff a psycho.

Restraining her forward momentum with his body, he kicks the office door closed and somehow manages to lift first one foot and then the other and insert it into underpants, slip, and skirt, and to pull all of these up her thighs. It is like dressing a four-year-old. It is like shoeing a horse. The instant her lower garments are in place he releases her and she propels herself through the door.

For the first few hours she stalks the campus, seething with rage, but then her rage becomes intolerable. She switches it off and decides what happened isn't his fault but her own. Something she did has turned him off. It can't just be that she called attention to what they'd been doing, it had to be something else. Something about what she was doing when he screwed her. Something about her reactions, perhaps. Making too much noise, or too little. Maybe he wanted her to do something to him and didn't know how to ask. If she can just find out what it is, perhaps she can get him back. It is critical to her sense of well-being and to her sanity that she somehow get him back.

Being in his class is now excruciating for her. Each time he looks at her, she recalls what their sessions in his office were like and she aches to have them back again, impersonal as they may have been. He scrupulously avoids calling on her in class. After class she hangs around, trying to talk to him, but he has become even more removed than before. She begs to speak with him in private. He tells her he doesn't wish to speak to her outside of class and he adheres to that.

When the course is over he gives her a B–, which is at least one full grade less than she deserves. It takes her two years to get over Austin Richards, if, in fact, she ever does.

She is terribly shy with men, and can make absolutely no small talk. To deaden her inhibitions she drinks. Usually two or three vodkas are enough to sedate the polite and prudish Jekyll and release the Hyde. When drunk she spends her evenings alone in her dorm room or else standing across the street from Richards's house at the edge of campus, watching him pass from one lighted window to the next, doing whatever it is that husbands and fathers do in their homes in the evening, alternately fantasizing winning him back and killing him for what he did to her. She cannot decide which is the more satisfying fantasy.

16

When Max and Caruso got back to the Two-Eight it was after three A.M. The sergeant seemed vastly amused.

"We talked to the gypsy cab driver," he said. "Nice guy from the Ivory Coast, speaks mostly French. He says he didn't see the shooting, but he did see the guy in the yellow tanktop throw something like a gun over the retaining wall. So the guy in the yellow tanktop is definitely our shooter. Funny thing is, the guy in the yellow tanktop is the only one who's now ready to give anybody up. He says the guy in the Lakers shirt did it."

"Did you tell that to the guy in the Lakers shirt?" said Max.

"Yeah," said the sergeant, chuckling. "He ain't giving up the guy in the yellow tanktop, though. He thinks it's just an old cop trick, which it is, except this time it just happens to be true."

By four A.M. the kid in the Lakers shirt was finally willing to make a statement naming the kid in the yellow tanktop as the shooter. The sergeant called the assistant D.A. who was catching cases that night, who gave permission to have the kid in the yellow tanktop formally arrested and taken downtown to Central Booking.

Max and Caruso went back to the Two-Five. They had a day tour beginning at eight A.M. in just four hours. It was too late to go home so they slept in the dorm. Max had phoned Babette earlier to say he might not make it home that night, but he'd awakened her and she was less than pleasant. He felt a mixture of guilt and resentment when he hung up the phone. As if it was his fucking fault he'd caught a fresh one on 110th.

As he lay in the dark of the tiny cop dorm Max couldn't stop thinking about Susan. He'd loved having her on the Petlin canvass and on the case up in Harlem. He'd loved showing her his work. It would never have occurred to Babette to ask to come with him on an investigation. O.K., O.K., when he'd first met her, Babette did help him catch a vicious killer, and had even saved Max's life. But that was then and this was now. Now was different. Now Babette didn't give a good goddam about his profession.

The rapport he had with Susan was something special. He sensed that she liked him. She probably didn't know he was married. Well, hell, the way things were going, he might not be married long. If he and Babette split up he was free to go out with Susan. Assuming she would want to date a cop.

He hugged the pillow, imagining it was Susan.

By eight A.M. they were back at their desks at the Two-Five, sitting at their IBM Selectrics, hunting and pecking and cursing as they typed out their printed forms in triplicate — "Unusual Occurrence Reports" and "fives" for the discovery of Billy's body in the park and for Petlin's on Eighty-second Street, "pink fives" and "five-As" for follow-ups on the Smiley case. The Selectrics had replaced their filthy manual typewriters about three years before and were now as grimy and unappealing as their predecessors.

Haggerty, a handsome detective whom they'd nicknamed Hollywood for his fashionable attire and the self-conscious way he was always checking his appearance in mirrors and other shiny surfaces, walked into the squad room, started to sit down, reached a hand in his pants pocket, and swore.

"Christ, I got my wife's keys," said Haggerty.

"What a coincidence," said Caruso. "*I* got your wife's keys too."

Haggerty gave Caruso the smile the joke deserved.

Max had a sudden lovely image of having his wife's keys and realized with shock that the wife in the image was not Babette but Susan.

17

In life Irv Smiley had been a minor television executive, a short man, a man distinguished by neither appearance nor personality nor accomplishment, a man not many of his co-workers at Manhattan Cable TV knew by name, a man few of the tenants who lived in his own building at 345 East Fifty-ninth Street even knew existed. In death Irv Smiley is the focus of a citywide homicide investigation that

No.

Somebody wanted Irv Smiley dead, and they wanted it so badly that it had not been enough for them merely to sever his carotid artery, which is a very bad way to die, they also saw fit, when Irv Smiley finally did bleed to death, to bash his

No.

On a desk in the entryway of Irv Smiley's affluent bachelor pad on East Fifty-ninth Street lies a bunch of letters. Bills, charitable solicitations, a catalogue from L.L. Bean, a printed report from his congressman. The man to whom these things are addressed will never open his mail, because sometime around midnight on Friday, April 8, someone who had other plans for Irv Smiley

No no.

In a cavernous and gloomy apartment on West 102nd Street sits Florence Smiley, an old woman in a faded blue terry cloth robe who had not expected to outlive any of her children. Her youngest son, Irv, the thirty-three-year-old television executive who was the apple of her eye, was murdered on April 8 in his affluent East Fifty-ninth Street bachelor pad, and now the cops are saying it was a gay S and M killing.

"How could they say he was a pervert?" she asks for perhaps the dozenth time since you entered the apartment on West 102nd Street.

83

"He never ran around with fairies or this type of element. He was a good boy, a clean boy, a boy who loved God. How can they think such things about him?"

You don't know what to tell the elderly mother of the thirty-three-year-old television executive, nor do you know

No no no no no.

18

"Maxie, bubbeleh! How ya been, kid?"

Max got hugged not by his mother or father but by Dr. Tony Natale, police shrink, one of Max's closest friends.

Tony Natale had been a longshoreman in Brooklyn at the age of sixteen, a foot patrolman at twenty-one, and at thirty-two — Max's age — a police shrink, the result of going to school at night for about a hundred years and earning his Ph.D. in psychology. Now, at forty-seven, Natale counseled burned-out cops and earned a fifth of what he could make in the private sector. Natale had enormous, contagious energy and enthusiasm, a hopeless Brooklyn accent, and happened to be the only adult male not a relative whom Max allowed to hug him. Max figured the hugging was an Italian thing — which was not to say the Jews weren't huggers, because they were — only with Tony it was different.

Natale's office had been moved from the ancient hole in the wall he occupied when Max first met him seven years before to a nice *modern* hole in the wall at One Police Plaza, the impressive fifty-eight-million dollar red brick building near the entrance to the Brooklyn Bridge. Max had brought along a brown bag lunch, hoping to pick Natale's brain about the Smiley and Petlin cases, although he frankly doubted that Natale was going to be able to suggest anything that Max hadn't thought of already.

"So, Max, how's the family?" said Natale. "How's that kid of yours, eh?"

"Terrific, Tony, Sam is just terrific," said Max. "You wouldn't believe the things he's saying now."

"And Babette?" said Natale. "How's she?"

85

"She's, uh, terrific too."

A wicked smile from Natale.

"Uh-oh," said Natale. "What's going on? Marriage on the rocks?"

Max shrugged.

"How long you guys been married now," asked Natale, "five years?"

"Seven."

A throaty chuckle.

"The old seven year itch, eh?" said Natale. "You playin' a little hide-the-pepperoni on the side?"

Max shook his head and managed a weak smile.

"No, no, nothing like that," he said. "It's just . . . I don't know . . . over, I guess. We don't seem to enjoy being with each other anymore."

Max was surprised. He hadn't intended to say that much to Natale. But then, he hadn't intended to say that much to Joanie Jarvis either. Natale was looking at him expectantly with an encouraging half-smile on his face.

"I don't know how something as great, as . . . *hot* as what I had with Babette could have degenerated into what we have now," said Max miserably. "I mean, I just don't understand how it happened. Do you?"

"Sure I do," said Natale cheerfully.

"Yeah?" said Max. "Tell me."

"It won't do you any good," said Natale.

"Why won't it?"

"'Cause you're not ready to hear."

"Tell me anyway," said Max.

"O.K.," said Natale. "Well, what happened was fear of intimacy. The old incest taboo. Things got a little too cozy, O.K.? Babette started looking a little too much like family, and you heard when you were a kid that you weren't supposed to hump a member of your family, so you stopped feeling sexy with her."

Max smiled on one side of his face.

"You don't like that explanation?" said Natale. "O.K., here's another way to look at it. You two got a little too close, O.K.? A little too vulnerable. Being vulnerable is scary. So, rather than risk being really hurt in case one of you ever dumped the other, you both pulled back to a comfortable distance, figuring if you ever got dumped it wouldn't

86

hurt so much. Only problem is, you can't maintain any marriage worth having from a safe distance. And the *real* irony is, pulling back didn't keep you from being hurt either."

Max slowly raised his eyebrows and spread his hands.

"I don't know, Tony," he said and sighed. "I just don't know. Maybe you're right. Who knows?"

"Meaning," said Natale, "you ain't buying either one of those, right?"

"It's just that . . . I don't know," said Max. "It's just that we used to be so much in love, and now we aren't. That's what kills me. I mean what happened to *love?*"

Natale looked at Max a moment, still smiling, his gaze stopping politely at the surface of Max's face. And then his gaze continued on through Max, right through the flesh of his face and through his skull and out the back of Max's head, back toward the wall at the rear of the hole-in-the-wall office. His smile faded slowly, like an orange sun sinking gradually into the ocean, as he waded into his own private torments.

"Love," said Natale, the smile now completely faded, "is the self-delusion we manufacture to justify the trouble we take to have sex."

Max said nothing, uncomfortable with the seriousness of Natale's tone.

"When we first meet a potential mate, we can see them quite clearly for a matter of minutes," Natale continued. "Then our view is obscured by a rosy fog made up of our own dreams, our fantasies, our expectations, our hopes. After we've been with that person for a while, for maybe a year, the rosy fog is replaced by another one, a gray one, made up of our collected hurts and grievances. After those first few minutes we never see the real face of our beloved again."

"Yeah," said Max. He felt he was talking not to his friend but to a dark entity that was using his friend as a medium, speaking through his lips.

Natale gradually pulled himself back from wherever he'd been. The smile returned to his lips, the twinkle to his eye.

"Hey," said Natale, "at least I ain't *bitter,* right?"

"Right," said Max. Natale's own marriage of twenty years had ended recently in a rather messy divorce. Max had been told it was Natale who'd done the splitting, but now he wasn't sure.

"I just follow John Dillinger's advice," said Natale.

"What's that?" asked Max.

"Never trust a woman or an automatic pistol."

"I wouldn't carry an automatic if they paid me," said Max, focusing on the more comfortable caveat.

"Good boy," said Natale. "And listen, if things with Babette don't get better, get the fuck out."

"You serious?" said Max. It seemed odd advice from a shrink, odder yet from someone who knew Babette and presumably liked her.

"Hell yes, I'm serious," said Natale. "Come and stay with *me*. I'm having the time of my life, kid."

"That so?" said Max dubiously.

Natale nodded, smiling wickedly.

"The singles world is a fucking seller's market for guys," he said. "I'm getting more ass than a toilet seat."

"Yeah?" said Max wistfully. He hated hearing about anybody who was having good sex. "Aren't you afraid of AIDS?"

"Nah," said Natale, shaking his head.

"You use condoms?" asked Max.

"I *hate* condoms," said Natale. "Fucking with a condom is like fucking inside a goddam scuba suit. I'd rather get AIDS than wear a condom."

Max frowned. Natale exhaled slowly.

"That was a stupid thing to say," said Natale. "I don't know, maybe I got an unconscious death wish. To punish myself for all the great sex I'm getting now."

Max shrugged. Natale brightened again.

"Seriously, Max," he said. "These girls are totally unself-conscious about their bodies. To them fucking is as natural as eating or sleeping or pissing. And they come in about thirty seconds. Do you know how long it used to take me to make Rochelle come?"

Max shook his head. He didn't know and he didn't want to. Before the Segal baby and the Natale divorce the two couples had hung out a lot together. And Natale's wife, Rochelle, had been like an aunt.

"Hey, Tony, I didn't come here to talk about making Rochelle come," said Max irritably. "I came here to talk about a couple cases we got."

Natale nodded.

"I'm sorry," said Natale contritely. "I get a little carried away sometimes."

"Right," said Max. "So listen, you been following the Smiley and Petlin cases at all?"

"Some," said Natale. "Enough to get the general drift."

"We've been proceeding with the idea it's the same perp," said Max. "And with the idea he's a fag."

"Sounds reasonable," said Natale, "seeing as how both victims were naked. It's unlikely the killer was a woman. Women don't tend to kill men. They aren't strong enough is the main reason. Now as I recall you never found a murder weapon, the cause of death in both cases was severance of the carotid artery, there was postmortem disfigurement of the face, and the killer is presumed to have taken his time before leaving the crime scene."

Max nodded.

"Yeah. So?"

"Well, let's see," said Natale. "Killers who bring their own weapons to a crime scene are what the FBI calls organized. They're planners, stalkers. They enjoy the hunt. Killers who disfigure their victims' faces tend to know them pretty well. Neck wounds are characteristic of homosexual homicides, by the way—"

"Yeah," said Max, "that one I knew."

Natale nodded.

"O.K.," he said, "murderers who kill sadistically and slowly are older — in their thirties, say. They feel some mastery of the situation. That's unlike teenagers and killers in their early twenties who feel threatened by their victims and need to dispose of them fast. Oh, and killers who spend lots of time at the crime scene usually live nearby.

"In mutilation murders, which are very common, as you know, whites kill whites and Blacks kill Blacks. And most killers by far are male and under the age of forty. So you're probably looking for a highly organized white male homosexual in his thirties who knows his victims well and lives nearby."

Max nodded, impressed.

"All this comes from profiling, right?" he said. "The FBI's Behavioral Science Unit."

"Right," said Natale, "but the idea behind profiling started a long time before that. You remember the Mad Bomber?"

"Sort of," said Max.

"In the 1950s a guy they called the Mad Bomber had been terrorizing New York City for years. Sixteen years, I think it was. A Greenwich

Village psychiatrist named James Brussel studied photos of the bomb scenes and letters the Bomber had written. Then he told the cops to look for a heavy, foreign-born, Roman Catholic, Eastern European man between forty and fifty years of age who lived in a city in Connecticut with a maiden sister or aunt, that when he was apprehended he'd be wearing a double-breasted suit, and — get this — that the jacket would be buttoned."

"So what happened?"

"The Mad Bomber was apprehended in Waterbury, Connecticut," said Natale. "His name was George Metesky. There was only one detail in his profile Brussel got wrong: Metesky was living with *two* maiden sisters, not one. And, yeah, at the time of his arrest Metesky was wearing a double-breasted suit. Buttoned."

Max chuckled appreciatively and shook his head.

"Anything else you can tell about my killer?"

"Yeah," said Natale. "One thing."

"What's that?" said Max.

"He ain't gonna stop at just two," said Natale.

19

Toward the end of her senior year of college Judy meets an accounting student named Teddy Greco in a campus bar called Bidwell's. Greco has curly black hair and a perpetual five o'clock shadow. He's a little too brash, a little too coarse, a little too short, a little too hairy for her tastes. She doesn't think him at all attractive physically, but finds herself unaccountably amused by his audacity. She allows him to court her, knowing she will never go to bed with him, rationalizing that she needs the ego support.

On their third date she allows herself one vodka too many, and before she knows it he has maneuvered her into his narrow, low-ceilinged, laundry-littered room in the attic of his dorm and finessed her jeans and sweater off.

"Listen, Teddy, I don't think this is such a good idea," she says, struggling to stand up and maintain her balance while inserting a foot into her jeans.

"But I want you so much," he says, smothering her with kisses. "You want me too, I can tell."

"You flatter yourself," she says, succeeding in inserting the first foot in her trouser leg and trying for the second.

"You can't refuse me, Jude," he says, dropping to his knees in front of her. "I'll kill myself if you refuse me. My blood will be on your hands."

She threads her second foot through her trouser leg, but when she starts to pull the jeans up her thighs he tugs them down again.

"I'll do anything to make love to you, Jude," he says softly, "anything in the world. Just name it and it's yours."

"Teddy, please," she says, trying to pull up her jeans again.

"Have pity on me, Jude," he says, "this is a desperate man you see before you."

Gazing up at her from his knees, he appears comical, harmless, vulnerable, and less hairy and unattractive than usual. She can't restrain a smile, which he takes as license to walk toward her on his knees. Before she can stop him, he has hugged his arms around her buttocks, pressed his face against her belly, pulled down her panties, and buried his mouth in her muff.

"What are you *doing?*" she says, panicked. She is totally unprepared for anything like this, having heard rumors of such things but not believed them, mortified to have anyone put his nose and mouth to her private parts, worried sick she might not smell so good, having no idea whatsoever why anyone would choose to do that to her or what reactions might be expected of her in such an unprecedented situation.

"Stop it!" she cries, trying to pull away from him. But he's as persistent as he is adept, and before she knows it she finds herself responding in spite of herself, shivering with pleasure, afraid she'll faint. She backs up against the closest wall and sinks to the floor, with Teddy's face fastened to her crotch like a blood-sucking leech.

It is the most exquisite feeling she has ever experienced, and by the time Teddy escorts her back to her dorm she fears he might have introduced her to something she's not willing to be without.

Their second night of sex is even better than the first. His technical ability is breathtaking and suggests unimaginable experience. She has no idea how somebody so unattractive could have found so many willing women to practice upon. She begins mentally whittling away at his shortcomings to prepare herself for feeling something romantic about him. But when he takes her home that night he seems preoccupied.

"Listen, Jude," he says at her dorm door, taking both her hands in his, "I want to say something, O.K.?"

"O.K."

What he has to say, she thinks, can't be good. People don't ask permission to say anything good. Maybe it has to do with the area of personal hygiene. She has always kept herself scrupulously clean down there, even before he started licking it, and much more so since, washing and douching and deodorizing several times a day; but you never knew, maybe when they were that close to it they could still detect an odor.

"I think you're a terrific girl, and a lot of fun in the sack and everything, but I'm starting to get a little worried."

"You're worried?" she says. "What are you worried about?"

"That you might be getting the wrong idea about what we've been doing," he says.

Oh, Jesus, she thinks. Here it comes.

"What do you mean?" she says.

"Well, I just don't want you to misunderstand. I mean, I love fooling around with you in the sack and everything, I'm not saying *that*. I just hope you don't, y'know, start falling in love with me or anything."

She begins to get dizzy. She wonders if she's going to be able to continue standing upright.

"You . . . don't want me to start falling in love with you," she says dazedly.

"No."

"Why not?"

"Why not?" He shakes his head. "It doesn't matter."

"No," she says, "tell me." Maybe it's something she can change, maybe it's something she can fix — how she reacts to him in bed or something. Maybe he's not ready for marriage and wants to make sure she isn't going to pressure him about that.

"Well," he says, "to be absolutely honest about it?"

"Yes?"

"To be absolutely honest about it, Jude, I don't know if I really find you all that attractive. Physically, I mean."

She is aghast, unable to believe what she's hearing. She tears open the door and stumbles into the dorm and sits down on the lobby floor. Two girls ask if she's all right. She doesn't even hear them. Somehow she's able to make it all the way up to her room before collapsing on her bed in tears. It is a horrid joke. She has managed to get rejected for not being attractive enough by someone she herself considered too unattractive to go out with, yet the pain of being rejected by this slimy nerd is every bit as intense as if she'd been rejected by the captain of the goddam football team. The nerve, the colossal gall of this short, hairy, sleazy little asshole! The *nerve!*

As much as she detests Teddy, she cannot face losing him or the addictive thing he does to her body with his tongue. She knows there's no way to get him back. It is simply not possible. She cannot become more attractive than she is.

She decides to commit suicide. Late that night when everybody has gone to bed, she takes a razor blade into the bathroom. She turns on the cold water and presses the blade lightly to the veins in her right wrist. She sees the edge of the blade depress the veins and begin to break the outermost layer of skin. She envisions the blade going in deeper, severing the veins, the blood spurting out, spraying the sink, her knees weakening from the loss of blood, dropping to the tiled floor, being found in a sticky puddle of half-dried brown blood the following morning.

She decides she can't go through with it.

She is so shattered by Teddy's rejection of her that she considers dropping out of college before graduation. Instead she gets drunk on vodka and remains there. Her suitemates beg her not to blow her degree. Somehow she pulls herself together in time to take her finals and graduate. When she gets her degree she goes back to Lake Forest to live with her parents.

The construction site at East Fifty-seventh Street again. Max and Caruso moseyed in, beyond the crude wooden fence meant to keep out the public. A hardhat saw them, sauntered over.

"I help you gentlemen?"

Not much help in the voice.

"We're looking for Albert Prince. He here?"

"Who wantsa know?"

"Police." The shield. "He here?"

"Uh, yeah, yeah. That guy right over there. Whatsamatter, he in some kinda trouble?"

"No trouble at all, we just want to talk to him is all."

"Prince? Yo, Prince! Someone to see ya."

A big guy, maybe six-one or six-two, with a yellow hardhat, hightop work shoes, sweatshirt with the arms torn out, arms big as Max's legs, came toward them.

"Him?" said Caruso. *"That's* Albert Prince?"

"Why do you ask?" said Max, savoring his partner's surprise.

"He don't look like no . . ." Caruso trailed off. "Albert Prince?"

"Right?" Low voice, two octaves lower than Caruso's.

"Police." The shield again. "We'd like to ask you a few questions."

"What about?"

"You wanna talk right here?"

"Here's as good as anyplace. What's this about?"

"We're investigating the Smiley and Petlin homicides. Maybe you heard about them on TV?"

"Uh, yeah, I think I heard somethin' or other. Two guys got their throats cut, that it?"

"Right. We wondered if you knew either one of them."

Long look. "Nope."

"Or you met one of them at some point."

Another long look. "Why you askin' me this?"

A shrug. "We thought maybe you knew somethin'."

"Why'd you think that?"

"Somebody said maybe you did."

Nothing.

"Somebody said maybe *you* said you did."

Long pause. "Who?" Just the one word, spoken quietly and clearly, but with the force of a sock in the belly.

"A guy at the Mindshaft."

Another long pause. "The Mindshaft?"

"Right."

Silence. "What's the Mindshaft?"

Max and Caruso exchanged glances. "Why don't you come back to the office and talk to us about it, Albert."

"I got nothin' to talk about."

If Prince didn't want to talk, they couldn't question him unless they arrested him. If they arrested him they had to Mirandize him. If they Mirandized him and he wanted an attorney, they couldn't talk to him.

True, they often bent the rules with crack dealers in Harlem who were obvious perps in homicides, but Prince wasn't one of those. And it was doubtful they could do in Midtown what they did in Harlem, particularly with a case being followed closely in the media.

It would be helpful to know if Prince had a criminal record, but if they called BCI, the Bureau of Criminal Identification, and found he had another criminal case pending it would mean he was already represented by an attorney, in which case Miranda warnings couldn't be waived and he couldn't be questioned even if he agreed to be. There would also be a record of their request for information, along with the date it was requested, so any attempt to question him after that would make it impossible to bring the case to court.

"C'mon, Albert, take a ride with us. Let's talk."

"I toldja. I got nothin' to talk about."

"*We* do."

"Then talk to yourself. I got work to do."

Albert Prince turned around and walked back to work. Max and Caruso watched him go.

21

Judy works in the office at Todd'ler Town, writing catalogue copy and doing drudge work. She takes a few graduate courses in literature at Northwestern University in Evanston. Outside of the small staff at the office she has no friends. When she isn't at the office she's locked in her bedroom at her parents' home, writing poems and stories, drinking vodka.

During the years at Todd'ler Town she loses a little weight and meets several men who seem to find her attractive, but she refuses to go out with them. They are too fat, too thin, too crude, too shy. She's suspicious of anyone who likes her.

She meets a handsome young doctor with blond hair and blue eyes. His name is Stuart Sherman and he's interning at Michael Reese. She is astonished when he asks her out, but she accepts. He takes her drinking at the Top of the Rock, the Chicago skyline twinkling below them, and tells her of the horrors of interning at a major metropolitan hospital. A few nights later he asks her out again. They go to Riccardo's, an old artists' hangout on the Near North Side, and then to a soft-lit bar on Rush Street. At one point he holds her hand. She cannot imagine what he sees in her. She cannot stop herself from falling in love with him.

On their third date he takes her on a moonlight cruise along the Chicago River on the Wendella tour boat. As they stand at the rail, holding hands and gazing at the floodlit buildings rising up on both sides of the river, he kisses her. She melts. It is all she can do to restrain herself from blurting out sticky declarations of love.

After the cruise he drives her in his ratty old Chevy to the shore of Lake Michigan. They share a flask of martinis. She gets fairly high. He puts his arms around her and kisses her with mounting passion. But the wounds from Teddy Greco and Austin Richards have barely scabbed over, so when he eventually slips his hand under her skirt and begins to caress her upper thighs, she pushes it away.

"What's wrong, Judy?" he whispers.

"I'm not ready yet."

"I understand," he says, kissing her hair, squeezing her shoulder. But a moment later the hand is back.

"Please, Stu."

"O.K.," he says, "O.K." But the hand slides up to her pubic mound and the fingers creep under the legband of her panties.

"I can't do this, Stuart, I really can't," she says, horribly ambivalent, pulling his fingers out of her panties, aching to have him inside of her but terrified of being hurt again.

"Why not?" he says.

"I'm just not ready," she says, hating herself for depriving them of what they both so desperately want. "I just can't do this now."

"I don't blame you a bit," he says, returning his fingers to her crotch, discovering the heat and the slipperiness and knowing that he's won.

"Please . . . stop what you're doing . . . right now, Stuart," she says, breathing heavily, beginning to writhe under his touch.

"O.K." he says. "I will. Very soon."

His love-making is so tender she surrenders to it totally. His touch is so affectionate she feels it safe to express verbally what he's told her tactilely.

"I think I'm falling in love with you," she whispers.

He is silent. Silence is not one of the possible responses she's imagined. Oh, no, she thinks, oh, no. Not again. Take it back. Is it too late to take it back?

"I guess," she says tentatively, "when I say I'm falling in love, what I actually mean is that it's just so wonderful being together. I think it's much too early to know if what I feel is love. What I love is our being together. I hope we can be together a lot."

Will that erase it? Can anything erase a declaration of love?

"Judy," he says, "I . . . wonder if you're aware of my . . . situation."

"Your situation?"

Oh, God, his *situation*. What in God's name is his situation?

"I've been seeing a girl from Northwestern for some time now," he says, "a Chi Omega. We're practically engaged, Judy, I thought you knew that. I mean I thought you *knew* that. Didn't you know that?"

She flings open the door and runs from the Chevy, from Stuart Sherman, from men altogether. He tries to catch up with her, to talk to her, to drive her home. She strikes him in the face, drawing blood. He lets her go.

She vows never to go out with another man as long as she lives. She spends hours in her room, writing stories about men who come to violent ends — falling off roofs and being impaled on iron fence posts, accidentally slicing off arms with electric hedge clippers, being decapitated by windows blown off construction sites, being burned alive in holds of torpedoed ships.

She spins out elaborate fantasies of revenge against Stuart Sherman, Teddy Greco, and Austin Richards. Sometimes she's a cat burglar, sneaking into their beds when they're asleep, slipping a pistol into their mouths, and blowing their heads off. Sometimes she wears a scuba outfit, sneaking up on them underwater when they're swimming in Lake Michigan, and stabs them in the heart. Sometimes she simply drives up next to them at stoplights and lobs hand grenades in the windows of their cars.

On weekends she borrows one of the family Cadillacs and drives to a succession of small towns in Illinois and has picnics in graveyards. In the graveyard of Mattoon, Illinois, she's fascinated to find the headstone of a girl who was born the same year as she. The girl had died at the age of two. Her name was Caroline Busey. At first Judy envies Caroline Busey. Then she begins having fantasies about her. Finally, she decides to become her.

Judy goes to the Mattoon Town Hall and asks for a photocopy of Caroline Busey's birth certificate. It is remarkably easy to obtain a copy of anyone's birth certificate, especially in a small town. Judy uses the birth certificate to apply for a learner's permit in Caroline Busey's name, and with the learner's permit she obtains a driver's license.

She doesn't know what she wants with a driver's license that identifies her as Caroline Busey, a resident of Mattoon, Illinois, but she likes the idea that she can become somebody else at will.

After living with it for so many years Judy decides she can no longer tolerate her father's drinking. She packs a single suitcase and moves to New York.

In New York Judy has a bad time of it at first. The city overwhelms her with noise, overcrowding, filth, fumes, and rudeness. Chattering jackhammers, whooping and yelping ambulance and police sirens, tractor trailer airhorns, crowds stuffed into the subway cars, garbage spewing into the streets, spray-painted graffiti on every wall, the hostility of salespeople.

She is desperately lonely. She is unable to make friends. She walks down the street and is terrified of passersby. She doesn't know what frightens her more, the possibility that they might attack her or that she might attack *them*. She becomes a hermit, staying alone in her small apartment for days at a time.

Badly in need of companionship, she goes to the A.S.P.C.A., where she is shown a homeless kitten who's about to be destroyed. She takes it home and spends hours talking to it and grooming it. It is her only friend.

She subsists on a generous trust fund her guilty father has set up for her. She still isn't dating. A few men ask her out, but she's too critical of them to accept. She feels unattractive and inadequate, but longs for a loving relationship with a gentle man.

She joins Sports Training Institute on East Forty-ninth Street and begins working out with a trainer there three times a week. She goes on a diet and loses twenty pounds. She gazes at her image in the mirror for hours. She no longer recognizes herself. She is slim and strikingly attractive. She feels beautiful and better than other women, but, strangely, also ugly and inferior. More men ask her out. Still socially awkward, she declines.

At her gym she befriends a wealthy middle-aged widow named Rose Brill, who takes the younger woman under her wing. Rose introduces Judy to Bendel's, Bergdorf's, Laura Ashley, Chanel, Courreges, Kenso, Kansai, and teaches her how to dress like a successful career woman. Rose takes Judy to lunch at Le Cirque and Grenouille and Judy memorizes everything Rose does — learns how to read a menu, how to order and taste wine, how to behave toward maître d's, how to tip, how to behave imperiously and get respect.

Judy uses her trust fund to move to a better apartment in a newly renovated brownstone on the East Side. Walter Barmack, the real estate agent who finds it for her, asks her out. When she tells him she loves him he stops seeing her. Alone in her apartment, Judy drinks vodka and has more violent fantasies of revenge, but she never gets around to acting them out. Never, that is, until Irv Smiley pushes her over the edge.

22

Solid thighs, like redwoods. A narrow waist, V-ing out to extraordinary lats and traps. Good arms, not bulky, but good triceps and decent biceps. Solid deltoids, and through the spacious armholes of the tanktop could be seen occasional glimpses of breasts — admittedly small, but definitely breasts, not pecs, with tight pink nipples on the ends. She stood and moved like a guy and she was proud of it.

"Oh, by the way, Judy," she said to the slim woman with the long black hair who was doing two-handed pull-downs on the Cybex lat pull-down machine, "I won't be here Friday, so train with Kim then and I'll pick ya up again on Monday, O.K.?"

"O.K.," said Judy. She relinquished the pull-down bar to her trainer and gazed upward to the double-height ceiling, with its exposed pipes and heating ducts and peeling paint that curled away from the plaster like badly burned skin. With what they charged you to train at this grim, pool-less, Jacuzziless, saunaless, steamroomless, subterranean torture chamber, you'd think they could at least paint the fucking ceiling.

Judy Wells admired her new trainer. Ronnie was stronger and had a better build than most of the male trainers at Sports Training Institute, and yet she was not a lesbian. She even had a boyfriend. You could bet Ronnie didn't take any shit from him either.

"Where will you be Friday, Ronnie?" asked Judy.

"Competing," said Ronnie.

"Really?" said Judy. "Weightlifting, you mean?"

"Nah, bodybuilding." This a little apologetically, as if weightlifting might have been more honorable.

"No kidding," said Judy. "That's great."

"Yeah, well, *I* get a kick out of it."

"Well, you ought to do very well in the competition. You've got a wonderful build."

"Yeah?" said Ronnie, trying on the compliment for size and deciding it was a poor fit. "This is nothin'. You oughta see when I *flex*."

"Good definition, huh?"

Ronnie nodded matter-of-factly.

"Also in competition I get to rub this dark-colored goop all over my body. It really looks terrific. I'll hafta bring in my pictures sometime to show ya."

"I'll bet you look great in them," said Judy, then wondered if she were expressing a bit too much interest in her trainer's body. She did admire the muscular young woman's physique, much more than her own, much more than any man's in the gym, but she certainly didn't want Ronnie to think she was hot for her.

"How often do you work out?" said Judy, hoping to put the conversation on a more technical track, but also entertaining a brief fantasy of building herself up like Ronnie if it didn't entail too much work.

"About four hours a day."

"Four hours a day," said Judy, deciding that looking like Ronnie was more trouble than it was worth. "How many days a week, though, three?"

"Seven."

"Seven?" said Judy. "I thought you weren't supposed to do that. I mean, I thought you were supposed to let the muscles recover for a day between workouts."

"I do," said Ronnie patiently. "I work on different muscle groups on different days."

A short, pudgy male client on the adjoining Nautilus machine let his weights fall back down too fast on the relaxation stroke. They made an embarrassing *clang* that resounded through the machine room and caused several heads to turn.

"Fuckin' asshole," said Ronnie under her breath, just loud enough for him to hear her. "Fuckin' fat wimpy faggot asshole."

Judy let her gaze travel to the client who had just disgraced himself. He *was* a fat wimpy asshole, she thought, although she doubted he was a faggot. He reminded her more than a little of Irv Smiley, the man she'd killed.

Irv Smiley had been a minor executive at Manhattan Cable TV when she went there to interview for a job. He'd tried to hit on her immediately, but she wasn't at all interested in him and pretended not to know what he was doing. He was short, obvious, and not very attractive. He told her she had the right qualifications for the job, but there were two other applicants with more experience. He said he'd let her know.

A week later he called to say that it was between her and another girl, and could they talk it over at dinner. She wanted the job and felt she could handle the pass when it came, so she accepted his invitation.

Dinner was at an unexpectedly tasteful Northern Italian place on the West Side, and Smiley surprised her by knowing something about Italian food. If only he didn't have such a crude sense of humor. "Ya know why God made whiskey?" was one of his jokes. "So fat women could get laid."

Judy resented the joke, having been fat herself as a girl, and ordered another Absolut on ice. The more Absoluts she had, the less obnoxious Smiley looked to her. At certain moments, and from certain angles, his face looked almost, well, not unattractive. *Ya know why God made whiskey? So short unattractive men could let laid.*

After an extremely tasty zabaglione and three more Absoluts, Judy began feeling horny.

"I've just had an amazing idea," said Smiley, as if he were about to invent gasohol. "What would you think of coming back to my place for a nightcap?"

"It's late," she said, hating herself for wanting to be talked into going home with him, "and you have to get up in the morning."

"It's not that late," he said, shooting a glance at the wrist with the Rolex. "Besides, you've never seen my place."

The temptation to see where he lived was less than overwhelming but, against her better judgment, she allowed him to talk her into going back for a nightcap.

Once they got there he became a real asshole, swaggering about the place, showing off, putting her down in subtle ways. He made her take off her clothes herself and watched while she undressed. It was a power thing and she resented it. With another man it might have been exciting. With Smiley it was demeaning.

Only when she had peeled off the last of her underclothes and stood there naked and vulnerable for him to ogle did he even begin to undress himself. When he was naked she realized why. Smiley had a soft, womanish body and his penis was disproportionately small. If she hadn't been seriously drunk she would have gotten dressed and gone home right then. But the vodka had deadened the part of her brain that registered distaste at short, pudgy male bodies. More importantly, it deadened her sober distaste for sex.

She pushed him down on the bed and began hungrily caressing him, reached for his rapidly stiffening little penis, and tried to shove it inside of her.

Her aggressiveness must have scared him because his penis went as limp as linguini. To assert his manhood Smiley slugged her, a hard close-handed punch to the jaw.

It was the first time anyone had ever struck her. Her head swelled with rage like a balloon filling with water. She scarcely felt the pain. She swung wildly at him with her fists, connecting only once, the punch bouncing ineffectually off his pudgy, feminine breast. He lunged forward, grabbed her wrists, and with unexpected strength pinned them behind her.

They were both breathing hard. Smiley was pleased at having over-powered her so easily. He must have felt this restored his errant man-hood, for his little prick grew stiff again. She was so enraged her head felt as if it might explode, but she realized she was no match for him in upper body strength. She stopped struggling and relaxed. He continued to hold her, her wrists pinned behind her back.

Trapped with her head against his neck, her eyes focused on objects atop his night table. A packet of letters bound with a rubber band wait-ing to be mailed. A roll of postage stamps in a clear plastic holder. A folded white cotton handkerchief. A mess of small change. A ring of keys. A small case the size of a pack of matches with a retract-able steel blade.

Her eyes irised down on the plastic case like lasers. She could feel her heart beating. She sighed loudly. She moved her cheek against his neck.

"You're very strong." A whisper.

"Shut up," he said, certain she was mocking him.

"I mean it. I had no idea you were so strong. It really turns me on." She didn't whisper this, she breathed it directly into the flesh of his neck.

This time he believed her. He laughed softly and pulled her down on top of him and entered her. He came within seconds, and when he was drained she held back the retch with her teeth and covered his face with kisses.

He sighed and closed his eyes and within sixty seconds was snoring softly. She moved her fingers softly over his neck and located his carotid, the artery her trainers at Sports Training Institute had taught her to use for taking her pulse while exercising. With an engorged excitement similar to sex, only greater, she stretched forward, palmed the small plastic case, extended the blade forward with her thumb, and thrust it swiftly into his neck.

The sudden pulsing geyser of blood caught her by surprise. She was bathed in it. Smiley awoke, hysterical, disbelieving, and thrashed around, screaming like a girl, unable to think of anything to do to prevent his life from pulsing out of him.

Judy watched him sink and twitch, her heart pounding. Just before his eyes glazed over, she explained it.

"Now we're even, you fuck."

Although he was probably dead, she was overwhelmed by another wave of rage. She battered his face with her closed fists until the anger was finally spent. Then she stared at him, quite fascinated with what she'd done.

She felt no remorse. She felt a tremendous feeling of satisfaction. Justice, she felt, had finally triumphed. After years of being degraded by men and raging in silence she'd finally killed one who'd hurt her. He had surely deserved it. He had to be punished.

She picked up the plastic case with the extendible blade she'd used to cut Smiley's throat. A nice little weapon. You never know when such a nifty little gadget might come in handy again. She dropped it into her purse. She was exhausted and still drunk and covered with Smiley's blood. She had even gotten blood in her eyes. She went into his bathroom and started cleaning herself up with a wet washcloth, then figured the hell with it. She ran a hot tub, climbed in, and soaked for at least half an hour.

By the time she finished her bath she'd sobered up a little. She went about the apartment, wiping fingerprints from everything she might have touched. She looked at Smiley's tiny, deflated penis and wondered if she could be identified from vaginal juices. She took a washcloth and wiped it clean.

She realized it might not be wise to be seen leaving Smiley's apartment looking as she did when she entered. Who'd seen her come in, the doorman? Other tenants? She remembered only the doorman. She wondered if he'd be able to describe her to the police.

She looked in Smiley's closet for something to wear. Everything was short, but she finally found a pair of slacks that fit her and a hat to hide her hair. She left quietly, pulling the door closed behind her. Halfway down the corridor she thought she heard somebody come out of another apartment into the hallway, a neighbor perhaps. She walked a little faster. She didn't look back.

At home she contemplated her deed. She still felt no remorse. In a way it wasn't even she who'd killed him. It was the dark entity within her, who'd raged in silence every time she'd been hurt since she'd been a little girl, an entity whom she alone knew existed, who only emerged when the pathway was lubricated with vodka.

Unlike Judy, her entity was powerful. Unlike Judy, her entity was vengeful. Like Stevenson's Mr. Hyde, only hers wasn't a Mr. She decided to call her entity Monty Black — Black for the black widow spider, Monty for the French pronunciation of "mantis," a species of insect whose females routinely bite their males' heads off after mating.

Monty Black had taken spontaneous revenge against Irv Smiley and drawn first blood, but Irv Smiley was not the only man who'd abused her. Others like Freddy Petlin . . . Walter Barmack . . . Teddy Greco . . . Stuart Sherman . . . Austin Richards . . . . Why should Smiley die and the others live? It made no sense. It wasn't fair.

Unless, of course, they'd changed. Some of them she hadn't seen in years. Conceivably they'd matured, mellowed, forsaken their venal ways. If so, when she saw them she would know. If so, they'd be spared. But if they were still driven by their cocks, they would have to die. She would track them down and give them a chance. God gave even the citizens of Sodom and Gomorrah a chance.

The phone rang. Max and Caruso, typing up their accursed fives, competed at not answering it. Finally Max, tired of the sound, caught it on the twelfth ring.

"Two-Five squad, Segal."

"Oh, is this Detective Segal?"

"Who's this?"

"It's Susan, Max. Susan Simon. It rang so long I thought no one was there. I do hope I'm not calling at an inconvenient time."

Max, she'd called him *Max*.

"Susan! Hey, how ya doin', Susan?"

Caruso looked up and scowled.

"Well, fine. I was just typing up my notes from our interview and I found I had a lot of questions. I wondered if it would be convenient for me to come back and ask you some more questions about the cases? Unless you think I'd be in the way."

"No, no, you wouldn't be in the way at all, Susan—"

"The *fuck* she wouldn't!"

Max interposed his body between Caruso and the phone, as if that would screen out his partner's vulgarity.

"You want us to pick you up?"

"Well, golly, that would be wonderful, Max, but I wouldn't want to put you to any trouble. I mean, I wouldn't want you to go out of your way or anything."

"No problem, Susan. In fact, we were going to drive down to Midtown to talk to somebody connected with the Petlin case anyway. Maybe you'd like to come along and listen in."

A terrific groan from Caruso.

"Oh, I'd love to."

"Great. Gimme your address again, huh?"

"It's 427 East Fifty-second, Max. That's just East of First. Should I wait for you outside?"

"No, wait in the lobby. I'll come in and get you."

"*No, wait* in the *lob*by, I'll *come* in and *get* you," mimicked Caruso in a high voice in the background.

Max made a vicious face at Caruso and protected the mouthpiece from further indignities with his cupped hand.

"How long do you think you'll be?"

"Uh, lemme see. About thirty minutes, that O.K.?"

"Thirty minutes would be wonderful, Max. Thank you."

Max hung up the phone.

"*No, wait* in the *lob*by, I'll *come* in and *get* you," said Caruso again in the high voice.

"Shut up, Caruso, for Christ's sake."

"Not *much* you don't want to get into that broad's pants, you phony, not *much*."

"She's a member of the press, Caruso. The boss told us to be nice to her."

"The boss said be *nice* to her, right. The boss didn't say pull down her pants and kiss her ass. Your nose is so brown from that phone call it looks like a fuckin' Hershey bar."

"Kiss my ass, Caruso."

"Kiss *mine*."

It took less than twenty minutes to whip down the FDR to the Fifty-third Street exit, and about two minutes more before Max pulled up in front of Susan's building. Susan wasn't visible. Had he said twenty minutes or thirty? Maybe they were late and she'd gone back upstairs.

"Your girlfriend is makin' you wait already, I see," said Caruso, lighting up a cigar.

"She's not my girlfriend," Max said and got out of the car.

Susan came out of the building. She looked even better than he remembered her. And now he noticed her scent, a fresh, young fragrance. Why didn't Babette ever wear anything like that? Susan was maybe five to eight years older than Babette, but she looked and smelled younger.

"Hi!" she said.

"Hi," he said. "Hope we're not late."

"You're not late at all. I just came down."

"Oh, good. Well, let's go, then."

He led her back out to the car.

"Where are we going?"

"There's a guy named Albert Prince who's a suspect in both the Smiley and Petlin cases. He's into the scene at the gay S and M clubs, and somebody told us recently he's been talking about Smiley."

"So we're going to talk to Prince?"

"No," said Max, opening the rear door of the Fury for her, "we already talked to Prince. I mean we tried. He's not willing to cooperate with us just yet, so we're going to see somebody else. Somebody who knows him."

"Somebody who's into the gay S and M scene?"

"Uh, not precisely," said Max.

He helped Susan into the car and then got in the driver's side.

"You remember Sal Caruso of course?"

"Hi, Sal."

Caruso merely nodded, then exhaled a cloud of foul-smelling cigar smoke toward the rear of the car.

"Mr. Wainwright will see you now."

Max, Caruso, and Susan got up from the couches in the waiting room and allowed the British secretary to show them into Wainwright's office. It was a large corner office and it had twenty-seventh floor views of the city to the East and South. You could have squeezed Max's entire apartment into it and had room left over for a walk-in closet.

"Detectives?"

Wainwright rose from the table in the center of the room which served as his desk. The desk was barren except for a speaker-phone and three photographs of his wife and children in silver frames. Wainwright had a face that looked like it was used to getting its way. High cheekbones, high forehead, long patrician nose, long thrusting jaw, bushy black eyebrows, aluminum-colored hair that lay on his forehead like bangs. Max estimated Wainwright's age at sixty.

"Mr. Wainwright," said Max, extending his hand, "I'm Detective Segal, this is Detective Caruso and . . . Detective Simon."

Max winked at Susan. She blushed.

"Scotty Wainwright," said Wainwright, shaking hands all around. "Please."

They took seats on wide chrome-and-leather Barcelona chairs facing Wainwright. Wainwright sat down on a corner of his desk, placing himself on a higher level than his visitors and in a decidedly more casual position. There was an uncomfortable pause.

"We're here to talk about your buddy Albert Prince," said Caruso, sensing Wainwright's positioning strategy and trying to shift the balance a little in the room.

Wainwright regarded them impassively.

"What is it you wish me to tell you about Mr. Prince?"

"How well do you know him?" asked Max.

"Quite well," said Wainwright.

"Well enough to know he's a suspect in the Smiley and Petlin homicides?" said Max.

A pause.

"What makes him a suspect?"

"He was reported talking about Mr. Smiley in a familiar way," said Max, "and he refused to talk to us when we asked him about it."

"I see. How does that make him a suspect?"

"Excuse me?" said Max.

"How does that make Mr. Prince a suspect?"

"Well," said Max, "the fact that he was unwilling to talk looks suspicious. It looks like he has something to hide."

"I imagine he *does* have something to hide," said Wainwright.

"You do?" said Caruso.

"I imagine so," said Wainwright. "I imagine you do as well."

"Huh?" said Caruso, suddenly flustered.

"I imagine everyone in this room has something to hide," said Wainwright. "I know *I* do. But that doesn't make us suspects in a murder case."

"Mr. Wainwright," said Max, "Irving Smiley was killed on Friday, April eighth, Frederick Petlin on Tuesday, April twelfth. Would you be able to tell us anything of Albert Prince's whereabouts on either of those nights?"

Wainwright appeared to be giving this some thought. Then he abruptly stood up and walked to the door. Max thought he'd taken offense at the question and was terminating the interview. Instead Wainwright opened the door and said in a loud voice: "Miss Earnshaw?"

The British secretary appeared in the doorway.

"Do you have my calendar, Miss Earnshaw?"

The secretary disappeared, then reappeared with a large, leatherbound calendar so fast she must have anticipated Wainwright's request.

"Yes, Mr. Wainwright."

"What do you show for the evenings of Friday, April the eighth and Tuesday, April the twelfth?"

The secretary flipped through the pages of the calendar. "On April eight you had dinner at '21' with Mrs. Wainwright, sir. On April twelve you had dinner alone at the home of Mr. Albert Prince."

"Thank you, Miss Earnshaw."

The secretary vanished. Wainwright turned to Max, Caruso, and Susan.

"Is there anything else you wish to know?" said Wainwright.

"I guess not," said Max.

He put his hand lightly on her shoulder as they were escorted out of the room.

25

"What do you mean you can't tell whether Smiley or Petlin had sex before they died?" said Max, breathing through his mouth to repress the stench of the autopsy room. "I thought we were taking that for granted."

Chernin, peeling Freddy Petlin's scalp carefully down over his face, flashed a patronizing smile.

"In forensic medicine, Max," he said, "one doesn't take anything for granted. There is honestly no way to tell if either Mr. Smiley or Mr. Petlin had sex before they exsanguinated. True, we may find dried semen on the glans penis, but that doesn't tell us much, because the semen might only have dribbled out post mortem when the sphincter relaxed."

Chernin peeled the rear portion of Petlin's scalp and folded it back over his ears. Max thought of bananas and rubber masks and wondered how bad it was that they could no longer say both victims had had sex before death. Pretty bad.

"Did you take oral and anal swabs of Smiley as I requested?" said Max, turning his irritation on Chernin.

The M.E. nodded, switched on the electrical autopsy saw, and inserted it into Petlin's skull.

"And?" asked Max, talking above the hideous sound.

"And," said Chernin, moving the vibrating blade across the top of the skull, producing a small shower of fine particles of bone and hair, "both swabs were negative for semen."

"So what are you telling me," said Max, "Smiley didn't have sex before he died?"

"No," said Chernin, reversing the saw's direction, "only that the killer doesn't appear to have ejaculated in Mr. Smiley's mouth or rectum."

Chernin turned off the saw and Max, knowing what was coming next, chose to look away.

He glanced over at the body on the next table. A light-skinned Hispanic woman. Early twenties. Slim, lovely body. Fiercely beautiful face, even in death. The elderly Russian M.E. who'd drawn her had yet to slice her crown and peel her down. Max wondered what she'd been like alive and what had led up to the seven gunshot wounds in her chest. He had a fleeting fantasy the young woman would be sewn up, brought back to life, and be annoyed that strange men had cut her open and stared at her nakedness. Max let his eye stray down to her thick black bush and caught himself having an inappropriate thought.

"Let's say the killer was giving Smiley a blow job," said Max, still looking at the young Hispanic woman and dreading the soft, sucking sound that would mean Chernin was pulling the sawed-out section off of Petlin's skull. "Or let's say Smiley was screwing the guy in the rear. Wouldn't there be evidence of that on Smiley's penis? Dried saliva or fecal material? Some shit like that?"

Chernin pulled off the skullcap and Max shuddered.

"There might be either of those,"said Chernin. "If he had fellatio performed on him we might very well find amylase from the killer's saliva on Mr. Smiley's penis. I didn't swab Mr. Smiley's penis when he was posted because you didn't ask me to, but I could certainly swab Mr. Petlin's. Would you like me to do that, Max?"

"*Like* it," said Max. "I'd fucking *love* it."

26

"O.K., gentlemen, what've we got?" said McIlheny looking around the squad at the ten homicide detectives sitting on desks and in the chairs.

"Albert Prince is a dead end for now," said Max.

"His boyfriend vouches for his whereabouts on the night of the Petlin homicide," said Caruso. "Course, that don't mean they couldn'ta done Petlin *together*."

"Who went to the funerals?" asked McIlheny.

A detective named Quinlan raised his hand.

"Myself and Tommy went to Smiley's," said Quinlan. "We took pictures of everybody."

"Get anything?" said McIlheny.

"Nah," said Quinlan. "But the family is ordering three eleven-by-fourteens, three five-by-sevens, and twelve wallet-sized prints, so we'll come out O.K. on the job."

Several guffaws.

"And the Petlin funeral? Who went to that? Hollywood?"

Haggerty raised his hand.

"Myself and Ruiz," said Haggerty. "Zilch. Not even a print order."

Some polite chuckles. Hollywood's quip was obviously derivative of Quinlan's, but he was popular enough for them to laugh anyhow.

"O.K.," said McIlheny, "who's running down Smiley's address book?"

Several detectives raised their hands.

"Anybody got anything yet?"

A chorus of uh-uhs, nos, nahs, nothins, nadas.

"Petlin's?"

More negative grunts.

"Who's got some forensic reports for me?"

Max raised his hand.

"First serology," said Max, looking at his notes. "Smiley had type O blood, Petlin type A. Blood samples from both crime scenes were respectively O and A and are presumed to be the victims'. There's no way to determine whether either Smiley or Petlin had sex before death, but anal and oral swabs for semen in both autopsies were negative, and a swab of Petlin's penis showed neither dried saliva nor fecal material."

"What does that mean?" said McIlheny.

"It means," said Max, "that so far we can't prove either Smiley or Petlin had sex with the killer before they died, but we strongly *suspect* it. Next, hair and fiber. Several hairs were found in the beds and in the traps of the sink and tub drains. Some of the hairs were characteristic of the victims and some weren't. Of those that weren't, some at the Smiley crime scene had root sheaths."

"That sounds good," said McIlheny. "Anybody analyzing them?"

"About the only thing you can do with it is DNA fingerprinting," said Max, "but there's nothing yet to match it to."

"What about latent prints?" said McIlheny.

"Yeah," said Hollywood, "we hear you and Caruso planted yours all over the Smiley crime scene."

More laughter. Max began perspiring slightly.

"One thing I can tell you," said Max, "is the prints CSU lifted from the S and M equipment in Petlin's apartment look very good."

"Yeah?"

"*Too* good, in fact."

"What do you mean?"

"The surfaces were too clean, the prints too clear, and the equipment itself looked too new," said Max. "I think the perp bought it for the occasion and staged the scene."

"To make us think what?" said McIlheny.

"That he was a gay S and M killer," said Max. "So either he's not gay, or else . . ."

"Or else?"

"Or else he's not a guy," said Max.

Everybody looked at Max.

"You sayin' it's a female, Segal?"

Max shrugged.

"Why else would the perp try so hard to make us think we're looking for a male?"

116

Stroke . . . stroke . . . stroke . . . stroke . . . stroke.

"Do you like that, precious?"

Stroke . . . stroke . . . stroke . . . stroke . . . stroke.

"Does that feel good, darling?"

Stroke . . . stroke . . . stroke . . . stroke . . . stroke.

"Yes, you like that, don't you, sweetheart?"

Keeping a tight grasp on its tail, Judy Wells pulled the stiff wire brush through the cat's thick fur, going against the direction of growth, collecting enough fluff to stuff a sofa, as the cat dug her claws into the twelve-hundred-dollar red-and-white Early American quilt that served as a bedspread, arched her back as though she were mating, and purred loudly enough to be heard in the next apartment.

There wasn't much furniture in the five-room co-op, but what there was had been selected with care. An Eames captain's chair with a molded plywood back and deep leather cushions. A couple of chrome-and-leather Breuer chairs. Several oak pieces that had been carefully stripped and waxed. A signed Steinberg print of a cat with thought bubbles above its head which read "The *Paris Review*?"

As she groomed her cat, Judy Wells let her thoughts wander. To Irv Smiley. To Freddy Petlin. To Walter Barmack.

Walter Barmack, the romantic real estate agent. Walter Barmack, who found her this very apartment, who took her dining and dancing at the Rainbow Room at the top of the RCA Building in Rockefeller Center and brought her a corsage and wore a white dinner jacket and ordered Dom Perignon at the table just as her father would have done and swept her out onto the dance floor and was so graceful and assured he made her feel for a moment they were Fred Astaire and Ginger Rogers.

Walter Barmack, who took her on a hansom cab ride in the moonlight in Central Park, who took her to Tiffany to browse through rings, who took her to bed—this very bed on which she sat grooming her cat. Walter Barmack, who, when she shyly told him he was the most romantic man she'd ever met and couldn't help falling in love with him, abruptly stopped seeing her. Abruptly stopped seeing her and, when she tried to telephone him at Greenwald Realty, refused to take her calls. Walter Barmack.

She stopped brushing the cat, went to the phone directory, looked up Greenwald Realty, and dialed the number.

"Greenwald, good morning."

"Hello, does Walter Barmack still work there?" said Judy. "This is his cousin Cindy from Denver. I was told to look him up when I got to New York, but I'm afraid this may be an old number."

"Who did you wish to speak with, ma'am?"

"Walter Barmack?"

"Just a moment, ma'am."

Click.

If he were there what would she do? Would she get him on the line? Actually talk to the bastard after all these years? What would she say?

"Ma'am?"

"Yes?"

"There is nobody currently employed here by that name. But one of the agents says there was a Walter Barmack who worked here a few years ago. He suggests you try Burnam & Bolls."

"Burnam & Bolls."

"Yes, ma'am."

"Well, thank you. You've been most helpful."

Burnam & Bolls was listed in the building directory on the twenty-sixth floor. Judy took the elevator up to twenty-six, got out, and walked down the hallway. At the end of the corridor were two glass doors on which was sandblasted the name *Burnam & Bolls* in a small, tasteful typeface.

Judy looked at her watch. Eleven-forty-five. Nearly lunch time. She got into another elevator and descended to the lobby. At twelve sharp she started checking the people as they emerged from the elevators. Nobody who even looked like Walter Barmack.

At seven minutes after twelve she spotted him. Tall, black hair, handsome face, widow's peak, horn-rimmed glasses, confident stride.

Her heart began to thunder in her chest. He was with an attractive, short-haired redhead, probably a client. Judy wondered whether Walter was fucking her.

Judy put on her mirrored aviator sunglasses and watched. The redhead and Walter went through the revolving door. Pulse racing, Judy followed them. Out on the street she kept half a block behind them. The sidewalk was thick with lunch hour traffic and Judy had to scurry quickly around clumps of people to keep Walter and the redhead in sight.

They stopped at an inexpensive restaurant and, after a moment's conference, went inside. Well, he wasn't fucking her, she decided. Not yet, at any rate. Maybe later, after he found her an apartment. Why don't we celebrate at the Rainbow Room. What a marvelous idea, Walter. Oh, the view is breathtaking. Care to dance? Holding the redhead loosely, confidently, in his strong arms on the dance floor, moving closer, ever closer as they danced, until their bodies were nearly touching. . . .

Judy entered the restaurant and looked around. It was early and not many of the booths were taken yet. Judy walked past them and took a seat in an adjoining booth, at Walter's back. A waitress brought menus.

"Will you be alone?" she asked.

Yes, thought Judy, for a lifetime.

"No, a friend is joining me," she said, fearful she'd be asked to surrender the booth if she told the truth. "But I'll look at the menu while I'm waiting for him. Do you have cocktails?"

"Yes, ma'am."

"Good. Bring me an Absolut on ice while I'm waiting."

"I don't know if we have that brand, ma'am."

"Any vodka on ice will be fine."

The waitress left two menus. Judy picked one up, pretended to peruse it, and stared over it to Walter's back. She looked at his neck, his thick manly neck where the hair curled ever so slightly over the top of his collar. She remembered pressing her lips to that neck. She imagined pressing a blade into it, feeling the blood spurt out, spattering all over her.

When Max's elevator arrived at the eighth floor of Four World Trade Center he could already hear distant shouting. He flashed his shield at the guard behind the security desk and then walked out onto the floor of the Commodities Exchange.

It was overwhelming. It was a circus. The room could have held a football field in either direction, which wasn't a bad image because both the level of shouting in the pits and the level of litter on the floor would have rivaled those of any stadium in the country.

Traders — thousands of men and scores of women — stood in twenty-three maroon-carpeted octagonal-shaped pits. They held order pads and wore numbered plastic badges and ill-fitting, unlined, Dacron trader's jackets — orange, yellow, blue, red, any color you could name, stripes, checkerboards — every company with its own uniform. The traders gazed upward at the video display terminals angled down at every pit from steel frames above their heads, flashing current commodity prices at them. They shouted bids at colleagues standing a yard away to buy or sell future contracts in sugar, cocoa, coffee, orange juice, cotton, gold, silver, copper, aluminum, crude oil, heating oil, unleaded gas, natural gas, platinum, palladium, dollar indexes, stock indexes, and CRBs.

Ranged around the pits were banks of phones in shallow beige cubicles, thousands of phones, which flashed rather than rang. Around the room up near ceiling level were enormous black screens with continuously crawling commodity prices and late-breaking trading news. There was too much going on — greed, fear, hysteria. Max thought of Vegas — the huge casino at Caesars Palace, the mammoth slot machine room at Circus Circus — except that wasn't quite it. Vegas was rather sedate by comparison.

Max had split up Petlin's address book among Caruso and several other detectives in the squad to run down all the female names. A woman named Melanie Sanborn, a commodities trader, was next on Max's list, although how he was going to find her in this chaos he couldn't imagine.

Two men in trader's jackets stood in the pit next to Max, two steps down.

"You *knew* the market was going down, motherfucker," said one in an orange jacket. "Why the fuck did you stuff me with them?"

"Because you fucking *bid* for them, motherfucker," said one in yellow.

If this discussion were taking place in the Two-Five, thought Max, one of these guys would now take out an Uzi and blow the other away.

"Excuse me," said Max, flashing his shield. "Either of you gents happen to know a young lady named Melanie Sanborn?"

The two men turned to look at Max, glanced at his shield, shrugged, and resumed their conversation.

"So where's the offer for the two-thirty-five puts?" said the one in the orange jacket.

"The two-thirty-five puts are at one-thirty," said the one in the yellow.

Max walked away. He asked six more people before somebody was finally able to point out Melanie Sanborn. She was nice looking. High breasts, bare legs, a short skirt under her red-and-white-striped trader's jacket. A slight snaggletooth and soft blond hair.

"Excuse me," said Max.

"How's July?" yelled someone in Melanie Sanborn's direction.

"I'm a half bid at sixty, twenty up," she said.

"Excuse me," said Max, walking down the two steps and touching her on the shoulder.

She turned and saw him, scanned his jacket, then looked down at his feet.

"You're not supposed to be in the pit without a badge," she said, pointing to the numbered plastic badge clipped to the lapel of her jacket.

Max took out his gold shield and showed it to her.

"Will this do?" he said.

She smiled, showing the snaggletooth.

"I guess."

"Can you spare a few minutes to talk?" asked Max.

"What about?" Still smiling.

"Freddy Petlin," said Max.

The smile faded.

"Sold five at double," yelled a man next to her in the pit. "How's the follow-up market?"

"I'll be fifty bid for the other five," she said, not looking at him. To Max she said "Why not?"

"This your first time at the Exchange?" said Melanie Sanborn, settling back into the booth of Limit Up, the low-lit traders' bar around the corner.

"Yep."

"Any questions?"

"Yeah," said Max. "What does Limit Up mean?"

"It's a traders' term. To prevent a commodity from going up or down too much, the CFTC has set a limit on how much a contract can move up or down in a certain day — to prevent panic in the pits. So if the price reaches the limit going down it's called limit down, and if the price reaches the limit going up, it's called—"

"Limit up," said Max. "I get it. Why is everybody screaming in the pits?"

"The form of trading in commodities is called 'open outcry.' As opposed to silent electronic trading, I guess. The rule is you have to make yourself heard by anyone who might want to compete. The shriller voices carry better."

The waitress arrived with two bottles of Dos Equis on a tray, a wedge of lime protruding from the top of each, and two glasses. The table top was worn and pitted, but the waitress dutifully put down coasters and set the bottles atop them before she withdrew.

"So," said Melanie Sanborn. "What do you want to know about Freddy Petlin?"

"Well, let's see," said Max. "First, what kind of a guy was he?"

She pushed her lime down into the neck of her bottle with a red lacquered fingernail, raised the bottle to her lips, and took several gulps.

"Freddy was a trader," she said when she'd put the bottle back down on the table.

"Meaning?"

"Meaning he was a little loud and a little vulgar, but not a bad guy," she said. "He was fair. People in the pit liked doing business with him.

Like if a trader found at the close he'd accidentally bought eighty contracts when he'd only meant to buy seventy, Freddy'd take back the other ten, even if they'd gone down."

"And that's legal?"

"Not technically."

"Why would he do that?"

"Traders help each other out that way," she said. "If they don't, after a while you find it hard to hear their bids."

Max nodded. Melanie was systematically stripping the wet label off the beer bottle with a shiny red thumbnail.

"And what was your relationship to Freddy?"

"You mean," she said, cocking her head and looking faintly bemused, "was I sleeping with him?"

"Yeah."

She took a long pull at her beer, then shook her head vigorously, swinging her hair.

"No way," she said. "I admit I did feel a little sorry for the guy, but I'm not into mercy fucks."

"I see," said Max. "Tell me, why do you think you were in Petlin's address book?"

"I *was?*" She looked genuinely surprised. "God, I don't know. The guy was always hitting on me, but I never took it seriously, you know? I mean guys on the floor are always hitting on us. Maybe he really liked me. Hey, wouldn't that be something?"

She seemed oddly touched that a loud, vulgar guy she worked with who was always hitting on her might actually have liked her. She continued stripping the label off the bottle, only now it was an obsession.

"The night of April twelfth, the night Petlin died," said Max gently, "do you happen to recall what you were doing that night?"

Melanie stopped stripping. Her face hardened like fast-drying cement.

"Oh, shit," she said, "is *that* what this is?"

"I'm just asking the question," said Max.

"Yeah, well, I'm just advising you to address all *further* questions about my relationship to Mr. Petlin to my attorneys at Dewey-Ballantine," she said.

She stood up abruptly, jarring the table and sending one of the unused glasses crashing to the floor. Max caught the other backhanded. She pushed past him, unavoidably brushing his shoulder with her buttock, and stalked out of the bar without looking back. The sensation of contact with her buttock remained on his shoulder, tingling.

Max sighed. He was sorry she'd gotten so angry and left. He'd enjoyed talking with her as he did with Susan. He had little reason to think Melanie Sanborn was a serious suspect. He wondered why she'd gotten so huffy when he asked if she had an alibi for the night of Petlin's death.

He doubted it would be worth anything but he reached into his jacket anyway, pulled out a Ziploc bag, fitted it over her beer bottle, and slid it into his pocket.

29

"So," said Joanie Jarvis, "how did you guys do on your assignment?"

"Not too well," said Babette.

"What happened?"

Babette looked at the floor. Max said nothing.

"Well," said Babette, "the one night we tried, Max came in after putting Sam to bed and said something like 'O.K., let's do the assignment.'"

Jarvis made a face and looked at Max.

"And I said, 'Boy *that* sounds romantic.'"

"Yeah?"

"So then," said Babette, "Max—"

"So then," said Max, interrupting, "Max went and got a whole lot of candles and arranged them all around the rim of the tub and filled the tub with bubble bath and got an ice bucket and some ice and put a bottle of wine into it and coaxed—*coaxed*—his wife into the bathroom and out of her clothes and into the tub, and then, thinking he might like a little encouragement for his efforts, made the *unpardonable* mistake of asking her, 'So how do you like it so far?'"

"And what did you say," said Jarvis to Babette.

"I . . . asked him if he wanted me to say how wonderful he was for putting it all together, but—"

"And what did you say, Max?"

"What did I say? I said *yes*. I *did* want her to say something nice to me. Is that some kind of fucking crime or what?"

"And what did you say, Babette?"

"I said . . ."

"You want to know what she said? I'll tell you what she said. She said, 'You spent six minutes setting this up, it's not like you've built me the Taj *Mahal* or anything.' Right?"

"Well, you *did* spend six minutes setting it up. What am I supposed to do, pee all over myself?"

"So then what happened?" said Jarvis.

"I apologized and he wouldn't accept it," said Babette. "He got out of the bath and kicked some of the glass candle holders onto the floor and broke them, and then he left the house and stayed out all night at some gay S and M club."

Jarvis, who rarely allowed her face to show surprise, this time couldn't hide it.

Max held up his hand.

"Before you get the wrong idea," he said, "I don't happen to be a fag. I was undercover on a homicide case."

Jarvis let out a relieved laugh.

Max had a sudden powerful yearning to be out of there, to be out of his marriage, to be in a bathtub with Susan, who would appreciate and treasure him.

"Guys, guys, guys," she said. "You have to learn to communicate with each other. You have to learn to forgive each other, to listen to each other, to listen to what each of you *needs* from the other. You are both so locked into a pattern of blame and guilt that you can't even *hear* each other anymore. You overreact with guilt to everything the other says, to every ounce of implied blame, and you escalate it right through the fucking ceiling. If you were the United States and Russia, you'd have bombed each other off the map by now. I want you to do me a favor."

"What?" said Babette dully.

"I want you to try it again. I want you to try another romantic experience, O.K.? Only this time I want you to *listen* to each other, to what the other is really saying, and then I want you to try and give each other that. O.K.? Will you try that for next time?"

Silence.

"Guys?"

"Sure," said Babette.

"Sure," said Max.

30

Promptly at seven minutes after five Walter Barmack emerged from the Burnam & Bolls building.

So, seven minutes after twelve he goes to lunch, seven minutes after five he leaves for the day — there's a man who loves his work, thought Judy, standing across the street.

This being Midtown, there was a chance he lived within walking distance. Judy followed him from across Madison Avenue. At the corner of Madison and Fifty-fifth, he turned east. Did he live on Fifty-fifth? She waited till he was well ahead of her before she fell into step behind him.

At First Avenue he headed north. She followed him all the way to Sixty-first. He turned east again and entered the corner building. Judy waited five minutes before she crossed the street and walked into the lobby of the building. She wasn't sure what she wanted to find out. Whether Walter was married might be a good place to start.

A uniformed doorman greeted her.

"Help you, Miss?"

"Oh, yes," she said, smiling self-consciously. "I'm Mr. Barmack's secretary. It's his birthday next Thursday and his wife asked me to help her plan a little surprise get-together for him. Would you happen to know if she's at home now?"

The doorman smiled.

"Yes, she is, Miss," he said, "but so is he. He just got home five minutes ago."

"Oh, shoot," said Judy. "I guess he didn't go to that drink meeting after all. Well, I'll just have to try another time."

Judy went through the revolving door.

Well, she thought, so he's married. So taking him back to his apartment to seduce him and kill him wasn't going to work. She certainly couldn't kill him in her *own* apartment. Where else could she do it? And was it worth the trouble?

31

"Dada, I put a hamburger in my ear," said Sam proudly.

Max looked to see if this were true and discovered that it was. His son's ear was crammed with chopped meat and ketchup.

They were in the Oracle, their neighborhood Greek diner on Second Avenue and Nineteenth Street. Chandeliers with orange bulbs shaped like flames hung by heavy brass chains from the fake stucco ceiling. Curlicued wrought iron served as privacy screens between the booths. Mirrors treated to look as if the mercury coating on the back was badly decomposed adorned the fake brick walls. The restaurant was a testament to the art of Greek diner interior designers.

Sam Segal was a celebrity among the waiters here, despite where he chose to put his food.

"Don't ever do this again, Sam," said Max wearily, scooping hamburger out of the tiny ear.

"Why not?"

"Because we don't put hamburgers in our ears," said Max.

"Why *don't* we?" said Sam.

"Because it's dangerous," said Max.

"And it's bad manners," said Babette.

"What's manners?" said Sam.

"Just don't do it anymore, O.K.?"

"O.K."

The waiter appeared, smiling at Sam.

"Nick, do you have a penis?" said Sam.

The red-coated waiter blushed and smiled and cleared away dishes, chuckling.

"Does Nick have a penis, Mama?" asked Sam.

"I expect he does," said Babette, embarrassed and trying to squelch a giggle.

"Yes or no?" said Sam.

"Yes," said Babette.

"Good," said Sam.

When the waiter left, Babette snorted laughter into the crook of her arm. Max disguised his as nose-blowing. Sam regarded them seriously, not sure what they were doing, and took off his shoes.

"Mama, are you laughing or crying?" said Sam.

"Mama is . . . laughing, Sam," she said.

"Oh."

Sam put his straw in his mouth and blew bubbles in his milk.

"Don't do that," said Max.

"Why not?" said Sam.

"Because I said so," said Max.

"Oh, let him," said Babette.

Max frowned at her.

"When I was a little girl my parents didn't let me do it either," said Babette. "But it was fun and I don't see the harm in it. I promised myself when I had a kid I'd let him do it."

Max exhaled loudly and looked away. Sam delightedly resumed blowing bubbles in his milk, but the no-longer forbidden activity soon paled and he stopped. Max looked up to see his son's latest experiment — eating saltine crackers from between his toes. How Sam had managed to get the crackers so quickly between his toes and, more to the point, *why,* Max couldn't fathom.

"Sam!"

Sam looked startled.

"Yes, Dada?"

"We do not eat crackers with our feet!"

Sam's expression revealed this advisory to be a genuine revelation.

"Why don't we?"

"Because we don't, that's why!"

Sam looked at Max a moment and then burst into tears. Babette glared at Max.

"Congratulations," she said, "you frightened a three-year-old."

Sam screamed as though his fingernails were being torn out. Other diners turned to stare at the obvious child abusers, as Max tried to pacify his son.

"Sam," he said, "I'm sorry I yelled at you. I'm really sorry, O.K.? Please don't cry."

Max reached over to caress Sam, but the boy pulled away as if Max's touch were leprous.

"No!" he shouted. "Don't touch me! Go away!"

"Honey, I'm really, really sorry," said Max. "Did I scare you with my loud voice?"

"What do *you* think?" said Babette, taking the wailing boy in her lap to comfort him.

"I didn't ask you, I asked Sam," said Max.

Nick the waiter came over to help.

"Whatsamotta, whatsamotta, Sammy?" said the waiter.

"Nothing," said Max, irritated at the friendly waiter's concern, interpreting it as a comment on his parenting.

"I have to go poopoo!" said Sam.

"C'mon, precious," said Babette, "I'll take you."

Babette got up and carried the still blubbering boy off to the women's room. A middle-aged woman at the next booth with pinkish-red hair continued to stare disapprovingly at Max. Max glared at her but the woman refused to break her gaze.

"Turn around," said Max finally. "Eat your goddam food."

The woman made a shocked and disapproving noise.

"Now I *am* going to report you to the management," she said, starting to get up.

"Save your breath, sweetheart," said Max. "*I'm* the management."

"What?"

"You heard me, I *own* this place," said Max, "and you're outta here *now*."

Max pointed to the door. All the other diners turned to stare. The woman's eyes grew so wide he thought they'd pop right out of her head.

"Don't even bother to pay the check, it's on the house," said Max. "Just get out now and don't ever come back."

The woman stalked out of the restaurant with as much dignity as she could muster. Nick came scurrying over.

"Whatsamotta, Mr. Segal? Whatsamotta?"

"Nothing, Nick," said Max, pulling out a twenty and throwing it down next to the woman's food. "That woman was a friend of mine and I told her I'd pay her check."

Sam returned, pulling a frustrated-looking Babette along behind him.

"Hi, Sam, did you go poopoo?"

"No, Dada, I didn't."

"He refused to use the women's room," said Babette. "He said he didn't see any urinals there."

"Dada, I'm a *boy* and I have a penis, and Mama's a *girl* and she has a vagina, so you have to take me to the *boys'* bathroom, not the *girls'* ."

Gratified that Sam had apparently forgotten his anger, Max took the boy downstairs to the men's room where, as usual, Sam insisted on touching everything.

"Don't touch things in here," said Max, putting toilet paper down on the seat, pulling down his son's pants, and installing him on it.

"Why can't I?"

"Because of the germs."

"What are germs, Dada?"

"Tiny little bugs. So tiny you can't even see them."

"Show me how big, Dada."

"I can't, honey, they're so tiny you can't see them."

"Are they this big?" said Sam, holding up two fingers close together.

"No, smaller than that."

"This big?"

"Even smaller."

"Dada, sometimes my penis goes way out and sometimes it goes way in — in and out, in and out, just like magic. Isn't that funny?"

"It is."

"Does your penis do that, too, Dada?"

"Sometimes."

"Dada, when I grow up I'm going to marry my mom."

"You can't do that, hon."

A sudden pout of defiance, as if he'd been told he couldn't watch Peewee's Playhouse.

"Why can't I?"

"Because Mom's already *got* a husband. Me."

"That's O.K.," said Sam happily, "I'll marry her too. Then she'll have *two* husbands. We'll be two dads together, Dada. Won't that be fun?"

"It doesn't work that way, Sam. Mama can only have *one* husband.

But by the time you grow up you'll meet someone you like just as much as Mama and you'll marry her."

Sam mulled this over, frowning. Squatting down beside the toilet in the cramped booth, Max's face was six inches from his son's. The boy stopped frowning and gazed into Max's face with a beatific smile.

"Hi, Dada."

"Hi, Sam."

Sam spontaneously leaned forward six inches and kissed his father on the mouth. Max was overwhelmed with a surge of love for his tiny son.

"I'm done now, Dada."

Max checked the bowl and saw that it was utterly empty. They washed their hands and went back to the booth.

"He didn't have to go," said Max.

Babette shrugged. They were both familiar with the phenomenon. Max left a big tip for the waiter and they proceeded to the cashier's desk.

The cashier, a twenty-year-old black-haired Greek beauty with a moustache, always gave Max soulful looks. She offered Sam after-dinner mints from a bowl.

"You can have two mints, Sam," said Max.

"I want six mints," said Sam, reaching for the bowl.

"Two is what you get," said Max.

"No, six," said Sam, screwing up his face, poised to bawl.

"Two," said Max firmly.

Sam exploded in tears and turned to Babette.

"Mama, Dada said t-t-t-*two!*"

"You can have six," said Babette wearily.

"*What?*" said Max.

Sam grabbed for the bowl. Max tried to take it away from him. Sam threw it on the ground, shattering it, scattering mints all over the floor. The black-haired beauty with the moustache looked terribly saddened, as if a tryst with the furious dad were no longer a possibility.

Sam threw a tantrum, kicking and screaming on the floor, and Max, babbling apologies, picked him up and carried him out the door.

By the time they reached home Sam had stopped screaming but periodically emitted short, involuntary, choking sobs, like an automobile engine that had been turned off but wasn't quite through.

Nobody was speaking to anybody. Sam was furious with Max because he didn't get his mints, Babette was furious with Max for escalating the scene at the restaurant, and Max was furious at Babette for undercutting his authority.

Max resented having to be the heavy, hated the role of disciplinarian, but, like the role of economizer in their finances, he felt he had to take it because Babette wasn't willing to.

Max started getting Sam ready for bed.

"I don't want Dada to put me to bed," said Sam, "I want *Mama*."

"C'mon, buddy, let's just take these clothes off."

"I don't want Dada, I don't *like* Dada, I want *Mama*."

Stung by his son's words in spite of himself, Max withdrew, trying not to feel hurt. Babette did the going-to-bed countdown, following which Max came in and asked for his usual goodnight kiss. Pleased at his apparent power over the supplicant dad, Sam said no.

When he was sure Sam was asleep Max crept back into the room and pressed his lips to the sleeping child's face.

32

"And how are you feeling today?" asked Dr. Glass.

"Pretty good," said Judy Wells. "No, actually not all that good, to tell you the truth."

She sat primly on the low polyurethane foam couch with the inclined pillow at the end near the window where you were supposed to put your head, although she had never put her head there and never would. She stared at the clean tissue that Dr. Glass had placed there in case she ever did put her head down, which he would crumple up and throw away unused after her session, a waste of money, but he could afford it, the bastard, with what he was probably pulling in.

"What seems to be the trouble?" he said.

"Well," she said, "it's just that I've been trying to decide something and I keep vacillating."

"What are you trying to decide?"

She looked at him and smiled. He was not the most perceptive person in the world, but he meant well. And he had helped her with certain things. Like the fears when she'd first come to New York that people on the street might attack her or that she might attack them. Like her obsessive need to return to bars and restaurants where men had taken her to see if they were there with other women, and if they were to see if the women were more attractive than she was and if they were touching each other. She had told Dr. Glass she was compelled to do these things, that she didn't have a choice. He'd tried to get her to see that she did.

He was so earnest, so supportive, so non-judgmental, so professionally unshockable. She wondered how he'd react if she told him what she'd been up to. She shook her head.

"I don't think I'm ready to talk about it yet."

"Perfectly all right," said Dr. Glass. "You can talk about it whenever you're ready."

"Thank you."

"Perhaps you can just tell me the nature of your dilemma without telling me its content."

"O.K.," she said. "Well, there's something I'd like to do, something I feel I *ought* to do, but it may just be too much trouble to do it."

"Would this thing afford you some satisfaction if you did it?"

"Oh, yes," she said. "Yes, indeed."

"You shouldn't do it if the only reason is that you think you ought to," said Dr. Glass. "But if it would please you, if it would really afford you satisfaction, well then, where's the harm?"

"I don't know," she said. "It might be a lot of trouble. And other people might not approve of what I want to do."

Dr. Glass smiled tolerantly.

"Other people," he said. "Don't always be so concerned about what *other* people think. What do *you* think? Would you approve of what you want to do?"

"Oh, yes," she said, "I certainly would."

"Then do it," he said.

"Yes?"

"Absolutely," he said.

"Well, thank you very much," she said. "I think I may just follow your advice."

"Good for you!" he said.

33

Early Sunday morning. Wearing her mirrored sunglasses, Judy stood on the corner of Sixty-first and First, reading *Vanity Fair*. It was a perfect New York day. Sunny, cool, dry, crisp, the sky an unfamiliar new blue, almost violet, the air so clear the images of buildings fairly snapped.

Even the garbage looked clean today, tied neatly in shiny black bags and placed in trim rows at the curb. If there was raw sewage in the East River, today it had surely sunk to the bottom and recycled harmlessly into the environment. If noxious gases escaped from idling truck or bus exhausts, today they dissipated harmlessly into the just-laundered air. Today cab drivers in improbably clean and undented vehicles slowed to stops at corners when the lights turned red, without swerving, swearing, honking, or hitting pedestrians. Today pedestrians, walking erect, passed on the sidewalks and risked smiles at absolute strangers. On a day like this you felt you could do anything in the world.

She hadn't been standing there for more than an hour when Barmack emerged from his apartment building. He looked so different in faded jeans and canvas sneakers. Younger, softer, more relaxed—almost boyish. The way she remembered him. He crossed the street to her side and went straight to the newsstand. There was a short line.

Still pretending to read the magazine, Judy strolled over and took a position in line right behind him. There he was, inches away, closer than the day at the restaurant, close enough to touch. What would he have done if he'd thought she was standing behind him? What if he'd turned around and seen her?

It wouldn't matter. He would never recognize her now. She looked quite different than when he had known her, than when he had his way with her. The sunglasses, of course, but also the blond hair. Even if she'd looked exactly the same, he still wouldn't have recognized her. We only recognize people we expect to see, and he certainly never expected to see her again, that was for sure.

The line moved forward. They mostly bought the *Times* in this neighborhood, maybe also the *News* for the sports and the comics. The *Times* had no comics and juiceless sports. Now the person in front of Walter was examining his *Times* to make sure he had all the sections. Sometimes they didn't put them all in and you didn't realize it till you got back to your apartment, and then you either had to drag yourself back to the newsstand and complain or go without the section you wanted and feel deprived.

Now Walter was at the head of the line, pulling his dollar and a quarter out of the right hand pocket of his jeans, inches away from her, his secret flesh inches away from her own. This man standing in front of her didn't realize it but he no longer belonged to his wife, his mother, himself, or anybody else. He belonged to her alone.

Now Walter had paid and was moving away. Turning, he let his gaze alight on her for just an instant — not, typically, on her face, oh, no, where there was one chance in fifty he might recognize her and possibly even, as a consequence, save his life. No, Walter's gaze was, predictably, on her body. On her buttocks. From her buttocks up to her breasts, and by then she was at the front of the line, paying for her own *Times,* and Walter had crossed the street and gone back to his apartment for the doubtlessly short time remaining to him on this earth.

When she got her *Times* she checked only one section, and it was there. The real estate section. The Sunday *New York Times* had the finest real estate section in the country. If you were looking for an apartment you had to look in the Sunday *New York Times*.

Scanning two-bedroom co-ops, she found something intriguing. Something on the eighteenth floor of a building on Ninety-second and Central Park West, overlooking the Reservoir and all of Central Park. The asking price was a million five. A million five! Somebody was actually going to cough up close to a million and a half dollars for that apartment! Not she, of course.

There was a phone number to call, the agent. The company was M.B. Sawyer Realty. She went to the phone booth on the corner, inserted a quarter, dialed, and told the person who answered that she was interested in the place on Ninety-second and Central Park West. The agent, a tough-sounding woman named Esther Cross, made an appointment to meet her in front of the building in forty minutes. Had she requested it, the woman would have picked her up in a cab. Had she requested it, the woman would have done her laundry. The commission on a million five was ninety thousand dollars.

The building at Ninety-second and Central Park West was one of the great old West Side limestone buildings with gargoyles and twelve-foot ceilings. A building the same height, if erected in that space today, would have had five more stories.

A stocky middle-aged woman with iron-colored hair was already waiting for her. You bet she was.

"Mrs. Black?" A big artificial smile.

"You must be Esther Cross," said Judy.

"Good to meet you, Mrs. Black," said Esther Cross. "It *is* Mrs.?"

"Yes, yes," said Judy. "I wouldn't need a two-bedroom apartment if it were just me, now would I?"

Esther Cross chuckled a little too enthusiastically over that. You'd have thought it was one of the three wittiest remarks she'd heard all week.

The doorman let them in and they took the elevator up to eighteen. There were large mirrors in the elevator and a red leather bench to sit down on. Judy wondered how long the elevator had been self-service.

"This is a lovely building," said Esther Cross, unlocking the apartment and allowing Judy to enter first. "They've made a lot of improvements and they plan to do a lot more. And the board is very strong. Tell me . . . what does your husband do?"

So casual. *Tell me . . . what does your husband do?* Never mind what *I* do. Never mind that I could be the CEO of a Fortune 500 company. If my husband's profession sounds impressive enough, then maybe I could pay for this place and we could pass the board and you could collect your ninety-thousand-dollar commission.

"Oh," said Judy offhandedly, "he's in money."

"Oh?" said Esther Cross, her eyes bright.

"Yes," said Judy, as if slightly embarrassed to be revealing just how wealthy they were, "he was at Manny Hanny for the longest time, and then he decided to get out. Now he just sits on the board."

She hoped she wouldn't have to do too much more of this. The insiders' nickname for Manufacturer's Hanover Trust was about the extent of her knowledge of banking.

"Ah," said Esther Cross, obviously impressed. "And, uh, what is your husband's, uh, first name?"

"Walter," said Judy.

"Walter . . . *Black*," said Esther, nodding, enormously impressed with the made-up name. "Of course."

Judy looked around the apartment. It was bare and filthy and it smelled of old people.

"I see this place is going to need a lot of work," said Judy, striding swiftly into the kitchen and glancing disapprovingly at the antiquated fixtures. "A whole new kitchen, new bathrooms, new plumbing, new wiring. . . ."

"It's a fixer-upper," said Esther Cross, "but the reason it's only a million five is it's an estate sale. Frankly — and I shouldn't be telling you this — I think they'd take a little less."

A fixer-upper! A million-and-a-half-dollar fixer-upper!

"How *much* less?" said Judy coolly.

Esther Cross looked at her adversary a moment, trying to decide what figure to give her.

"I think if you offered them a million three, all cash, they'd go for it," she said in a low conspiratorial voice, as if the executors of the estate were waiting in the next room, as if she and Esther were secret allies against them.

Judy exhaled with faint amusement and turned away, shaking her head, as if the figure were so preposterously high she could no longer take the agent seriously, which was, in fact, the case. Judy relished her role. If she had really been interested in the apartment rather than acting a part, she'd have been passive, self-deprecating, and apologetic.

"You never know with these estate sales, though," said Esther Cross, deciding she had underestimated her mark, desperately trying to save the situation, "you offer them something really low, they might just be so hungry to get it off their hands they'd go for it."

Judy chortled and walked through the rooms. The large bare dining room and living room with the too-small windows overlooking the fabulous view. The two bedrooms with dust balls on the parquet floors. The terrace. Judy opened the terrace door and stepped outside.

The view was enough quite literally to take your breath away. It hardly seemed as though you were in a busy, filthy city. You felt like you were somewhere in the country with woods, meadows, and a lake.

If I lived here, thought Judy, I would do nothing all day or night but stand on this terrace and look at the view.

Then she examined the terrace itself, which was, of course, her only reason for being there. The railing around it was ornate but rusted iron-work. There were four rusting white metal chairs, a collapsed striped awning badly in need of repair, a round white metal umbrella table without the umbrella, and a chaise longue with plastic basket-weave webbing in better condition than the other furniture. It was perfect for her purposes.

She walked back inside.

"I'm afraid it isn't quite what I had in mind," said Judy.

Esther Cross looked at her a moment, knowing she'd blown it by quoting the stupid million three figure, wondered whether she ought to tell her what the estate would really take for it — seven hundred and fifty thousand — and then figured the hell with it, why not cut your losses.

"Frankly, my dear," said Esther Cross, "I didn't *think* you'd care for it. It's much too depressing and it needs too much work. But I have something right across the park on Fifth which you . . . are . . . going . . . to . . . *die* for."

34

"Why do I have to wear this? I don't *like* this. I'm not a baby, I'm a big boy."

"I know you're a big boy," said Max, "but if you wear this they'll think you're a *little* boy, and then we won't have to buy a ticket for you."

"What's a ticket?"

"It's what you need to buy to get into the circus," said Max.

"Max, this is stupid," said Babette. "Nobody is going to believe he's under two."

"Sure they will," said Max. "He's small for his age. And why would you want to spend the money for a third ticket if you didn't have to?"

"I don't want to *wear* this," said Sam, pulling at the toddler jumpsuit, "I *hate* this!"

"Listen, Sam," said Max sternly, "do you want to go to the circus or not?"

"Not," said Sam.

"How do you know?" said Max, chagrined at having been out-bluffed by a three-year-old. "You've never been to one before."

"Max, let him wear what he wants to wear," said Babette.

"I thought you *liked* dressing him younger," said Max.

"I do," she said, "but not that young. This really looks stupid on him."

She opened the refrigerator, started to take out the mocha éclair she'd bought and been saving for herself for lunch, then decided there wasn't time to enjoy it properly and closed the refrigerator door.

"Babette, just humor me this once, will ya?" said Max. "We can save eighteen dollars."

"Max, if we don't leave right now it doesn't matter *what* he wears because the circus will have started without us."

In the crush of parents and children at Madison Square Garden Max shouted above the noise, coaching Sam not to talk near the ticket takers, or if he did talk, to say nothing but "Dada" and "googoo." He needn't have worried. The besieged ticket takers were far more worried about being trampled to death than they were about the possibility that a three-year-old masquerading as an under-two was sneaking in without a ticket.

Although Max had paid top dollar for the tickets — characteristically nullifying whatever savings he had achieved by the age deception with Sam — by the time they reached their seats they were so high up they could scarcely see anything at all.

The circus *had* already started, but it hardly mattered. There was so much going on, even Max didn't know where to look first. In one ring several Asian gentlemen in white pants and spangled shirts were jumping off the ends of high-tech teeter-totters, doing unreasonable numbers of somersaults in the air before they came down. In another ring an endless procession of clowns was climbing out of a tiny Volkswagen. Max wondered idly how they could all fit inside it, and then realized he didn't care.

In the third and closest ring, a trained bear was riding a unicycle.

"Sam, *look*," said Max excitedly. "A bear is riding a unicycle!"

Sam looked happily in the wrong direction and nodded, content with his father's enthusiasm.

"No, no, right down *there*. See?" said Max. "See that bear down there? He's riding a unicycle!"

Now Sam saw where his father was pointing, but he still only nodded politely. He had never been to a circus before, but he was little more than mildly amused by bears riding unicycles. In his Richard Scarry books bears rode unicycles all the time. They also drove bulldozers, flew biplanes, and baked birthday cakes.

The bear unicycled out of the ring and, with a great to-do, was replaced by a fellow in a leopard skin with a shaved head who, the ringmaster announced, was about to wrestle vicious man-eating alligators. But instead of vicious man-eating alligators, out came a succession of smallish creatures who were nearly comatose on tranquilizers. The Mr. Clean–type went through a lot of melodramatic moves designed to show

how risky a venture he was engaged in, but the drugged gators undercut his performance by barely struggling. One crawled to the edge of the ring and, before Mr. Clean could get to him, fell asleep.

"I don't know about that guy," said Max dubiously. "It's not much of an act. Maybe the regular guy got sick and this is a temp."

Irritated as she was with Max, Babette couldn't resist laughing. Seeing her laugh, Sam laughed as well. Soon all three of them were roaring with laughter. It felt good.

When the big lion act came out Sam advised everyone within earshot that he had to go poopoo. Heaving a tremendous sigh, Max picked him up and carried him down the crowded row of children and parents toward the aisle.

They returned from the circus in the late afternoon. Despite having missed the big lion act, Sam had had a marvelous time, but now he was exhausted and cranky. The circus flashlight with the fiber-optic brush sticking out of the lens end which they'd bought worked till they got inside their apartment door, then quit forever, which made the napless three-year-old burst into tears.

As Babette set about putting Sam down for a short nap, Max went into the kitchen, looking for something to eat. In the refrigerator was a tempting mocha éclair. Without thinking about it, he picked it up and began to eat.

Babette strolled into the kitchen, sighing, saw Max, and stopped dead in her tracks.

"What are you doing?" she said, disbelievingly.

"Eating a mocha éclair," said Max, his mouth full of mocha filling. "Want a bite?"

"That . . . was . . . *my* . . . mocha . . . éclair," said Babette, instant icicles forming on her wordstream.

"Yeah?" said Max. "Sorry. I didn't see your name on it."

"How *dare* you eat my mocha éclair?" she said.

"How *dare* I?" said Max. "Is that what you said — how *dare* I? How *dare* you say 'how *dare* you' to me?"

"I have been saving that mocha éclair for myself," said Babette, ignoring the argumentative-redundant syntax. "That éclair happened to be about the only thing in this house that was mine, and what did you do? You came right in here and, without even *asking* me if it was mine, you ate it."

"It's not the end of the fucking world, Babette," he said tiredly.

"Isn't it?" she said. "I think it is."

"What?" he said.

"I said I think it *is*. I cannot abide your . . . your selfishness and your . . . thoughtlessness and your utter disregard for my *feelings* a moment longer."

"Meaning what?" he said warily.

"Meaning that I will not take it any longer. Meaning that I have *had* it with you!" she said and burst into tears.

"You've had it with me, have you?" said Max. "Well, I've fucking well had it with *you!* I'm fucking sick of the way we've been living lately. This isn't a marriage, this is a fucking prizefight!"

"Good," she said, "because it's now over and we both lost. I'll just go and get Sam out of bed and we'll find ourselves some other place to live."

He stared at her, his heart beginning to pound. Nobody was pulling back. They were allowing it to escalate. This fight looked like it could go all the way. Did he want it to? Was he willing to end the marriage right then and there over a mocha éclair? He thought of Susan. The notion of Susan getting into a lather over a mocha éclair was unimaginable.

"Don't be absurd," said Max, "you can't move out of here."

"No?"

"No. *I'm* the man, *I'll* move out of here."

"Fine," she said, "move out, then."

"Fine," he said, "I will."

He strode to the closet and yanked a suitcase out of a pile residing precariously on the top shelf, which sent them all cascading down on top of his head. There was no dignity in pathos. All tragedy was farce.

He grabbed one of the suitcases, strode into the bathroom, and threw in all his toilet articles. Then he strode into the bedroom and threw in an armload of his clothes. Then he went to the door and opened it.

"I am going now," he said, his voice shaking. He didn't know what he wanted from her. To be told not to go, he supposed.

"Fine," she said. "Go."

"Fine," he said, and walked through the door.

35

"Holy shit," said Tony Natale, opening the door, looking Max over and seeing the suitcase in his hand. "You really did it. You left Babette."

"That's right," said Max, "I did."

"I can't believe you actually did it."

"Well, believe it," said Max, "because you've got a new roommate."

"Son of a bitch," said Natale. "What finally did it? What was the last straw?"

"A mocha éclair," said Max.

"A mocha éclair," said Natale, admiringly. "Perfect. A mocha éclair is certainly a valid issue over which to end a marriage. C'mon in. Make yourself at home."

Home was a small one-bedroom apartment in the West Village. Natale had been separated from his wife for almost a year, but his apartment looked like he had just moved in. There were no pictures on the walls, no curtains on the windows, no homey touches. Unopened cartons of books stood everywhere.

Natale thought it best to lay out some ground rules: he and Max would go fifty-fifty on groceries and liquor. If Max stayed past a week they would split the rent and utilities. Natale would sleep on the waterbed in the tiny bedroom, but Max could reserve it on twenty-four hours' notice for sleep-over dates. The rest of the time Max would occupy the Castro convertible with worn armrests in the small living room.

"So," said Natale, studying his new roommate eagerly, "ya think this is really split city, or you might get back together?"

"How the fuck should I know?" said Max. "I've only been here ten minutes!"

"You're right," said Natale. "Max, bubbeleh, you've done the right thing. You are not gonna regret it, mark my words. There is so much pussy out there waiting for you, in six months you won't even want it anymore."

"I don't want it *now*," said Max.

Natale looked at Max, alarmed.

"Tony, I didn't leave my wife and child because I wanted pussy, I left because my marriage was intolerable."

"Of course, of course," said Natale. "But wait till you see what's out there. Have I told you about Cheryl?"

"Cheryl?" said Max. "Who's Cheryl?"

"Who's Cheryl?" said Natale and cackled wickedly.

He went to an ancient desk, opened the top drawer, withdrew a thick stack of Polaroids, and thrust them at Max.

"This is Cheryl," said Natale.

Max looked at the Polaroids. They were all taken with a flash and they were all close-ups. Some featured a woman's small but nicely shaped breasts, with and without a lacy black brassiere. Some featured a woman's nicely shaped buttocks, with and without black bikini panties. Some featured perhaps the same woman's pelvic area, with and without the panties. Some featured internal views of a vagina, which could have only interested a gynecologist. There was not one picture of the woman's face.

"These are all Cheryl?" said Max.

Natale nodded proudly.

"These are all tit, tush, and pussy shots," said Max. "Why aren't there any pictures of her face?"

Natale frowned, walked over, took the pictures out of Max's hand, and looked them over with great interest.

"You're right," he said. "There aren't any pictures of her face."

"Why is that?" asked Max.

Natale sighed.

"I dunno. I guess I must be unconsciously depersonalizing her to distance myself from her and any chance of deeper involvement."

Max nodded, as if he understood.

"Why distance yourself?" he said after a while.

"Because I know how seriously to take her," said Natale.

"How seriously?" said Max.

"Not at all," said Natale. "She's a nice girl and a great fuck, but she's . . ."

"Yeah?" said Max.

"Kind of trashy," said Natale.

36

It was not a call he looked forward to making, but one he couldn't avoid. He hunched forward with his elbows on his battered metal desk and dialed. After six rings she answered.

"Hello?"

"Hi," said Max, "it's me."

No response.

"I, uh, just wondered how Sam is doing."

A long pause.

"Sam is fine."

No emotion in her voice whatever. He got the same hostile blankness from crack dealers in Harlem. You don't reach me on any level, was the message, you do not exist in my world.

"I'm glad he's fine," said Max. "Is he . . . upset I'm not there?"

"What do *you* think?" she said.

As if *he* had been the one to suggest splitting up. O.K., crack dealers were warmer.

"Uh, yeah. Well. Uh, is he there? Can I talk to him?"

No response, but he heard her put down the receiver and call to Sam. Sam answered something he couldn't make out, and then he heard her say it was Dada calling and did he want to talk to him. There was further discussion that he couldn't decipher, and then she got back on the line.

"He doesn't want to talk to you," she said.

There didn't seem to be anything leading away from the remark. Dead air hung in the phone.

"Right," he said. "Well, I'll try again later."

Nothing.

"Nice talking to you, too," he said, hanging up the phone.

37

Nine-thirty Monday morning Judy put through the call.

"Burnam & Bolls, good morning."

"Good morning," said Judy. "May I please speak to Walter Barmack?"

"May I tell him who's calling?"

"Monty Black."

"And will he know what this is in reference to?"

"Not until I tell him," said Judy evenly.

There was a click. After a moment Walter picked up.

"This is Walter Barmack," said the familiar voice.

Judy felt the pulse surge in her throat and had to wait a moment before she could speak. Please, God, she prayed, let me be able to do this smoothly. Let me not stammer or make a complete fool of myself.

"Mr. Barmack, my name is Monty Black," she said. "I am interested in purchasing a two-bedroom co-op with a high-floor view of the Central Park Reservoir on either Fifth Avenue or Central Park West. Do you have any such listings?"

Walter Barmack's tone grew instantly sunny.

"As a matter of fact I do," he said. "I happen to have a beauty on Fifth. Tenth floor. Recently renovated. Reservoir view from all rooms but the kitchen."

"Yes," said Judy coolly, "I've seen it. Have you anything else?"

"Yes. I have another at Central Park West at Ninety-second. Reservoir view from living room, dining room, master bedroom, and master bath, and a twenty-foot terrace. It's an estate sale, so I think we could get it well below market."

"That sounds promising. When may I see it?"

"How about today?"

"Excellent," said Judy. "I'll meet you out in front of the building at one P.M."

"One P.M.," said Walter Barmack. "See you then, Miss Black."

When she hung up the phone, Judy was shaking so badly she could barely get the receiver back in its cradle. One P.M. That gave her more than three hours to get ready. More than enough time. Before she went into the bathroom she went to the liquor cabinet and poured herself a shot of Absolut just to steady her nerves.

By twelve-forty-five P.M. Judy was standing on the park side of Central Park West at Ninety-third Street, one block north and across the street from the building where she was to meet Walter Barmack. The nearly three hours she had spent in preparation had paid off. She looked, she thought, absolutely perfect. Tan business suit, the shoulders a bit wider and the skirt a bit shorter than need be. White silk blouse, opened one button lower than need be. No bra. Stockings with seams. Spike heels. Beige calfskin gloves, although the weather was a bit too warm for them. Blond hair falling casually across her forehead. And the mirrored sunglasses, of course.

Three shots of Absolut had failed to calm her down sufficiently to pull this off in exactly the way she wanted. She opened her purse, withdrew the flask, raised it to her lips, and slowly drained it.

At ten after one Walter Barmack appeared. He seemed surprised she wasn't there, ducked into the lobby, consulted with the doorman, came out again, looked up and down the street.

He deliberately came ten minutes late to make me wait, not because he knows who I am but because I'm a woman, she thought, and now he fears he's blown it.

Barmack looked at his watch, then stood in front of the building, waiting nervously.

Good, she thought, let the bastard wait. He's not about to leave so long as there's a chance I'll show up and buy an apartment from him.

A cab passed, heading north on Central Park West. She flagged it down and got inside.

"Ninety-second and Central Park West," she said.

The cab driver turned around to look at her as though she were crazy.

"That's one block back that way, lady," he said.

She handed him a twenty-dollar bill.

"Drive around the block," she said.

The cabbie shrugged, took the money, and put the car in gear.

When she pulled up in front of the building at Ninety-second and Central Park West it was nearly one-twenty. Barmack was still there, of course. Getting out of the cab, Judy allowed him a swift glance up her skirt before she adjusted it.

"I'm Monty Black," she said, extending her gloved hand, choosing not to mention how late she was.

"Walter Barmack," he said, taking her hand, also choosing not to mention it.

Neither complain nor explain, she remembered from somewhere. Where had she heard that? It was obvious that Barmack didn't remember her.

"I'm anxious to see the place," she said. "Shall we go right up?"

"Of course," he said.

They went into the lobby. Barmack nodded to the doorman and led her to the elevator.

"Warm day," he said.

"Mmmm," she said.

The elevator arrived. He allowed her to enter, then followed her in. The mirrors were familiar, the leather bench. The doors closed. He pressed the button marked 18. The elevator rose. Neither of them spoke. Her pulse was pounding in her temples, in her throat, in her breasts. Just before they arrived at eighteen he risked a swift survey of her body.

The doors opened. They got out. She followed him down the hall to the empty apartment. He opened it with his key and showed her in.

"So," he said, "here it is. As you can see, it needs a bit of work, but the views are fantastic."

Judy walked into the kitchen, looked around briefly and came right out.

"We'd have to tear out the entire kitchen, of course," she said.

"Well, I don't know if you'd have to do anything *that* drastic, but . . ."

Judy walked into the dining room.

"The windows facing the park are much too small," she said. "They'd all have to be torn out and replaced. And, naturally, the apartment would have to be completely rewired."

"I suppose that a certain amount of rewiring might be necessary, but . . ."

She stuck her head into the bathroom off the living room.

"And the bathrooms would obviously have to be torn out too."

"Some of the plumbing does need redoing, however . . ."

Judy walked into the hallway that separated the bedrooms from the entertaining area and disappeared.

Expecting the woman to return immediately with more dire pronouncements, Barmack stayed in the entryway. Three minutes passed. Five. He grew curious. He walked into the hallway. It was dark and he nearly tripped over something lying on the floor. One of her shoes? How does somebody lose a shoe and just leave it there?

He walked farther on down the darkened hallway. Another shoe. Farther on his foot snagged something soft. He picked it up and looked at it. Her suit coat. What the hell was going on here?

He walked farther and found something else. Her skirt! His face grew hot. Little beads of perspiration sprang out of the pores in his forehead, his neck, and the areas above his mouth and beneath his eyes. He walked into the master bedroom, not knowing what he'd find next.

On the floor of the master bedroom was a trail: Her blouse. Her slip. Two stockings. And, just at the threshold of the terrace door, a pair of black silk panties.

He could now feel a muffled pounding in his ears. Slightly dizzy, he walked to the terrace door and looked outside. In a casual pose on the chaise longue lay Miss Black, wearing only her mirrored sunglasses.

Barmack was speechless. The woman's body was superb. And completely naked. Far below them on Central Park West he could hear the sounds of traffic, a horn, a distant siren, some kids yelling. It was extremely warm out on the terrace. He supposed there was no chance now of selling her the apartment.

"Come here, Walter," she said.

"What is this," he said when he was able to speak, "some kind of a joke? Is this a what-do-you-call-it, a Strip-o-gram? Who put you up to this?"

Walter Barmack was very uncomfortable. Aroused, certainly, but sure somebody was setting him up for a huge laugh at his expense. He hated being the butt of anybody's practical jokes.

"It's not a joke, Walter," she said, "not remotely. And nobody knows about this but you and me."

"Who are you?" he said.

She took off her sunglasses. There was something vaguely familiar about the face now that he looked at it.

"You don't recognize me?" she said.

"No. Who are you?"

"Judy Wells," she said.

She got up off the chaise and walked slowly over to him.

Judy Wells. Oh, God. The broad he'd boffed in the apartment he rented her. The one who'd fallen for him so pitifully.

"I remember you now," he said. "The other name was what threw me."

"You do remember me then," she said, stopping two inches away. "How touching."

She caressed his perspiring neck.

"What are you doing?" he said. "What is the point of all this?"

"I just wanted to see you again," she said.

She moved her hands down to his belt and unbuckled it. My God, did she want to do it right here, outside on the terrace of one of his listings?

"Now listen," he said, but he didn't know what he wanted her to listen to.

She unzipped his fly and pulled his trousers down below his waist. He was getting extremely excited in spite of himself.

"I've thought about you a lot, Walter," she whispered, brushing his lips with her own. He thought he smelled something on her breath — liquor, maybe — but he wasn't sure.

Her arms snaked around his neck, pulling him forward, pulling him toward the chaise.

"I can't do this," he gasped. "I have a wife, a family . . . I'm afraid this will . . ." — he felt his undershorts sliding gently but firmly down below his turgid groin — ". . . simply have to stop."

He allowed himself to be led the last few steps to the chaise, hobbled by the trousers and undershorts now down at his ankles, and to be pulled down on top of her.

He wanted to stop her. He couldn't. Nothing this exciting had ever happened to him. He hadn't remembered her being exciting before. How the hell could she have become such a . . . . What was she doing

154

now? She had hold of his cock was doing something to it — trying to roll a condom onto it. Of all the . . . . And then she abandoned the condom and was stuffing him inside of her and he no longer resisted at all.

She was an animal, an absolute animal! It was unbelievable! When he climaxed, he groaned with gratitude. He opened his eyes and reached out to caress her, to thank her, and saw something in her hand that didn't at first register. Something small. Something with . . . *a blade!* She was coming at him with a fucking razor blade!

He jolted backward as her hand shot forward with the blade, just grazing the tip of his nose. She lunged again and he lost his balance, falling off the chaise to the terrace floor, his bare buttocks bruising on the rough concrete. Now she was getting up and coming at him again.

"Are you *crazy?* What the fuck are you doing?"

"Just something I needed to do."

He lurched to his feet, his ankles still trapped above his shoes in his pushed-down trousers and undershorts, and backed away from another lunge, his lower back landing hard against the rusted terrace railing. And then she came at him again.

He threw up his arms to cover his face and leaned as far backward as he could and . . . the railing gave way. He heard it groan, then snap, and then he was falling! Falling through the air! Falling eighteen stories downward! He finally started screaming when he reached the seventh floor.

Walter Barmack hit the pavement like a load of wet wash. Judy heard screams from passersby and shuddered. She hadn't figured on the railing giving way. It had ruined her moment of triumph completely, denying her her real climax.

She knew she had to get dressed and out of there fast. She went inside and began picking up articles of clothing, hopping on one foot in the musty, furnitureless apartment, dressing as quickly as she could. Well, Barmack had been just as cock-driven as Petlin. He could have saved his life by showing he'd changed, by resisting her, but he chose to fuck and die instead. She was little more than the instrument of his self-destruction. Like the mantis, she was just part of the natural order.

When she was completely dressed she looked around to see if there was anything she'd forgotten. Fingerprints! She put on her gloves, took out a handkerchief, walked back through the apartment, and carefully wiped every surface she remembered touching — doorknobs, light switches, moldings, everything.

On the floor by the door to the terrace Barmack had left something made of leather. She picked it up. His black leather Filofax. She turned to the calendar section and started to rip out the page with her name on it, then realized the pages below it might retain the impression of the pen or pencil; she thought better of it and put the whole Filofax into her purse.

She walked to the entryway and the door to the hallway and heard the first sirens approaching down on the street. She opened the apartment door, stepped into the corridor, and pulled the door shut behind her.

She pushed the button for the elevator and waited. And waited. And waited. She glanced impatiently at her watch but was too distracted to register the time. What could be keeping the accursed elevator? What if there were somebody in it when it arrived? She briefly considered walking down the full eighteen stories, then decided she couldn't risk being trapped if there were a locked door at the bottom.

The elevator arrived and groaned to a stop. The doors opened in a mechanical stutter. Mercifully, there was nobody inside it. She got in.

When the doors opened at lobby level she could hear the commotion out on the street. A huge crowd of people, very noisy. Screams. More sirens. A throng of people blocked the door, standing on tiptoe, chattering away in tones of spectators at an athletic event, excited in some darkly erotic way. She pushed past them, praying nobody would notice her. She needn't have worried.

Three blue-and-white patrol cars had pulled up, turret lights flashing. Six swarthy officers who couldn't have been more than twenty years old were trying to push back the morbidly fascinated, carnivorous crowd. Between bobbing heads and gesticulating arms she strained to catch a glimpse of the body. And then she saw it.

The blood. The gore. The sickly glistening internal organs. The bodies. *Bodies.* Yes, more than one. Walter's and . . . a young woman's! My God, Walter's body must have hit a young woman when he fell, and . . . oh no, a *stroller!* A stroller and . . . a little *child!* She'd killed a mother and a child!

She was overcome by waves of dizziness and nausea. She fled across Central Park West, gagging, partially digested food threatening to back up through her esophagus. She narrowly missed being hit by a battered yellow cab whose driver screamed curses at her in an unfamiliar Middle Eastern tongue.

Judy wandered through Central Park in a daze, overcome by guilt and remorse, trying to deal with the deaths of the mother and her child. Crossing a bike path, she was nearly run down by three cyclists on ten-speed bikes who cursed at her as they passed.

She staggered to the reservoir. Leaning against the hurricane fence, staring into the water as joggers loped past her, she finally succeeded in getting some perspective on what had happened.

What had happened was a horrid accident. Who could have known that the railing would give way before she could cut Walter's carotid and that he'd plunge to his death? Who could have known that a mother and her child would be passing underneath the building at the precise moment that Walter fell? The deaths of the mother and the child were not her doing, not her responsibility, not her fault. The deaths of the mother and the child were an accident. A hideous coincidence. An act of God. Was she to blame for acts of God? She was not. She could feel bad, but only as an observer, as an outsider. It had simply not been her responsibility.

She took several deep breaths and tried to pull herself together. She was still shaking. She probably looked a mess. She walked back across the running track and located a public women's room and took a look in the mirror.

Just as she thought, a complete mess. Her hair, her makeup, her clothing, all a disaster. She went into the toilet stall and locked the door behind her. She took out a hairbrush, removed the blond wig, tucked it inside her purse, and brushed out her long black hair. Then she opened her contact lens case, carefully removed the two blue lenses, put them inside their individual compartments, and put those into her purse as well. Then she applied fresh makeup and straightened her clothing.

40

By the time Detectives Rodriguez and Maloney of the Twenty-fourth PDU arrived on the scene, the first EMS bus had pulled up. The uniforms had spread tarps and sheets over as much of the mess as they could, but it was everywhere. While covering up the little girl Patrolman DeSantis had puked up his lunch, which didn't make things at the Central Park West scene any more appetizing.

"We got an i.d. on the male from his wallet," said Sergeant McKenna, the supervisor, "one Walter F. Barmack, d.o.b. February fourteenth, 1946."

"Valentine's Day," said Maloney. "You call the Crime Scene Unit, sarge?"

Sergeant McKenna shook his head.

"Why the fuck not?" said Maloney.

"There wasn't no *crime*," said McKenna.

"You're sayin' he was a jumper?" said Rodriguez.

"Nah," said McKenna, "jumpers are pretty careful, they look before they leap. I never heard of a jumper landed on anybody. This guy Barmack had his pants and skivvies down around his ankles. We figure he was standing on one of the terraces, exposing himself, and somehow lost his balance."

Maloney shook his head.

"Still shoulda called in the CSU, sarge," he said. "This ever gets reclassified a homicide, you're up shit's creek without a paddle."

"It gets reclassified," said McKenna, "I'll make out the blue fives for ya myself."

"It gets reclassified," said Maloney, "you'll be making out more than blue fives, sarge, you'll be making out fuckin' *parking* citations on Staten fucking *Island*."

The M.E. got out of his Mercedes 190SL and hurried over.

"Dr. Chernin," said Maloney, "what brings you here, sir?"

"Heard it on the radio, happened to be in the neighborhood, and thought I'd drop in," said Chernin.

Rodriguez laughed darkly.

"That's what Barmack did," he said. "Dropped in."

"That the male?" said Chernin, pointing.

"Yeah," said Rodriguez.

"And there were two females? An adult and a little girl?"

"Yeah," said Rodriguez, shaking his head sadly. "Jesus."

Chernin walked over to one of the tarps and pulled it back. A collective *ahhh* went up from the onlookers. They strained forward to see the mess. Chernin turned around to look at them. Goddam ghouls, he thought. Then he let the tarp drop back in place.

"The adult female broke the male's fall," said McKenna. "The angle he hit her, I'd say she just telescoped inwards. She's probably no more'n three feet tall by now."

Chernin laughed.

"Her spine was probably pushed up through her skull on impact," said the M.E., taking another look, "but whatever telescoping there may have been wouldn't make her that much shorter."

"How come he didn't break apart on impact?" asked Rodriguez, talking to take his mind off his queasiness. "Was it because the female broke his fall?"

"Bodies don't break apart unless they hit an obstruction on the way down." said Chernin. "In physics we're taught things fall at thirty-two feet per second per second. But a falling body encounters so much wind resistance, you'd land with about the same force whether you fell from a tenth-story window or from a DC-10."

"C'mon, doc," said McKenna. "Remember that construction worker fell from the fiftieth story of that building on Seventy-ninth Street last March? They found his head and chest in one location, his right hip and thigh in another, and his workshoe with a foot inside it all the way down the block at *Eightieth* Street."

"I remember that," said Chernin. "But he tumbled, right?"

"Right," said McKenna, "he hit a waddayacallit, a scaffolding or something."

"That's what I'm saying," said Chernin. "If he hadn't tumbled, he wouldn't have broken apart."

A second EMS bus pulled up. For indoor deaths, morgue vehicles or "meat wagons" capable of holding many bodies removed the D.O.A.s. But outdoors on a public thoroughfare, EMS buses were used and they could only accommodate one body apiece.

"O.K.," said McKenna to the EMS men, "let's start mopping up."

"You're makin' a big mistake not having the CSU take pictures of this," said Maloney. "Mark my words."

41

"You seem quite pensive this evening, Miss Wells."

"Do I?" she said. "Yes, I suppose I do."

"What's troubling you?"

"Nothing really. I was troubled before, but not now."

"Does it have to do with the matter we discussed in our previous session? The thing you were trying to decide whether or not to do?"

"In a way."

"And did you decide to do it?"

"Yes."

"Excellent. And how did it turn out?"

"Not the way I expected."

"Better or worse?"

"Worse. Much worse."

"What happened, can you tell me?"

"Not just yet. Let's just say that there were unforeseen complications."

"I see."

"But I'm starting to think that they weren't really my fault, doctor. I mean, they happened as a result of wheels that I may have put into motion, but I don't believe that makes them my responsibility, do you?"

"I'm afraid I can't answer that without knowing the particulars. We *must* take responsibility for everything in our lives, of course . . ."

"Of course."

"But it's often hard to see how something which happened only as a consequence of something that we did was something that we should take the blame for and feel *guilty* about. Guilt is not a useful emotion."

"I couldn't agree with you more," she said.

He was a nice man, she thought, a really nice man. Such a kind, patient face. If she had a long enough backswing, she wondered if she could split his face with an ax.

Stroke . . . stroke . . . stroke . . . stroke . . . stroke.

"Yes, precious, you like that, don't you?"

Stroke . . . stroke . . . stroke . . . stroke . . . stroke.

"It feels good, doesn't it, darling? And it's making you look so sleek."

Stroke . . . stroke . . . stroke . . . stroke . . . stroke.

It was late Monday night. Judy was grooming the cat and thinking about her progress as a writer.

When she first moved to New York and became a hermit she'd begun writing a novel. It was about a shy, sensitive girl from an affluent suburb of Detroit who'd been tragically misunderstood and abused by the men in her life and who finally got fed up and began paying them back. The girl's father, Rodd Kelton, a self-made tycoon in the auto wrecking business, was a major character in the novel, but Judy had so much trouble writing him, making him alternately too virtuous or too nefarious, that she eventually abandoned the manuscript after scarcely fifty pages.

She took the same material and tried to write it as a stage play, but once more her ambivalence about the character of Rodd Kelton stymied her and the play never proceeded beyond the first act.

She thought she might do better with nonfiction, so she wrote a few articles on women's subjects on spec and sent them in over the transom and, to her surprise and delight, sold them to *Good Housekeeping* and *Family Circle*. She surveyed the writing styles of the competition and developed her own harder and more subjective style. She adopted the pen name of Susan Simon, which she felt sounded more New York–writerish than Judy Wells, and began to get assignments from the slick general service magazines. Judy Wells might have been a failure as a fiction writer, but Susan Simon had begun to make a name for herself as a journalist.

43

Salvatore Caruso walked into the reception room of *New York* magazine and looked around. The receptionist appeared to be busy on the phone. Caruso began to mosey on past her desk.

"Yes? May I help you?" she said, swiveling around in her chair.

Caruso flashed his shield.

"Uh, yeah. You got a female working for you by the name Simon? Susan Simon?"

The receptionist looked blank.

"I don't believe so."

Caruso nodded, apparently pleased. She *was* a phony, just as he'd suspected.

"Would you like me to check?" said the receptionist.

"Sure, go ahead and check," said Caruso.

The receptionist buzzed the managing editor on the intercom.

"There's a police officer here who wants to know if we have anybody working here named — I'm sorry, was it Simon?"

"Yeah. Susan Simon."

"Susan Simon," said the receptionist on the intercom. "I told him I wasn't familiar with the name. Uh-huh. O.K., thanks."

The receptionist hung up.

"Susan Simon is a freelance journalist on assignment to us for a story on some homicide cases. Is that the information you were looking for?"

"Yeah," said Caruso, "thanks, doll."

The receptionist thought it odd the policeman looked disappointed.

44

"Segal, Caruso, I got a job for you."

"You got a fresh kill for us, boss?" said Caruso hopefully. "I been prayin' for one." Caruso hated all the cases he was currently working on.

"Almost fresh," said McIlheny. "I just got a call from a detective in the Two-Four PDU, name of Maloney. Did you hear something yesterday about a guy falling off a terrace of a building on Ninety-second and Central Park West?"

"A jumper, wasn't it?" said Max. "He hit a young mother and a little girl."

"That's the guy," said McIlheny, "but he wasn't a jumper. Maloney's been doing a little canvassing in the building and it's starting to sound funny. He thinks he might want to reclassify."

"To homicide?" said Max.

McIlheny nodded.

"Go see him. I think he's onto something."

"Sergeant McKenna, the supervisor at the scene, thought Walter Barmack fell off a terrace while exposing himself," said Detective Maloney, who was driving.

"Right," said Max.

"That didn't make no sense to me," said Maloney. "I mean, who would he be exposing himself to? It didn't make sense to me he'd be exposing himself to somebody way the hell across the street in the park. Then I found out Barmack wasn't a tenant in the building, he was a real estate agent with a firm called Burnam & Bolls that's tryin' to sell this vacant apartment on the eighteenth floor."

"And that's the apartment he fell from?" said Caruso.

"The day Barmack died," said Maloney, "he took a blond female up there."

"What's your theory," said Max, "that he was having dangerous sex with her out on the terrace, he accidentally fell, and she was so scared she split?"

"Either that," said Maloney, "or she pushed him. The railing was pulled away from the wall though, so it coulda been an accident."

Maloney eased into a parking space near the building at Ninety-second and Central Park West. They got out of the car.

"It shouldn't be too hard to find out who he took up there," said Max. "Don't they write down their appointments?"

Maloney nodded.

"They said at his office Barmack kept his appointments in something called a Filofax. Very expensive, made in England. Except his is missing. Didn't leave it at the office and it wasn't recovered from the scene."

Caruso and Max looked at him.

"The blond broad took it," said Caruso.

"That's how it looks to me," said Maloney. "Which means she doesn't want us to know who he showed the apartment to."

"Didn't a couple people say they saw Petlin with a blonde the night he got it?" said Max.

45

These were some of the books in Judy Wells's bookcase: *Women and Love: A Cultural Revolution in Progress,* by Shere Hite. *Women Who Love Too Much,* by Robin Norwood. *Men Who Hate Women and the Women Who Love Them,* by Susan Forward and Joan Torres. *Men Who Can't Be Faithful: How to Pick Up the Pieces When He's Breaking Your Heart,* by Carol Botwin.

Intercourse, by Andrea Dworkin, in which the author says most men make love to women to make war on them, because intercourse is "the means of psychologically making a woman inferior; communicating to her cell by cell her own inferior status . . . shoving it into her, over and over . . . until she gives up and gives in." *Fire and Ice,* by the same author, in which a character declares "coitus is punishment."

Sleeping with the Enemy, by Nancy Price, in which the author says that if you sleep with men you're cursed with one set of names, and if you don't you're cursed with another. *Female Men,* by Joanna Russ, in which a female character kills a male and then confides that "The best way to silence an enemy is to bite out his larynx."

On a bulletin board above her desk were several quotations: "A woman without a man is like a fish without a bicycle." "All men are rapists and that's all they are" — Marilyn French. "Love is the victim's response to the rapist" — Ti-Grace Atkinson. "The male is an incomplete female, a walking abortion" — from the manifesto of SCUM (Society for Cutting Up Men), whose most famous member, Valerie Solanas, attacked Andy Warhol with a knife and nearly succeeded in slashing him to death.

* * *

The New York Public Library has telephone directories for most towns in the country. Judy's interest was towns in Illinois. Chicago, Champaign-Urbana, Danville, Rockford, Cicero, Aurora, Evanston, Wilmette, Glencoe, Deerfield, Highland Park.

Stuart Sherman, the young intern who'd dumped her for the Chi Omega, had come from Deerfield, studied in Evanston, and interned in Chicago. Teddy Greco, the accounting student who'd decided after bedding her that he wasn't attracted to her physically, had come from Rockford and studied in Champaign-Urbana. And Austin Richards, the tweedy English instructor who'd deflowered her in his office, had grown up in Cicero, gotten his B.A. and M.A. in Champaign-Urbana, then became an instructor and might be there yet.

She found four Stuart Shermans, but only one had an M.D. attached to his name, the one in Highland Park. She found a business address for him on the fashionable Near North Side of Chicago.

She found only one Theodore Greco, in Wilmette, but no business address for him in Chicago. She telephoned his home in Wilmette and told a harassed woman with a nasal voice that she was from the University of Illinois Alumni Association and needed Mr. Greco's business address. The woman with the nasal voice gave her an accounting firm in the Hancock Building on Michigan Avenue.

She found seven men named Austin Richards, but only one of them was in Champaign, and it had to be the one she'd known in college.

She consulted her calendar. It was now April 26. April 28 through 30 were completely clear. She went to the phone and made several reservations for the period of April 28 through 30 under the name of Caroline Busey. A round-trip plane ticket to Chicago. A room at the Drake. And a rental car—a Mustang convertible, if they had one. There was no reason why research trips, even those to plot murder, had to be dreary.

46

"Forensic science is based upon the Locard Principle," said Dr. Kaprilian of the NYPD Crime Lab, pushing a forefinger against the bridge of his glasses to tighten them on his nose, "which is the theory that when two bodies make contact there's a transfer of material from one to the other — blood, hair, fibers, pollen, saliva, whatever."

"Right," said Max.

"Now I believe that hairs uncharacteristic of the victim were found at both the Smiley and Petlin crime scenes."

"You *believe?*" said Max.

"Well," said Kaprilian, "I've seen the ones recovered from the sink and tub traps, but not those recovered from the bodies."

"Why don't you call Chernin?"

"As you know," said Kaprilian with tiredness in his voice, "the M.E.'s office is separate from the Crime Lab. We don't normally interact. We process trace evidence from the crime scene, they process evidence from the body. They could call in the Crime Lab, but so far Dr. Chernin hasn't seen fit to do so."

"I'll talk to him," said Max. "What could you tell from these hairs if I could get Chernin to lend them to you?"

"Well," said Kaprilian, "that depends on whether they're scalp hair, pubic hair, or axillary — armpit — hair, and on whether or not they have root sheaths. As you know, we lose a hundred to a hundred and twenty-five hairs a day from our scalp — those that fall out are in the telogen phase, which is the last stage of hair growth. Hairs in the telogen phase have lost their root sheaths, of course, so all you can tell about them is whether they're human or animal, what part of the body they came from, and whether they're Mongoloid, Negroid, or Caucasian."

"If there *were* a root sheath," said Max, "could you tell the sex of the person it came from?"

"If the hair was plucked and the root sheath intact?" said Kaprilian. "Possibly. You could examine the hair for the presence of a Y-chromosome. If you found a Y-chromosome you'd know you were dealing with a male, of course. Only males have Y-chromosomes. You could do a fluorescent stain and look at it under a microscope. It would stain only the Y-chromosomes. If it didn't fluoresce at all, it would mean it was probably a female."

"Probably?"

"Well, if you didn't find a Y-chromosome it wouldn't *necessarily* mean it was from a female. It could just mean the cells had deteriorated, lost their ability to pick up dye."

"Is there a better test for a female?"

Kaprilian nodded.

"If you found a structure called a Barr body."

"What the hell is a Barr body?" said Max.

"A structure — named, incidentally, after its discoverer, Murray Barr — which is a condensed, inactive X-chromosome. Females have Barr bodies, males don't. There weren't any Barr bodies in the hairs we recovered from the sink and tub traps, but I'd like to see the ones recovered from the autopsies."

"Wouldn't Dr. Chernin have checked for Barr bodies?"

Kaprilian shook his head and gave a patronizing smile.

"If I could get Chernin to part with some hairs," said Max, "you'd check them out for Y-chromosomes and Barr bodies?"

Kaprilian nodded.

"But Dr. Chernin would officially have to request our doing so."

"Got ya," said Max.

"Dr. Chernin, Max Segal. I tried to catch you at work, but they said you'd already gone home for the day. I hope I'm not calling at a bad time."

"Well, Max, we do have some people over and we're just about to sit down to dinner. . . ."

"Good. I've been talking to Dr. Kaprilian at the crime lab and he'd like to take a look at some of the hairs recovered from the Smiley and Petlin autopsies."

"Max, I don't think this is the best time to —"

"He says that unless you call in the crime lab he can't do anything, his hands are tied."

"What does he want with the hairs?" asked Chernin.

Kaprilian had seemed so sure Chernin wouldn't test for Barr bodies, Max decided not to mention them and tempt Chernin to disparage the process.

"I don't know," said Max, "it's a little technical for me. But he'd really like to see them. And I'd consider it a personal favor, Doc."

"Sal, I think I got something!" said Max excitedly when Caruso picked up on the seventeenth ring.

"What the fuck time is it?" said Caruso through lips thickened and parched by sleep.

Max looked guiltily at his watch. It said one-forty A.M.

"I don't know," said Max. "A little after midnight. I tried calling you before but your line was busy. You want to hear what I got or not?"

"Do I have a choice?" said Caruso.

"No," said Max. "Aram Kaprilian at the crime lab just examined hairs under a microscope recovered from the Smiley and Petlin scenes and he says at least two of them have Barr bodies."

"The fuck are Barr bodies?" said Caruso.

"Barr bodies?" said Max, as if surprised there was still someone who didn't know. "Condensed, inactive X-chromosomes. Females have Barr bodies, males don't. So that suggests our perp is a female."

"No," said Caruso, more irritated at being awakened and one-upped than pleased to be progressing on the case, "that suggests a female took a bath at Smiley's or Petlin's apartment once," said Caruso. "Don't mean dick."

"One of these hairs," said Max, "was recovered from combing Petlin's crotch at autopsy."

Caruso thought this over for fully five seconds before he allowed his mouth to widen in a grin.

47

"I tell you about this new girl I met?" said Natale, cautiously wedging two more dirty dishes into a sink already stacked above the rim and teetering precariously.

"Cheryl, you mean?" said Max.

"No, no, Cheryl was the one I showed you Polaroids of," said Natale. "This one's Cathy. I met her last week at the salad bar at the Korean grocery around the corner."

"I don't think you've mentioned Cathy to me," said Max patiently.

"Anyway, I gave her my number at the Koreans and she's been calling me practically every day. She's taking me to the opera tonight. *La Bohème*."

"No shit," said Max. "I didn't know you liked opera, Tony. I see there's a whole side of you I know nothing about."

"You kidding me?" said Natale. "I *hate* the opera. But afterwards I plan to take her back here and fuck her eyes out."

"Ah."

"So, if you wouldn't mind, kid," said Natale, "I'd appreciate it if you could arrange to be elsewhere between, say, ten-thirty and, I dunno, two o'clock."

Max sighed.

"Sure, Tony."

"Thanks, Max. I appreciate it, I really do."

"Hey, it's your apartment. I'm the guest."

"No, it's your place too, kid, I mean that," said Natale, continuing half to himself, "I figure after I fuck Cathy I'll kind of sound her out about the possibility of having a threesome."

"With who?" said Max, frowning, trying to gauge the parameters of Natale's hospitality.

"With Cheryl," said Natale.

"Oh."

Max was both relieved and disappointed.

"Tell me something, Tony."

"Yeah?"

"What if you go to the opera with Cathy, you come back here, you go to bed with her, and you discover you really *like* her? What happens then?"

Natale shook his head emphatically.

"Never happen," said Natale. "She'll either want me to make some kind of commitment to a relationship which I'm not ready to make, or else she'll want me to spend money on her which I don't have. I just want to get into her pants and then into a threesome with Cheryl."

"You know something?" said Max. "This is women's worst fantasy of how we talk about them."

At about the time Max figured *La Bohème* would be getting out he left Natale's apartment and began a leisurely stroll around the neighborhood.

He wasn't quite sure how he wanted to kill the three and a half hours and he resented having to do it. Being asked to leave while Natale entertained ladies in bed was something Max didn't have time for in his life. If the separation continued he was really going to need a place of his own, even though he couldn't afford to rent two apartments. Maybe he could handle a sublet.

Max realized there was time now to see a movie, which he hadn't done in months. Hell, he had time to see *two* movies, but he wasn't really in the mood for movies tonight.

He walked along Sixth Avenue and turned east on Eighth Street, making his way past the largest assemblage of shoe stores in the free world, through throngs of people who by day sold insurance and airline tickets in New Jersey and by night put on black leather and chains and pretended they were heavily into kinky sex.

Max was depressed. The investigation of the Smiley and Petlin cases was going nowhere. If the killer was an attractive blond woman, that cut the number of suspects in the tristate area down to maybe fifty thousand. The only way they were ever going to find her was by an act of

174

God. Murder, as homicide cops often said, *was* the easiest crime to get away with.

His separation was a source of constant anxiety. He was handling it with his parents by avoiding the subject with them altogether. If it progressed to divorce he supposed he would have to say something sooner or later. He did not relish explaining it to them.

He missed his son. He missed holding the boy on his lap and reading to him and inhaling the fragrance of his newly shampooed hair. When Sam wasn't being a complete pain in the ass he was unbearably wonderful. Max was always trying to sneak hugs, kisses, and feels with him in the same way he had with girls when he was in high school.

When he got home late from work he often woke Sam up to take him to pee, not so much to prevent bed-wetting — Sam had never wet his bed since he was toilet trained — but because it was a chance to cuddle with the sleepy child while carrying him to and from the bathroom. At such times Max propped up his dozing son at the toilet, aimed his weewee hard-on down toward the toilet bowl, and contemplated the not-so-far-off time when the boy would be using his erections for more than pissing.

He was all too aware how critical a period this was in the molding of Sam's personality. Although Max and Babette were struggling with their own present, it was their son's past they were now forming, the foggy period Sam would look back on decades from now in order to discover the sources of his unhappiness as an adult. Max wondered just how badly his leaving home would damage Sam.

He wondered what it would do to *him*. He wondered how he'd survive if the separation became permanent. He wondered how long it would take for Babette to acquire a lover and how he'd feel about it. He wondered how he'd feel if Babette's lover moved into the apartment. *Their* apartment. *His* apartment, for Christ's sake, which was his before he'd even met Babette. He wondered how he'd feel about another man marrying Babette and trying to play father to Sam.

This thought made Max's forehead tighten, his chest constrict. The image of his son with another father was infinitely more painful than that of his wife with another husband. If another man tried to cuckold him with his son, Max would tear the fucker to pieces for his presumption, literally drag him out of the apartment and kick the living shit out of him.

Maybe Babette wouldn't remarry. Maybe she wouldn't even rush to find another lover. Despite the way she'd been acting toward him, underneath all the hurt and anger, he suspected she still loved him. Underneath all the hurt and anger, he loved her as well.

He thought about how they'd met. Another serial killer, a weirdo who called himself the Hyena, had been stalking and killing young women. Babette had gone downtown to One Police Plaza — an unexpectedly contemporary and tastefully designed red-brick building with a landscaped sculpture garden — with information about the killings, information that she claimed to have gotten psychically. She walked past Max in the courtyard of One Police Plaza, their eyes met and — whammo! — the thunderbolt struck them both. He'd never been so immediately or so strongly attracted to anyone in his life.

Then he'd made the unpardonable blunder of observing that she was staring at him. She'd fled, hurling herself into a taxi. He saw the cab start up and knew he couldn't let her ride out of his life. So he threw himself across the hood of the cab. The vehicle screeched to a stop, the driver burst out of it, ready to clobber him, so Max shoved his shield in the guy's nose and told him if he didn't shut the fuck up he'd fucking book him for harassing an officer of the fucking law, which shut the guy up and made Babette giggle and get out of the cab. If ever there were such a thing as love at first sight, that had certainly been it.

So where had love gone? How had the passion and the tenderness they'd both felt in that first year descended to the banal and ugly scenes that now comprised their marriage? How had a king-sized bed, prized for the opportunities it afforded for sexual acrobatics, degenerated into a convenient place to hide and not risk accidentally touching while sleeping?

Perhaps it was just that the fresh white excitement of romance and lust had shriveled under the scorching banalities of running a household and raising a child. Or maybe Natale was right. Maybe love *was* merely the self-delusion we manufacture to justify the trouble we take to have sex.

Max went into a bar on Sixth Avenue and had several beers. When he finally got back to Natale's apartment it was after two, and Natale was alone and looking pensive.

"So how was *La Bohème?*" said Max.

"Terrific."

"And how was Cathy?"

"Terrific. She just left."

"So you got into her pants."

176

Natale nodded without much enthusiasm.

"Was it fun?"

Natale nodded.

"It was fun," he said. "Predictable fun. No surprises, Max. I already knew everything she was going to say, before, during, and after fucking. I'm too old for surprises. I already knew how she was going to smell, to feel, to sound, to taste. In the unlikely event I get to like her, I know how it'll go bad too — the hurts, the guilts, the resentments, the accusations. I know the dialogue, Max, I know every fucking word — I've heard it that often. I swear to God, I walk down the street and see a cute girl, I don't just have a sex fantasy about her like other guys, I have a fucking *Reader's Digest* condensed version of our entire affair, complete with breakup, before we've reached the end of the block. It's a special curse that comes with experience."

"Well, at least it saves a lot of time and money," said Max, hoping to lighten his friend's mood.

"Yeah," said Natale, unlightened.

"So did you sound her out about threesomes?" asked Max, the dutiful high school buddy pumping for details.

"Yeah," said Natale. "She didn't go for it."

"Awww," said Max.

"She *did* allow me to handcuff her to the bed before we had sex, though. That was no surprise either, by the way."

"Why'd you cuff her to the bed?"

Natale shrugged.

"I dunno. I got two pairs of cuffs is why, I guess. You know something? I ask every girl I take back here if they want me to cuff them to the bed." Natale turned to look at Max. "So far not one has said no, Max. Not *one.*"

"Really?" said Max, impressed.

"Really," said Natale. "I don't understand that. I mean, we're talking first date situations here. I'm a guy they don't know. I could be anybody. I could be a sadist, O.K.? I could be a fucking *killer*. Not one of them said no, Max."

"Strange," said Max.

"I mean," said Natale, "is that due to their desire to surrender responsibility for the act of sex, or is it due to an unconscious desire to be violated? You tell me that."

"I don't know," said Max.

"Neither do I, Max," said Natale, "neither do I."

48

On Thursday evening, April 28, Judy Wells dropped her cat off at Rose Brill's apartment and flew from La Guardia to Chicago's O'Hare airport. She was able to upgrade to business class on her frequent flier card. She picked up her rented Mustang convertible from Avis, drove it to the Drake hotel, and checked in as Caroline Busey.

From room service she ordered the tuna steak very rare and lightly braised, and a bottle of Far Niente Chardonnay. After switching back and forth between Carson and Koppel for twenty minutes — one was too light for her mood, the other too heavy — she turned off the TV and went to sleep.

The next morning, after a breakfast of cranberry juice, plain yogurt with honey, whole wheat toast with margarine, and Red Zinger herbal tea, she left the Drake and walked to the Hancock Building. In the building directory she found a listing for Gordon & Graubart, Certified Public Accountants.

She took the elevator up and loitered in the corridor until people began to leave Gordon & Graubart for lunch. The instant Teddy Greco emerged, she knew him. He still had the same five o'clock shadow, the same curly black hair, only now it sat higher on his head. He was with another man and they were involved in a lively discussion about max tax, proposed regs, passive losses, and PIGS.

Judy entered the elevator first so that she could stand behind them. Pressed up against Greco's back in the crowded car, she could feel his buttocks against her belly. The sensation repelled her, but she found it interesting. Only six layers of cloth — his underpants, his trousers, her skirt, her slip, her pantyhose, and undies — separated her flesh from his. In just two weeks, there would be no separation at all.

* * *

Thirty years ago, the house had probably looked daring. Soaring planes of glass, double-height ceiling, rakishly tilted roof. Now it just looked dated. Moneyed, to be sure, but dated. The hardware was all obsolete.

An attractive redheaded matron opened the door with a preoccupied expression on her face.

"Mrs. Sherman?"

"Yes?"

"Avon calling, Mrs. Sherman. I'd love to come in and chat, if you have a moment."

"Uh, well, I was just about to get some things together for the cleaners. . . ."

"Oh, I *always* put off trips to the cleaners. Would you believe they charged me sixty-five dollars to clean a coat? Sixty-five dollars!"

"Not really. Listen, Miss . . . ?"

"Black. Monty Black."

"Miss Black, I don't truthfully have the time to chat now. Maybe some other time."

"Perfectly understandable, Mrs. Sherman. I wonder if I could ask you an embarrassing favor, though. I think I've eaten something that disagreed with me at lunch, and I have a rather urgent need to . . . use a powder room."

"Oh, by all means. I'm afraid the commode in the powder room isn't working very well, but why don't you use the one in our bedroom? It's right through there."

"Thank you so much. I can't tell you how grateful I am."

To be allowed to enter their bedroom was an unexpected stroke of luck. Judy glanced left at the double-height living room with the over-sized hearth, the possibly original Dubuffet print framed above it with the wrong mat. She turned right and walked down a hallway and through the bedroom. She noted the large-screen Mitsubishi TV, the VCR underneath it, the library of films with clearly printed labels — at this distance she could make out only one title, *The Day the Earth Stood Still,* ironically one of her favorites. She noted the bed that Stuart Sherman shared with this bitch he'd chosen instead of her, with whom he watched films like *The Day the Earth Stood Still,* hugging under the covers, hearing Michael Rennie tell Patricia Neal that if anything happened to him to go to the robot and say, "Gort, Klatu morada. Miktu."

She entered the master bathroom.

Being in Stuart's bathroom was exciting. Like suddenly being a part of his life again. Like being in his clothes. There was a black Jacuzzi bathtub at one end, a big stall shower with clear glass doors at the other. There was a black toilet and a black bidet and two oval black sinks in a marble counter. She wondered whose decision it was to go with black fixtures.

She opened the mirrored medicine cabinet. The usual. Viadent toothpaste, angled toothbrushes, toothpicks, dental floss, Bufferin, Tylenol, Midol, 1000-mg. buffered vitamin C, lots of physicians' free samples, and enough Halston after-shave to last several lifetimes.

Oho, a prescription for Valium, issued by another physician. For whom? Why, it's Jennifer Sherman, the *missus*. How nice. Maybe she's a nervous wreck and they have a rotten marriage. What else? Oho, Imodium — also for the missus. A nervous stomach, maybe an irritable bowel. Jennifer has chronic diarrhea. Does he call her Jenny? And what does he call her in bed?

Better not take too long. A pity Jennifer won't look at the samples, purchased at great expense from a *real* Avon lady. Well, perhaps somebody else will place an order. A shame to leave without at least taking a souvenir, something to remember Stuart by until we meet again.

She picked up an expensive-looking pair of men's nail clippers and slipped them into her purse. She sat down on the toilet and urinated. She started to pull up her underpants, then had an idea: Why not leave the Shermans a souvenir? It was only fair — take something, leave something. She took off her panties. She straightened her clothes, washed her hands, then opened the door.

The coast was clear. Passing through the bedroom, she noticed a pile of clothes on a chair, probably what Jenny was about to get ready for the cleaners — she could think of her as Jenny now, having invaded her privacy. She took out her panties and slipped them into a pocket of Stuart's slacks, then left the room.

"Thanks so much for letting me use your bathroom, Mrs. Sherman."

"Not at all. I hope you feel better, Miss Black."

Sorting the pile of clothing for the cleaners, Jennifer Sherman went through pockets for loose change and felt something slippery in a pair of her husband's slacks. She withdrew the slippery thing and stared in disbelief. A woman's nylon underpants. Certainly not hers.

Her breath started coming very fast. This was unimaginable. This was not possible. Stuart had been faithful to her for so many years, so many years. True, their sex life hadn't been good of late. She used her frequently upset stomach as an excuse, but they both knew that wasn't it. She didn't blame him for taking a mistress.

She turned the underpants inside out. The label said Bloomingdale's. They were clean. She raised them to her nose. They'd been worn. She smelled the scent of the woman who'd stolen her husband.

Tears sprang to her eyes. She'd confront him about the underpants when he got home tonight. There'd be an ugly scene. No—she'd throw them away. Throw them away and say nothing. Throw them away, say nothing, and try to be a better wife.

49

Although the receptionist said that Dr. Sherman's last appointment of the day was at five-thirty, he didn't emerge from his building until almost seven. Judy nearly missed him because he looked so different. The gray in the once blond hair. The horn-rimmed glasses. The Armani suit. She followed him to the garage but didn't risk going in because there weren't many other people around. She waited till he drove his car out—a sleek black Mercedes 560SL. As an intern he'd seduced her in a battered Chevy.

Immediately after breakfast the following morning, Judy telephoned Sherman's office and made an appointment for a full physical examination for Monty Black on May 13. Then she called Gordon & Graubart and asked for Mr. Greco. He came on the line fairly quickly. She took a deep breath and reminded herself she was only playing a role.

"Hello?"

"Mr. Greco?"

"Yes?"

"Mr. Greco, my name is Monty Black."

"What can I do for you, Miss Black?" A smug, faintly condescending tone.

"I'm CEO of Black & Barrington in New York, Mr. Greco, and we're about to open an office in Chicago."

"Yes." More respect now, definitely more respect.

"We're interviewing accountants and we've heard good things about you."

"You have?" Some surprise in the voice. Didn't he think enough of his work to have good things said about him?

"I'm planning to be back in town on May twelfth. I'd like to have drinks with you after work. Would that be possible?"

"Uh, sure. May twelfth, you say?"

"Correct. I'll meet you at a bar on Michigan Avenue called the Tack Room."

"The Tack Room, you say?"

"Six sharp."

"How will I know you, Miss Black?"

"You won't have to, Mr. Greco. I'll know *you*."

"Can you tell me what is currently the best French restaurant in town?" she said.

The elderly concierge pursed his lips and frowned.

"Best or most expensive?" said the concierge.

"Most expensive."

"That's easy. Le Manoir."

"And is that walking distance from here?"

"Yes, but I hope you don't want to dine there today. The waiting list is at least two weeks."

"Two weeks is perfect," she said.

Le Manoir was impressive looking, although perhaps not by New York standards. She liked the fresh flowers on the tables but couldn't believe they'd chosen anything as downscale as carnations. The banquettes were a tasteful green leather, but the carpet was a swirling abomination that looked as if diners had been sick on it.

She stood at the bar and ordered an Absolut on ice. After drinking half of it, she asked the way to the women's room.

On the way to the women's room she was able to get a fairly good idea of the general layout. A table at the back in the little alcove there would be ideal for her purposes. She went into the restroom and washed her hands.

Before ringing for a bellman she telephoned Le Manoir.

"Le Manoir, bonjour."

"Bonjour," she said in her haughtiest voice. "I am calling for Miss Black of Black & Barrington. She would like me to make a lunch reservation for May thirteenth at twelve-twenty P.M."

"I will see, madame, if we have any openings on the thirteenth."

"Miss Black has specified that she would like the table at the back in the little alcove, and that she be able to complete her luncheon by two-thirty, as she has a board meeting at Merrill Lynch."

"May thirteenth at twelve-twenty will be fine, madame."

By the time she checked out of the Drake and drove the Mustang down to Champaign-Urbana it was close to five P.M. It was strange to be back, sad but also sweet. She remembered the smell of the trees, the look of the quad, the Alma Mater statue, the student union, Altgeld Hall, Greg Hall and Lincoln Hall, but there were so many new buildings, and the students all seemed about twelve years old.

She parked the car and went into the administration building. Yes, Austin Richards was still on staff in the English department, she was told. He was a full professor now. He still had the same office.

She checked his home address and then drove out to the modest house at the edge of campus and parked the car across the street and waited. Scarcely two hours passed before he drove up, parked in the driveway, and emerged from the car. He'd aged, she noted with satisfaction. He'd gone gray and lost a good deal of crown and forehead hair. He was much heavier around the middle, even had something of a paunch. There was resignation and weariness in his formerly energetic and purposeful stride. But he still wore a tweedy jacket with elbow patches and he still smoked a pipe. Some things, she thought, never changed.

When he went inside she took a drink of vodka from her flask, drove to the corner drugstore, stepped to the public phone, and called him. She had a moment of panic when she first heard his voice, but then she got into character and the moment passed.

"Hello?"

"Professor Richards?"

"Mm-hmm."

"Professor," she said, controlling her voice with difficulty, "my name is Monty Black, and I'm calling from *Mademoiselle* magazine in New York. We're doing a feature on college professors who've significantly influenced their students' professional lives, and your name has come up several times."

"Is that so?"

"Yes."

"Well, I'm extremely flattered, extremely flattered."

"I plan to be in Champaign-Urbana on May fourteenth. I wonder if I might interview you then?"

"May fourteenth? What day of the week would that be, do you happen to know?"

"A Saturday."

"A Saturday, huh? Sure. I don't see why not."

Assuming there aren't any coeds I'm trying to hump, that meant.

"Marvelous. I'll telephone you when I know what time I'll have available, Professor."

"I look forward to meeting you, Ms. Black."

"Not as much as I, Professor Richards."

50

"Tonight," said Natale, "is Cheryl's birthday."

"That's why you're wearing the suit?" said Max.

"Yeah," said Natale. "You know, I realized in all the time I've been seeing her I never once took her anywhere decent. So as a surprise tonight I'm taking her to a real fancy Italian restaurant, Toscana."

"That's nice."

"Yeah. She's getting all dressed up. She's really excited."

"That sounds really nice. You know something, Tony, underneath you may not be such a bad guy after all."

"Thanks, Max," said Natale. "By the way, you think it might be possible for you to kind of disappear from about ten-thirty to, say, one o'clock?"

Max nodded and heaved a mighty sigh.

"No problem," he said.

Max returned at half past one, figuring to give the birthday girl an extra half hour in the cuffs. Natale was sitting on the Castro convertible in his suit, his tie undone, looking drunk and dazed.

"Uh-oh," said Max. "What happened? Dinner a disaster?"

Natale shook his head.

"No, as a matter of fact, dinner was great," he said. "Cheryl was knocked out by Toscana. I've never seen her happier."

"Then why are you looking like that?"

Natale shook his head almost imperceptibly.

"I don't know," he said, "maybe there's something wrong with me. We were both drinking champagne and having so much fun, I suddenly got this perverse idea. I told her to take off her panties under the table and hand them to me."

186

"Yeah," said Max, trying to visualize it.

"She did, of course. Just reached up under her dress and slid them down and handed them to me. Which got both of us very turned on."

"I'll bet," said Max.

"But after a while I started feeling bad about it, you know? I felt like I'd degraded her and I wondered why I'd done it. I figured it was because we'd begun to get kind of intimate in the past couple weeks and it was too threatening to me, you know? I needed to do something to cheapen what I'd started to feel for her."

"Yeah."

"So I had another glass of champagne. But the more I drank, the guiltier I felt. I couldn't stand the feeling, so I started rationalizing. I rationalized that she *deserved* being degraded because she was trash."

"Yeah."

"Problem is, when my patients do that I call it 'retroactive deserving' and I don't let them get away with it. I can't let myself get away with it either."

"O.K."

"So to make up for degrading her . . . I asked her to marry me."

Max's eyes widened.

"You're kidding me."

"Oh, no, I'm quite serious. She accepted, of course. We toasted our engagement with more champagne. I called over the owner and told him I had just proposed. He sent over another bottle on the house. Cheryl is more deliriously happy than any human being has a right to be. I think I just made the worst mistake of my entire life."

51

This was going to be difficult, he knew it, but he owed it to his son. Although it was his own apartment he rang the doorbell before using his key to open the door. Why did I do that, he wondered, to warn her in case she's in the sack with the dishwasher repairman?

Babette raced up to the door just as he opened it, nearly colliding with it.

"Oh, it's you," she said. "Why did you ring the bell?"

"I don't know," he said.

They looked at each other awkwardly for a moment.

"So how you doing?" he said.

She shrugged.

"B*abette!*" yelled Sam from the other room, "is that *Max?*"

Max looked at her questioningly.

"Since you've been gone," said Babette, "he's been referring to us only as Babette and Max. He's stopped calling us Mama and Dada."

"You're kidding me."

"I'm not kidding you," she said. "Do you think I would kid about something as serious as that?"

"As serious as what?" said Max.

"He's denying we're his parents," said Babette.

"Oh, I don't think it means that —"

"No? What *do* you think it means?" said Babette. "He has also started having nightmares about lobsters and seals and he's started asking to sleep with his pacifier again. Last night he wet his bed for the first time in I don't even know how long."

"Oh, Jesus," said Max.

"Ba*bette!* Is that *Max?*"

"No," said Babette, "it's not Max, it's *Dada.*"

Sam slowly walked into the living room.

"Hi, Max," he said.

"Hi, buddy," said Max, sweeping him off his feet, but Sam straight-armed him before he could plant a kiss.

"Babette, is Max taking me to the park?" said Sam to his mother.

"Yes," said Babette.

"I don't *want* to go to the park."

"O.K.," said Max, "where do you want me to take you?"

"I want to stay here with Babette and play with my Brio trains."

"Well, you've been playing with Mama all week," said Max. "Today is Saturday and it's my day off and I came to take you to the park."

Sam considered this information for a moment.

"Why is it your day off?" he said.

"Because every week I get two days off, and sometimes one of them is a Saturday."

"Why do you get two days off?"

"Sam," said Babette, interrupting what Max recognized as the beginning of a compulsive, almost Talmudic line of inquiry about days off. "Dada hasn't seen you all week and he has come specially now to see you and take you somewhere to play with him, isn't that nice?"

"Why hasn't he seen me all week?" said Sam.

Babette looked at Max for help.

"Well," said Max lamely, "because my friend Tony Natale asked me to stay with him."

"Why did your friend—" Sam began, but Max cut him off.

"Sam," he said, "just now I happen to be staying with my friend Tony Natale, but I have really missed you and I have come over today to take you to the park to play on the slides, and after that maybe we'll go to FAO Schwarz and buy you a present."

At the word *present* Sam immediately forgot the fact that his parents were in the process of a possible divorce. Bribery with toys or sweets had never failed them in moments of duress.

"What kind of present?" said Sam, his eyes sparkling.

"Well," said Max, "we'll have to see what kinds of things they have there."

* * *

189

It was a warm, sunny day in Central Park, the fine weather having sucked hordes of people out of the buildings and into the greenery. Mimes, jugglers, and violinists walked against the wind, kept twelve spinning hatchets floating in the air, and sawed away at Paganini. Two full-blooded Apaches in feathered headdresses did war dances for loose change.

They headed toward Sam's favorite slide near Sixty-seventh Street, a beautifully sculpted, gracefully curving marble affair that always had a backlog of at least a dozen sliders waiting on line, clutching scruffy pieces of corrugated cardboard to sit on for greater speed.

In an adjacent play area a young Black man dressed as a clown was fashioning animal shapes out of long, skinny balloons. Max took Sam over to join the three toddlers raptly watching the demonstration, but soon detected something slightly off in the clown's patter and steered his son over to a huge construction of blocks, steps, and additional slides.

They hadn't been on the construction for more than five minutes when a child's cry caught Max's attention, and when he returned his gaze to Sam not ten seconds later the boy had vanished.

Max was alarmed. He raced around the back of the construction. No Sam. He raced around to the front. No Sam. He climbed to the top of the construction and looked down inside of it. Still no Sam. He panicked.

Oh, God, no, please no, don't let this happen to me, God, he prayed as he searched. The clown! He looked over to where the clown was making balloon sculptures, but he had vanished as well. The clown had taken Sam! Somehow, when Max wasn't looking, the fucking pervert clown had snatched his son!

Why hadn't he paid more attention to the clown to begin with? Especially when he'd sensed something off about his patter. John Wayne Gacy, the pederast and serial murderer who'd sodomized and murdered three dozen boys and then buried them under his porch, had often dressed up as a clown to entertain children at hospitals. How could Max, a homicide cop who worked in Harlem with Black crack-dealer killers, allow his attention to stray long enough for a fucking Black pederast killer clown to grab the person he loved most in the entire world?

He ran out of the play area and began to shout Sam's name. Calm down, he told himself. Get hold of yourself. Please, God, don't let this happen, just bring him back to me safe and sound and unbuggered by perverted Black killer clown cocks and I'll do anything you want me to, anything at all.

"Max, can we go back to the big slide now?"

Max spun around at the sound of his son's voice. He couldn't believe his prayers had been answered.

"Sam! Oh, thank God!"

Max rushed to the boy and hugged him so tightly he nearly strangled him, aware that this was the point in the old joke where he was supposed to look heavenward and say, "Where's his hat?"

"Where's the clown?" he said instead.

"Where's *what* clown?" asked Sam.

"The clown that was making the animals out of the balloons?" said Max.

"What balloons?" said Sam.

It was clear there was no connection between Sam's brief disappearance and the disappearance of the Black clown, and Max had to deal with the fact that he was a prejudiced racist honky bigot.

Max took Sam to FAO Schwarz and bought him a tiny car, then dropped him off at the apartment. He decided there was no point in mentioning Sam's brief disappearance to Babette.

"Did you have fun at the park with Dada?" said Babette, obscurely relieved that Max had returned him rather than spiriting the boy off to Nevada and suing for custody.

"We went to FAO Schwarz and Max bought me a car," said Sam.

"How wonderful," said Babette.

"So O.K.," said Max. "I'll pick him up again tomorrow morning around the same time, O.K.?"

"No, tomorrow is Sunday," said Babette. "Pick him up about eleven-thirty. I'm taking him to ten o'clock mass."

"Oh, yeah? How come?"

"It's just something I've decided to do now. Take him to church with me on Sundays."

"Maybe we ought to discuss this," said Max.

"There's nothing to discuss," said Babette. "It's what I've decided to do now."

Max stared at her for a moment, struggling with complex and contradictory emotions. They had always talked about exposing Sam equally to both Catholicism and Judaism. To keep Sam's religious education in balance, Babette's unilateral move toward Catholicism would have to be answered by a corresponding move toward Judaism. But Max had no interest in going to synagogue, and dragging Sam along with him didn't make it any more appealing.

"I'll pick him up tomorrow," said Max and left.

52

"Two-Five squad, Segal."

"Max? It's Susan. Susan Simon."

"Susan. *Hi.*"

"Am I calling at a bad time?"

"No, no. I mean," he laughed ruefully, "it's not what I would call a *good* time exactly, but it's not an inconvenient time, if that's what you're asking me."

"What's wrong?"

"Oh, nothing. Personal stuff. What's up?"

"Well, I was just calling to say hello and to find out if there are any new developments on the Smiley and Petlin cases."

"Nothing earth-shattering, no. How's your article coming?"

"So-so. I thought maybe we could get together and talk about it."

"Sure. You want me to pick you up and bring you back here?"

"Sure. Or if you have time later, after work, maybe we could have a drink and discuss it in a slightly more relaxed atmosphere."

"I'd like that," said Max.

"Oh, that would be fun," she said. "How about this evening?"

"Sure," said Max. "I get off at four today. I could pick you up at five."

"Wonderful, Max. I'll look for you at five then."

Susan was surprised at how glad she was to see him. Max seemed glad to see her too, although that was probably just wishful thinking. He selected a booth at the back of the moodily lit bar which would have been romantic if not for the fact that it was right next to the men's room and guys were constantly coming out zipping up their flies, which meant there was no way they'd washed their hands.

"So," he said, leaning back against the red tuck-and-roll Naugahyde booth, "where did we leave off last time?"

"Well, let's see," she said. "Mr. Wainwright had just given Albert Prince an alibi for April twelfth, the night of the, uh, Petlin murder, and . . ."

"Oh, right," he said. "Well, a lot *has* happened since then."

"Really? What?"

"Well, for one thing, we've pretty much dropped the idea the killer is a sadomasochistic fag."

"You have?" she said. She looked past him at the old Wurlitzer jukebox in the corner, the bubbles rising slowly up its colored tubes, and wondered what was in there, colored water or glycerin or what, and whether it would kill you if you drank it.

"Yeah," he said. "We're now fairly sure we're looking for a woman."

Breathing seemed suddenly more difficult, as if her lungs had lost some of their capacity to expand.

"A woman," she said, frowning.

"Yes."

"But what about the S and M equipment you found in Petlin's apartment?"

"Who told you about the S and M equipment?" said Max, regarding her oddly.

"Who told me?" she said, and the floor gave way beneath her feet.

"Yes."

Oh Jesus, she thought, oh dear sweet Jesus Christ.

"Why, was it a secret or something?" she said, trying to sound innocent.

"In a way," he said. "It's one of the things we deliberately kept from the press so we could screen out the nuts who confess to major homicides."

"I see," she said.

I have just confessed to being the killer, she thought. What do I do now, run? Feign an epileptic seizure? Lean forward and strangle him and run out of here?

She could feel her heart beating. She felt as though she were running uphill. She began to sweat in unexpected places.

"You look upset," he said.

"I do?" she said. It was barely a whisper.

194

"Yeah," he said. "Look, don't worry about it. It doesn't matter who told you, just so long as you promise not to write about it, O.K.?"

Dear sweet God in heaven, he was just afraid I was going to *write* about it, she thought. Her heart rate slowed.

"I promise," she said. The back of her blouse was stuck to the space between her shoulder blades. Drops of sweat slid silently down her sides from her underarms.

"Good," he said. "O.K., where were we? Oh, yeah, so they think it's a woman. An attractive blond one. A number of people have recalled seeing an attractive blond woman just before or just after the homicides. Did you hear about this guy Barmack?"

"Barmack?" she said, her heart beginning to race again.

"The guy that fell off the balcony on Central Park West and Ninety-second."

"Oh, yes," she said, thinking quickly. "There was something about that on the news. He killed that mother and child when he fell? Horrible, just horrible."

"Yeah, well, there's some feeling here now that he didn't fall, that he was pushed, which would make it a homicide, of course. And . . ."

"Yes?"

He shook his head. "Never mind."

"What?"

Max looked intently at her, took another swallow of his drink, then smiled uncertainly. He took a deep breath.

"If I tell you this, you've got to promise me you won't write about it," he said. "Not till I say it's O.K. You promise?"

"I promise," she said.

"Well," said Max, leaning closer, lowering his voice, "my own feeling is that the Barmack case is tied in with the Smiley and Petlin ones."

"Really?" said Susan thickly. "You mean you think it's . . . the same killer?"

"Well, the m.o. isn't the same, of course — Barmack wasn't found naked on the bed in his apartment, his carotid wasn't cut, and his face wasn't bashed. But, like both Smiley and Petlin, Barmack probably had sex with someone shortly before he died. And an attractive blond woman was seen with him too."

"Not really," said Susan.

Max nodded.

"Going up with him in the elevator to look at this apartment," said

Max. "What if they struggled and he fell to his death *before* she could slash his throat? What if she just didn't get the chance?"

Susan nodded, staring at him intently.

"That's very . . . interesting thinking," she said at last.

"Thank you."

"But if that was how it happened," she said, realizing she was dancing close to the precipice again but this time intentionally, "wouldn't there be at least some kind of cut on him, on his face or hands, from her knife?"

"Defense cuts. I've thought of that," said Max. "It didn't show up in the initial autopsy report. But I've asked Chernin to take another look."

"So let's say he finds something, and let's say you can then tie the Barmack case into the other two," she said. "Would that make it easier for you to find the killer?"

Her breathing ceased as she waited for his reply. He looked at her with a half-smile on his face and exhaled slowly.

"We've taken the doorman from the Barmack building and the concierge from the Petlin building over to a police artist," he said. "They've tried to put together a composite drawing of the blond woman and . . ."

"And?"

"Well," said Max, "see for yourself."

He reached into a thick manila envelope lying on the seat beside him, withdrew a sketch, and handed it to her. She took it from him and looked at it.

She held the sketch in both hands, her elbows planted firmly on the table to steady them. The woman in the drawing looked nothing at all like her.

"It's not much to go on, is it?" said Max.

"No, it isn't," she said at last.

Max seemed to cave in a little at this.

"Between you and me," he said, "I don't think we're ever going to catch this bitch. Not unless she keeps on killing guys and starts making some really big mistakes."

She looked at him and smiled. Her panic once more dissolved. A wave of relief engulfed her. Max looked genuinely beaten.

"You seem so . . . well, dispirited," she said. "Are you really taking this investigation that personally?"

"Yeah," he said, "and . . ."

196

"And you're having some personal problems now as well?" she said gently. "You indicated as much on the phone."

He nodded.

"Would you like to . . . talk about them at all? I don't mean to pry, but, well, sometimes it helps to talk. I'm a good listener."

She smiled encouragingly. He looked at her for a moment, trying to decide what, if anything, to tell her.

"My wife and I have just split up," he said.

She felt as though she had just been given a marvelous gift.

"Oh, I *am* sorry," she said, managing to work her features into a sympathetic frown.

"Yeah," he said.

"Have you been . . . together long?" she said, trying to calculate how long it might be before he'd be in the mood to ask her to dinner.

"Seven years," he said.

"Seven years," she said, shaking her head. "And are there . . . children?"

Max nodded, looking at the table top, spreading out the ring of moisture from his glass.

"A little boy," he said. "Three years old. That's what makes it so awful."

"How is he taking it?" she said.

"He's having nightmares about lobsters and seals and calling us by our first names."

She risked a sad smile.

"Are you feeling guilty?" she said.

"Yep."

"You know," she said, "I don't know if this will help you, but many child psychologists claim that children, even very young children, younger than three, can sense when their parents aren't getting along. They claim that it may actually be more harmful to the child to see his parents in a bad living situation than if they separated."

"Well, thanks for telling me that," he said.

"Does it relieve your guilt at all?" she asked.

He smiled at her and shook his head. They both laughed.

"Tell me," she said, "do you think you'll . . ."

She waved the rest of the question away.

"Do I think I'll *what?*" said Max, "Get back together with her? I don't know, Susan, I really don't."

She nodded. I'm becoming transparent, she thought. He knows I'm interested in him and I'm about to be pitifully obvious. Please let me shut up now, please just let me shut up.

"Max, I don't know if you have anyone to talk to about this, and I know you don't know me very well," she said. "But if you ever want to discuss anything with a sympathetic listener . . ."

She wrote down a number on her cocktail napkin.

"Here's my home number," she said. "Call me anytime. Anytime at all. Day or night."

Giving him the number is brilliant, she thought. Saying day or night is pushing it.

"Thank you," he said and took her hand. "That's very sweet. I really appreciate it."

When Max opened the front door of Natale's apartment he was startled to see the girl. She, on the other hand, did not seem at all surprised to see him.

"You must be Max," she said.

"Must I?" he said.

"Yes," she said, giggling.

She was maybe in her early twenties, slim, blond, and rather pretty.

"And who must you be?" said Max.

"Cheryl," she said.

Cheryl. His roommate's fiancée. It was not surprising he hadn't recognized her. He'd seen photographs of her, but they had not been of her face.

"Cheryl," he said. "I've heard a lot about you."

He was unable to look at her without being bombarded by subliminal flashes of the Polaroid nudes.

"Did you hear our news?"

"Yes," said Max, intrigued to hear that the engagement was still on. "Congratulations."

It made him uncomfortable that he'd seen her bare breasts and buttocks and a split-beaver shot of her vagina before he'd even met her. He felt an intimacy with her that might prove awkward, that might tempt him to behave toward her in an inappropriately sexual manner. He wondered if she knew Natale showed the pictures to his buddies. He wondered if she cared. Maybe she didn't. Maybe, as Natale had said, she was trash.

"I just think Tony's such a wonderful guy," she said.

"Really?" said Max. "Why do you think that?" They both looked startled, then laughed simultaneously. He hadn't meant the question to come out in quite that way. But he was often mystified why male friends of his who consistently pooped on women were so adored by them.

"I mean," said Max, "I know Tony in a much different way than you know him."

"Well, I should hope so," she said, giggling.

"Yeah. But what I mean is, what is it that you like so much about him?"

She furrowed her brow.

"Well," she said, "he's real thoughtful. I mean, to propose to me he took me to this real expensive Italian restaurant and everything."

"Yeah," said Max, tempted to point out that it was the only place he'd ever taken her, and that the proposal had been the fruit of guilt, not planning. "What else?"

"He's real smart about what makes people tick. He's told me stuff about myself that's been real helpful."

Natale entered from the bathroom.

"Hey, Max, I didn't know you were here."

"Yeah," said Cheryl, "we've been having a nice talk. Max has been asking me what I see in you."

"If you can't get your best friend to run you down," said Natale, "who can you get?"

54

"We got a fresh one," said Caruso as Max approached the car, carrying two slices of mushroom-and-pepperoni pizza and two cans of Coke Classic.

They were parked on First Avenue and Eighty-second, having just completed another interview from the seemingly inexhaustible pool of women in Freddy Petlin's address book, and come up with yet another zero. Nobody suspicious sounding, and no linkages to either the Smiley or the Barmack cases.

"Where?" said Max, maneuvering his way into the car without dropping dinner.

"In the Two-Three," said Caruso, pulling out into early evening traffic on First Avenue and heading uptown. "Two Black males shot a male Hispanic in a drug dispute. The identities of both the shooter and his accomplice are known."

"Sounds like a grounder," said Max, wishing Smiley and Petlin had been grounders too. "Hey, did you tell Susan Simon about the S and M equipment we found in Petlin's apartment?"

"Fuck no," said Caruso. "Why?"

"Because she knew about it," said Max, "and I sure wasn't the one who told her."

"Well, it sure as shit wasn't me," said Caruso. "I wouldn't give her shit. I wouldn't piss on her if her pants was on fire."

Max handed Caruso his pizza and inadvertently dripped hot oil and melted cheese on his partner's slacks.

"Oh, sorry," said Max.

"*Shit,*" said Caruso, holding both his pizza and the steering wheel in his left hand, reaching for his handkerchief and dabbing at his trousers with his right. "How many times I gotta tellya, hold the fucking pizza *up* when you pass it to me?"

"I *said* I was sorry."

"Yeah, well *sorry* don't fucking pay the fucking cleaning bill, does it?" said Caruso.

"Here's for the fucking cleaning bill," said Max, holding his own slice of pizza in his left hand, putting his can of Coke under his left arm, Caruso's can under his chin, reaching with his right hand into his pants pocket for a five-dollar bill, and thrusting it in Caruso's face.

"Put your money away, shmuck," said Caruso, temporarily losing control of the wheel, nearly sideswiping a van in the right lane, and hitting the yelp under the dashboard as if it had been the van's fault.

By the time they got to the scene at 106th and Second a large crowd had gathered. Caruso parked the car and they shouldered their way through the gapers and under the fluorescent pink plastic tape.

The victim, Perfecto Gomez, a Hispanic boy of about seventeen, sat crumpled forward on the sidewalk, one arm under his stomach at an improbable angle. He wore a black tanktop, acid-washed designer jeans, and the requisite brand new hightop Reebok basketball shoes. A pool of sticky, dark brown blood spread out from under his chest and ran off the curb into the gutter where it collected in a little pool.

A uniform saw Max and walked over.

"I was first on the scene, O.K.?" he said. "I hear a Hispanic male's been shot. I come up and here's this huge fuckin' crowd of people all around him. I figure they're tryin' to help him, give him CPR or somethin'. You know what they're doin'?"

"What were they doing?" said Max.

"Ripping off his fuckin' gold chains," said the uniform, shaking his head. "Can you believe that?"

"I can believe it," said Max.

Paul Pafko, a Twenty-third PDU man, recognized Caruso.

"There's good news and bad news," said Detective Pafko.

"Yeah?" said Caruso, who had wearied of good-news-bad-news jokes a generation before.

"The good news is," said Pafko, "is we've i.d.'d the shooter — one Jamal Stevens, street name Jimmy Feet, a Black male, about fifteen or sixteen years of age, and his accomplice, one Darnell Washington.

The bad news is, that whereas Washington has several priors and is known to us, Stevens don't and nobody knows what the fuck he looks like. We can reach out for someone to finger him, but I don't think we're gonna find anybody willing to give him up."

"I thought this was supposed to be a grounder," said Max petulantly.

Pafko shrugged.

"Looks like the ball took a bad hop," he said.

When Max and Caruso had first rolled up on the scene at 106th and Second it was about nine P.M. By shortly after midnight their canvassing had netted a witness, a young Black woman named Kimberly McCue, who lived on 106th and Second. They assured her all she'd have to do was identify the suspect in a line-up at the precinct; she would not have to go to court and risk recriminations from the accused or his friends.

They were lying. If Kimberly McCue failed to testify against Jamal Stevens in court they had no case. They always lied to witnesses. They both felt bad about it, but if they didn't lie they'd never get anyone to testify and they'd never clear a case.

They'd also gotten the name of another witness, a Hispanic girl named America something-or-other who lived in a project in the Bronx. They drove to the address in the Bronx, parked the car, and entered the smelly building, spider-webbed with graffiti. An obviously stoned Black man with rheumy eyes stared at them insolently.

"How ya doin', bro," said Caruso cheerily. "You know a Hispanic girl in this building name of America something?"

"You be de*tec*tives," said the man, chuckling at a private joke.

"You're a shrewd observer of your fellow man, sir," said Max.

"You be de*tec*tives, you best be carryin' *guns*," said the man unpleasantly.

Max and Caruso brushed past him to the elevators.

They went up to the twelfth floor and began banging on doors. When residents asked who was there they answered "Police" or "Policía." By now it was one A.M. and they were into overtime, which both of them needed badly — Max even more so, now that he was separated.

Max always thought it was a miracle more people whose doors they banged on at this hour didn't go into cardiac arrest. Even if you *didn't* have anything to hide, being dropped in on by the police at such an hour had to be traumatic, and Max doubted there were many people in the buildings they canvassed who had nothing to hide.

The thirty-seventh door they banged on was opened by a short, plump Hispanic woman with a pretty face and a belly that looked like it was going to give up its contents at any minute.

"Policía, señora," said Max, exhausting most of his Spanish vocabulary. "May we come in?"

"Si, si," she said, ushering them into the small apartment and closing the door behind her.

There were two religious paintings, one of Jesus and one of somebody else not readily identifiable, framed on the wall above the sofa, and two night views of the Manhattan skyline executed on black velvet. The TV was on and tuned to a movie starring John Wayne as a fairly young man. There was a playpen on the floor and numerous toddler toys.

"We're looking for America," said Max, aware of the absurdity of his words. "That you?"

The woman nodded vigorously many times.

"No," she said. "Iss my daughter."

"Your daughter," said Max. "And does your daughter live with you?"

The woman shook her head just as vigorously. "We los' her three years ago to crack," she said.

"I don't understand," said Max gently. "You're saying your daughter is no longer alive?"

The woman began to babble to Max in Spanish. Max turned helplessly to Caruso, who began to talk to her with surprising assurance in her own tongue. After a while he turned back to Max to translate.

"She says the daughter is alive but she'd be better off dead," said Caruso. "The daughter weighs seventy pounds and earns enough to buy food and drugs by hooking. She don't know where the daughter lives, and she says she threw out all photographs of her three years ago, which I find doubtful, but we're wastin' our time here in any case."

When they got back to the Two-Three, it was nearly two A.M. A detective named Paccione was sitting at his desk, interviewing an enormously fat light-skinned Black woman dressed in a white nurse's uniform.

Paccione's partner, Mano, took Max and Caruso aside.

"The broad is a sister of Jamal Stevens," he said sotto voce.

"The shooter?" said Max delightedly.

"She just come in off the fuckin' street all by herself," said Mano, raising his eyebrows. "She's gonna give the guy up."

"Why the fuck would she give us her brother?" said Caruso suspiciously.

"Some shit about how she's the outsider in the family," said Mano. "Whole family's into selling crack, including her twelve-year-old sister, including her mother. Including everybody but *her,* right?"

"Right," said Max.

"She hates her mother," said Mano. "It's gonna fuckin' *kill* her mother to have Jimmy get sent up on a twenty-five-to-life."

Caruso and Max walked over to Paccione and the nurse.

"Venus," said Mano, "this here's Detective Caruso and Detective Segal."

"Hi," she said.

"Hi," said Max. "Venus, where do you think Jimmy is now?"

"I don' know," she said. "He mos' likely be over to the project now."

Max looked at his watch. Ten after two. He had a day tour starting at eight. He and Caruso could work a couple more hours on overtime and then sleep in the dorm. When Max was still living with Babette such decisions had made him feel guilty. Living with Natale he didn't need to feel that way. He wondered how he'd feel living with Susan. Would she grow as jaded and disinterested in his work as Babette?

"If we drove you over to the project now and your brother was outside," said Max, "could you point him out to us?"

Venus nodded.

"You wanna take the van?" said Paccione.

They had access to a surveillance van with a periscope. If Venus were going to finger her brother and not risk being killed by the family for doing so, she'd have to remain undetected. The periscope would be useful.

"Sure," said Caruso, "let's take the van."

"Oh, one thing," said Mano. "Her brother's already got an attorney — I think the family's got Freberg on retainer for drug busts — so remember, if we *do* pull him in, we can't question him."

* * *

205

They pulled up across the street from the project where Venus and Jimmy lived. It was a large project, slightly less gone-to-hell than others Max had seen. In the Plymouth Fury ten yards down from the project entrance sat Paccione and Mano. In the van twenty yards up from the entrance sat Max, Caruso, and Venus. Caruso was in the driver's seat, Max and Venus were in the back of the windowless vehicle by the periscope. The Fury and the van maintained radio contact through their Motorola walkie-talkies. If Venus spotted Jimmy, all four detectives would converge on him for the collar.

It was two-forty A.M. Max had never quite gotten used to the fact that life uptown in the projects and on the street continued at about the same pace during all hours of the day and night. Max showed Venus how to move the periscope around and then they just sat and waited.

"They fixin' to have a war this summer," said Venus, making small talk. "You hear 'bout that?"

"No, I hadn't," said Max, hoping she was referring to rumors of a drug war in Harlem rather than a hot CIA tip about something in the Persian Gulf.

"Oh, yeah," she said. "They be many possies of shooters comin' up here this summer makin' hits, many possies. They be bringin' in lotsa nine millimeter submachine guns already. It gone be quite a lively summer."

"I'll bet it will," said Max. "What's this war supposed to be about, crack?"

"Crack and coke," she said. "Dominicans, Rastafarian Jamaicans, Puerto Ricans, Cubans, Colombians. The Dominicans be the worst, though."

"What about heroin?" asked Max. "They still use that or is it out of fashion now?"

"Oh, no, it not out of fashion," said Venus. "They sniff heroin to come down off smokin' crack."

Max nodded and moved the periscope down the block. Six Black teens were swaggering up the street now toward the project. They were about a hundred yards away.

"Max," said Caruso.

"I see them," said Max, peering through the periscope.

Max didn't recognize any of the boys. He knew Darnell Washington, a tall, heavyset bastard, and Washington was not among them.

"Hey, Venus," said Max, "take a look through here. See if you recognize your brother."

206

Venus looked through the periscope.

"I don' know," she said. "The dude with the hat *could* be him, I cain't tell."

"Keep looking," said Max.

The portable crackled. Paccione and Mano had seen the boys as well. The boys came closer. Before they got to the project they would pass the van. Venus kept peering at them through the periscope.

"I jus' don't know," she said. "It *look* like mah bruthuh, but I cain't be sure."

"Keep looking," said Max.

The boys kept coming. They wore flat-top haircuts, baggy shorts, hightop Reebok basketball shoes. Now they were ten yards from the van. Now they were five yards from the van. Now they were passing the van.

"Venus?"

"I jus' don' know," she said again. "It *look* like mah bruthuh, but I cain't be sure."

"You're not *sure?*" said Max incredulously. "How could you not be sure?"

"How the fuck could you not be *sure?*" said Caruso. "Don't you know what your fucking brother looks like?"

The radio crackled again.

"She's not sure," said Caruso into the radio.

"Don't you live with your brother?" said Max.

"Yeah, I lives with him."

"But you can't be sure if the guy in the hat is him?" said Max. "I don't understand."

"I jus' cain't be sure," she said.

"I say we take him," said Max.

"What if it's the wrong guy?" said Caruso.

"Then we're fucked," said Max. "But you gotta play the cards you're dealt, and this is what we're being dealt."

"O.K.," said Caruso, "let's take him."

"O.K.," said Max into the radio, "let's take him."

"You stay here," said Caruso to Venus. "Whatever happens, don't show your face if you want to stay alive."

Venus nodded. Max and Caruso got casually out of the van. Paccione and Mano got casually out of the Fury. All four cops strolled toward the six Black teenagers who were lounging in front of the project entrance.

The detectives were acting as if there were nothing the slightest bit unusual about four white men in sportcoats and ties going to visit a friend in the exclusively Black and Hispanic building at three A.M., and the six boys pretended to not even notice them. It was more than likely that the boy Venus was having trouble recognizing was the shooter. It was more than likely that all six boys were armed.

Max caught himself thinking about Susan, wondering if she'd be concerned about his safety if she knew what was going down, wondering if she'd mourn if he died. Would Sam? Would Babette?

Caruso and Max strolled on past the six boys and then, almost as an afterthought, turned to greet them.

"Howya doin', gentlemen?" said Max.

The boys nodded, their faces blank blackboards, wiped clean of all messages.

"We were going to pay a visit on someone in this building," said Max, making it up. "His name is Coco. Maybe you know him?"

The boys looked at each other, shrugged, then shook their heads. Everybody in Harlem knew at least three guys named Coco, but if you had to ask, the answer was no.

"This guy Coco lives on the sixth floor," said Max helpfully, looking at the boy he believed to be Jamal "Jimmy Feet" Stevens. "You know him?"

The boy shook his head. He was about six feet tall. He was slim, nice looking, and was wearing baggy shorts, an Adidas shirt, enormous hightop Reebok basketball shoes, and a white peaked cap with the bill off to the side. His face was soft, innocent, sweet and childlike, and it wore a bemused expression. If you were not a cop and had not seen such a face thousands of times before it would have been impossible to imagine this sweet boy as a killer.

"What's *your* name?" said Max.

"Me?" said the boy.

"Yeah."

The boy looked briefly at his friends, then back to Max.

"Jimmy," he said.

Caruso moved slowly and casually around until he was standing almost behind Jimmy. Paccione and Mano moved too, in a slow-motion pattern that reminded Max of the shift in the backfield before the football is snapped.

"Jimmy what?" said Max, as if the question were borne of idle curiosity and had no practical import.

"Jimmy Stevens," said the boy.

It was as if the ball had suddenly been snapped. Three revolvers emerged instantaneously from their holsters. Caruso took one final step, grabbed Jimmy's wrists behind him and cuffed them together.

The other five boys were utterly motionless, utterly impassive. If anything had happened, they had simply failed to notice it.

"Hey," said Jimmy, even more cool and bemused than previously, "what's goin' down, man?"

"Nothing to worry about," said Max. "We just want to talk to you is all."

"What about?" said Jimmy.

"Nothing important," said Caruso, "just murder."

Jimmy and his buddies exchanged cool, bemused looks, as if these hopelessly silly white men were playing a foolish game and they were choosing to indulge them just for a goof.

Caruso led Jimmy over to the Fury, put him in the back seat, and then climbed in after him. Max looked at the five remaining boys and judged that there wasn't going to be gunplay. Neither Babette nor Susan would have to mourn. He nodded to Paccione and Mano.

"Why don't you guys . . . take the other vehicle," said Max to the two detectives, implying that they drive Venus somewhere and drop her off, "and we'll meet you back at the Two-Three."

Paccione and Mano holstered their guns and headed toward the van. Max got into the driver's seat of the Fury and started up the car.

Jimmy observed that the cuffs were tight and politely requested that Caruso loosen them up a little. Caruso obliged. Jimmy said that his hat was crooked and politely requested that Caruso adjust it. Caruso again obliged. Jimmy politely asked if he was going to have to spend the night in jail.

"That's the least of your worries now, son," said Caruso. Then, perhaps feeling sorry for him, he added, "Don't worry, though, you've got a good lawyer, the top drug lawyer in the city. He'll have you outta there in no time. You got no priors, right?"

"Right."

"You'll either never go to jail or else it'll be a very short sentence," said Caruso. "Tell me somethin', Jimmy. You know, we can't ask you anything because you got a lawyer, but I'm just wondering. Why did you shoot him? Why did you shoot Perfecto? Did Darnell put you up to it or was it your own idea?"

"Why I shoot *who?*"

"Perfecto Gomez."

"I didn't shoot nobody," he said. "I don't even *know* nobody by that name you said."

"That right?" said Caruso, heating up. "Tell me something, Jimmy, you got a girlfriend?"

Jimmy laughed.

"Well, Jimmy," said Caruso, "you ain't gonna get your cock sucked by no girl for about two years, you know that? But Perfecto Gomez, the boy you shot, he ain't gonna get his cock sucked again *ever.*"

Jimmy stopped laughing, confused by Caruso's vacillation between friendship and hostility. Perhaps sensing his own ambivalence, Caruso added, "Hey, bro, this ain't nothin' personal between us, you understan'? It's just business. It's just my job."

At the Two-Three PDU Max and Caruso fingerprinted and Polaroided Jamal "Jimmy Feet" Stevens and then put him into the small, barred holding pen in the squad room.

"You know somethin'?" said Caruso sotto voce to Max. "He's not a bad kid. I'm sure that scumbag Darnell put him up to it."

"I know," said Max, looking at the boy in the cell, "I kinda like him too."

For a moment both men said nothing.

"So," said Caruso in a different tone, "should we call Silver and get him to authorize a formal collar or go get some witnesses and put together a line-up first?"

Silver was the assistant D.A. who was on call tonight, "catching" cases. A line-up would consist of half a dozen Black male volunteers who looked similar to the suspect and who'd be paid five dollars apiece to be in it.

"What witnesses you want to get?" asked Max.

"Well, Kimberly McCue," said Caruso. "We might also get this broad America — I think I know where she hooks. Plus we got that detestable scumbag Darnell Washington. I want to bring him in here just to break his dick."

"He'll never come in voluntarily," said Max.

"He don't come in voluntarily, we'll make him a material witness, lock him up in a fuckin' hotel room," said Caruso. "He refuses to comply we'll pull him in for contempt."

"You know where he lives?" said Max.

"Fuck *yes,* I know where he lives," said Caruso. It was as if Max had asked if Caruso knew where his *mother* lived.

Max shrugged.

"O.K., I'll call Silver."

Max dialed Silver's number and waited a long time until it was answered.

"Hello, Shel?" said Max. "Max Segal at Manhattan North. Sorry to wake you, but we just nailed Jamal Stevens, the kid who shot Perfecto Gomez? Can we make a formal arrest or do you want us to do a line-up first?"

"What time is it?" said Silver.

Max looked up at the clock on the wall. It said three-thirty.

"I dunno," said Max.

"Christ, it's three-*thirty!*" said Silver. "Where the fuck you going to get six guys for a line-up at three-*thirty?*"

"The men's shelter," said Max. "All we have to do is show up there, they'll be all over us like lint. They'd fucking sell their *mother* for that five bucks."

"You got witnesses?" said Silver.

"Three of them," said Max, stretching the truth.

"You're positive you've got the shooter?" said Silver. "You're absolutely *positive?*"

"On my mother's head," said Max. "He verified his name when we asked him, and his own sister i.d.'d him from the van. You need a line-up or not?"

There was a brief silence at the other end.

"I don't need a line-up if you can get a positive i.d. from one of the witnesses from a photo array."

"Thanks, Shel," said Max delightedly. He hung up the phone and turned to Caruso. "Let's go show Kimberly McCue some pictures."

At four A.M. they woke up Kimberly McCue and showed her an array of six Polaroids. She immediately picked out Jamal Stevens. At four-thirty they picked up Stevens from the holding pen at the Two-Three, put him in the car with two PDU detectives, Sharkey and DeMarco, and drove him downtown to One Police Plaza to Central Booking.

The booking process used to tie up detectives for up to forty-eight hours. It was simplified now, but still took too much time. The suspect had to be printed and Polaroided again and given an arrest number, and a determination had to be made if he were eligible for bail. The clerks who typed up the affidavits seemed determined to complete no more than five forms per hour. Sharkey and DeMarco, who were working the one A.M. to eight A.M. night watch, would process Stevens. Max was free to go back to the dorm and dream about Susan.

Before leaving the busy, dirty, crowded central booking area, both Max and Caruso walked up to Jimmy Stevens. He looked so young, so fucking young.

"Well, take care now, Jimmy," said Max warmly.

"Yeah," said Caruso, squeezing Stevens's shoulder, "there ain't nothin' personal about this, Jimmy. It's just business. It's just our job."

55

"I got to be honest withya, Max," said Tony Natale, "I'm very disappointed."

"In what?" said Max, his mouth full of linguini and clam sauce.

He'd had only about two hours of sleep between the night tour, in which he and Caruso had cleared the Perfecto Gomez case, and the following day tour, in which they'd unsuccessfully interviewed four more women in Petlin's address book. They were looking for the blonde, looking for anyone at all that Smiley, Petlin, or Barmack had known in common and they had come up with a big fat zero. Max was not in the mood for any of Natale's disappointments, whatever their source.

"I'm disappointed in the fact that you met my fiancée right here in this very apartment two whole nights ago and you haven't said word *one* about whether you liked her."

His *fiancée*. Referring to her not as Cheryl but as his *fiancée* was a bad sign, Max thought, a very bad sign indeed.

"I like her," said Max. "I do like her. I mean, what's not to like? She's young, she's pretty, she's, uh . . ."

"Yeah?"

Max tried to think of more selling adjectives, then shook his head.

"I'm sorry, Tony," he said. "You just can't show a guy split-beaver shots of a girl and tell him she's trash, then suddenly announce you're engaged to her and expect him to accept her as this — what? — this virgin *goddess* or something."

"Maybe you're right," said Natale. "Yeah, you're right. I never shoulda shown you those pictures. I don't know why the hell I did that. No, who am I kidding? I *do* know why I did it."

"You do?"

"Yeah," said Natale, "it's the classic male-bonding ritual — depersonalizing the female by focusing on her body, *guaranteeing* there'll be no personal connection by having no pictures of her face. It's the perfect misogynistic act, I swear to Christ. It's absolutely the perfect misogynistic act."

"If you say so."

"No, it absolutely is," said Natale. "The greater the threat, the more extreme the measures we mobilize to combat it. And this young woman, Cheryl, is quite a threat, Max, quite a threat indeed. She's young, she's beautiful, she's sexy, she's smart —"

"She's smart?"

"Oh, yes, Max," said Natale, "she's very smart. At times she's even profound. You oughta hear some of the things she comes up with."

"O.K., tell me some."

"O.K., let me think," said Natale, looking up and off to the side, doing a high-speed search of everything Cheryl had said in the past few days, editing for the trailer. "Well, just yesterday I said to her, 'God bless you, Cheryl,' and she answered, 'She has already.'"

Max regarded Natale warily.

"'She has already,'" Natale repeated, a look of fond reverence on his face.

Max nodded, prepared to let it go, but then decided he cared too much for his friend to do so.

"Tony, I've got to tell you something," said Max, "and it may come as a big shock to you in view of the state you're in, because I see now that you're a very sick puppy. Calling God 'she' isn't smart or profound, it's stupid. It wasn't even smart or profound twenty years ago in the sixties when *other* people were doing it. I mean, I was twelve years old and I knew that calling God 'she' was neither smart nor profound, it was only cute — spelled k-u-t-e — like signing your name with a little smiley face. Does she do that too, sign her name with a little smiley face?"

"Why are you doing this to me?" said Natale, a pierced Julius Caesar to his Brutus. "Why are you being so cruel?"

"I'll tell you why," said Max. "Because I'm your best friend, Tony. Because I'm worried about you. I think you're in terrible trouble. You've divorced your wife and you've found a cute young girl who's a quarter-century younger than you who's good to you in bed, and instead of just enjoying that situation for what it is, you've blown it up into something unreal which is going to burst right in your face and hurt the hell out of both of you. Frankly, I was a little uncomfortable when you started showing me naked Polaroids of Cheryl and obsessing about getting Cathy into a threesome with her, but you know what I am now, Tony? I'm *nostalgic* for those discussions. Do you remember what you told me in your office about love? 'Love is the self-delusion we manufacture to justify the trouble we take to have sex,' you said. You couldn't *possibly* have picked a better illustration of your point."

Natale stared at Max a moment, then laughed a mirthless, bitter laugh.

"This is really ironic, Max," he said, "you know that?"

"What is?" said Max.

"Your attacking my union with Cheryl so cruelly, tonight of all nights."

Union? His *union?* It was even worse than he thought.

"And why is that so ironic tonight of all nights, Tony?" said Max gently.

"Because tonight was the night I had planned to ask you to be—" Natale paused briefly for dramatic effect, "an usher at my wedding."

An usher at his wedding. An *usher* at his wedding. As stupid and kute as he thought Cheryl was, and as unutterably opposed as he was to their marriage, Max was absolutely devastated that Natale considered inviting him to be an *usher* at his wedding and not his best man.

"Max, is this your church or Babette's?"

"Shhh," said Max, whispering, "try to whisper, honey. It's *my* church, only we don't call it a church, we call it a synagogue."

"A what?" said Sam loudly.

"A synagogue," said Max, still whispering.

Sam looked around at the three dozen people in the upholstered seats with tiny brass plaques on the backs who were chanting in unison from the Saturday morning prayer service, then turned back to Max.

"Where's the baby Jesus?" he said in his loud voice.

Several heads turned to stare at him.

Max pushed him down in the seat and whispered hoarsely in his ear.

"Whisper, honey, please. People are trying to pray, and when you talk out loud it bothers them."

"Why are they trying to pray?" said Sam.

It was a question that Max himself was unable to answer.

"Because that's why people come here," said Max.

"But where is the baby Jesus?" said Sam, and more heads turned.

Max pulled him in close to his body, as if to absorb all the sound waves emanating from his tiny mouth, and continued to whisper to the child.

"The baby Jesus doesn't live here, the baby Jesus lives in *Mama's* church, and if you can't whisper we're going to have to leave," said Max, instantly realizing it was one of those bluffs that he always lost with his son, except that this one never had the slightest chance of succeeding since the boy clearly didn't want to be there in the first place.

"I don't *want* to whisper," said Sam loudly. "I'm *tired* of whispering."

A few people said "shhh," and Max nodded and threw them strained, apologetic smiles.

"I've got an idea," said Max, reaching into his pocket, taking out a fistful of Matchbox cars, and putting them on the floor. "Why don't you play with these?"

At the sight of the cars Sam's mood changed dramatically. He immediately got down on the floor with them and began silently arranging them in claustrophobic, urban parking lot arrangements.

Max returned his attention to the service. At an intricately carved podium on the *bimah* or platform at the front of the synagogue stood a rabbi and a cantor. The rabbi had a full brown beard but looked younger than Max himself; the cantor was an even younger woman with short blond hair and a heavy bosom. Things had changed dramatically since Max had last been in a synagogue.

A skinny bar mitzvah boy in a suit and fringed white *talis* was standing at the other podium, having trouble with the microphone, chanting the prayers that precede the reading of the *haftorah*, the section of the Torah that the boy himself would chant on this special day of his life. The lad looked so preposterously young, it was hard to imagine that patriarchs of old had ever chosen thirteen as the age boys were to be initiated into the tribe and considered to be men.

Max had the briefest flash that boys the age of the one on the *bimah* were at this moment buying and selling crack and killing each other up in the Two-Three and the Two-Five precincts, and then he pushed it away.

Listening to the familiar melody that the boy was chanting, Max recalled his own bar mitzvah at the shul in the Bronx, found himself deeply stirred in some tribal way, and had another uncomfortable flash — that Sam, who was now parking cars on the synagogue floor, would never have a bar mitzvah of his own, and that the line of Judaism which had been carried forward from generation to generation in the Segal family would finally die out with him. Max would be the last Jewish Segal. It made him miserably guilty.

He toyed with the rationale that at least centuries of anti-Semitic persecution against the Segal family — the persecution that led Max's paternal grandparents into the gas chambers of Dachau — would end as well. But he knew it was only a rationale and not even true, and it comforted him not at all. Future persecutors of Segal heirs would not be dissuaded by the fact that their victims were no longer Jewish. The martyrdom of Max's grandparents would be diminished—it mattered not how slightly—by the termination of the Jewish tradition in the Segal family, and history's finger would be pointed back down the ages toward Max for all of eternity.

57

On Thursday afternoon, May 12, Judy dropped her cat off again at
Rose Brill's and flew business class to Chicago. The flight attendant
apologized for not having Absolut on her cart. She gave Judy two little
bottles of Stolichnaya instead, which Judy accepted graciously.
  "Is this trip business or pleasure?" asked the flight attendant.
  "Actually, a bit of both," said Judy pleasantly.

She picked up the black Mustang convertible at the Hertz lot at
O'Hare and drove it to the Ritz-Carlton hotel on Michigan Avenue.
A car-hop held the door for her and welcomed her to the hotel, and
a bellboy sprang forward to extract her luggage from the Mustang's
small trunk and trundle it up to the reception floor.
  Letting her eyes sweep the nearby tables where elegantly dressed
men and women sipped elegant cups of tea and nibbled elegant cream-
filled pastries, Judy signed the register as Monty Black and allowed the
bellboy to show her up to her room.
  When the bellboy had departed, she unpacked her clothes and toilet articles in the spacious, mirrored and marbled dressing room and
took a short drink from her flask of vodka. She re-entered the bedroom. Admiring the view of the boats on the Chicago lake front fourteen floors below, she dialed nine for an outside line, then called Teddy
Greco's secretary and confirmed their drink date at six o'clock at the
Tack Room.

The Tack Room had an equestrian theme. English saddles, bridles,
riding crops, and other paraphernalia adorned the walls, along with
framed photographs of horse shows and ribbons which someone had

won and decided that a bar on Michigan Avenue was the best place to display them. The waiters and waitresses were dressed in riding habits.

Judy arrived early and chose a table in the back. To settle her nerves she ordered an Absolut on ice, which she had all but finished when Teddy Greco appeared. He was dressed in a far better outfit than the one she'd seen him in on her research trip, so he obviously believed this to be a hot job interview. He looked around the crowded bar, trying to figure out who Monty Black was, and she enjoyed his nervousness for several minutes before she raised her arm and signaled to him. When he approached the table she registered his admiring reaction to her appearance with appropriate pleasure.

"Miss Black?" he said hesitantly.

"Hello, Ted," she said, subtly patronizing him by countering with the first-name address, and offered him her hand.

He sat down. They spent a few moments trading observations about the weather and traffic conditions, and then she got him to talk about his background, to sell himself to her. She ordered drinks and remained impassive throughout the recitation, which caused him to sell harder than he'd meant to. She ordered another round and, finally wearying of his discomfort, held up her hand.

"Thank you, Ted," she said. "I don't need to hear anymore. As a matter of fact, I know quite a lot about you already."

"Oh?" said Greco, disconcerted.

"Yes," she said. "I realize you don't remember it, but we've met before. Many years ago."

He looked at her blankly.

"At the University of Illinois," she said. "We went out a couple of times."

His face remained blank, his eyebrows lowering and contracting.

"In fact," she said, "we had sex."

She watched him.

"It was not very *good* sex," she said, "but I didn't know any better at the time. I was a little heavier in those days, and my hair was black, but my name was different. It was Wells. Judy Wells."

His eyes grew slightly larger, his brows expanding and climbing.

"Judy Wells," he said softly after a moment. "Holy Christ. I think I *do* remember you."

"*Do* you," she said. "I'm sure the recollection isn't flattering."

"You weren't at all as . . . attractive as you are now," he said.

He was, at least, honest enough to tell the truth.

"Thank you, I suppose," she said.

He stared at her.

"Jesus Christ," he said. "Judy Wells. I never would've recognized you, not in a million years. You have certainly changed. You're . . . very beautiful now."

"Thank you," she said. "I wish I could return the compliment. In point of fact, you were never very good looking, Ted. And since I've seen you last you've put on a roll of fat at your waist and you're losing most of your hair."

He was obviously unprepared for her candor, but too dumbfounded to withdraw. Like many men accustomed to inflicting pain, he was unprepared to deflect it when it came from others.

"Oh," he said, his face getting flushed, "*I* get what this is now."

"No, you don't," she said, starting his test. "Because, despite your unattractiveness, I find you remarkably sexual."

"Oh, is that so?" he said, intending this to come out nasty, but inadvertently betraying his surprised and grudging pleasure in her compliment.

"Yes," she said, "it is. There is something about you that, unfortunately for me, arouses me enormously. For the past hour all I've been able to think about is the idea of going to bed with you."

He swallowed. Then his face took on an oily grin.

"You're serious about this?" he said.

"Quite serious," she said. "I assure you, I wouldn't be revealing such a thing if I didn't have to."

His oily grin got oilier.

"For the past hour I've been thinking a lot about going to bed with you too," he said.

She smiled at him and waited a beat, pleased he'd failed his test, just as she'd known he would.

"Where do you live?" she said, knowing the answer.

"Uh, in Wilmette," he said, "but we can't go there. I have a wife and kids."

She nodded.

"Well," she said, "I happen to be staying with my folks in Lake Forest, so *that's* out."

"We could go to a hotel," said Greco.

She shook her head.

"Why spend the money?" she said. "No, I've got a better idea."

"What's that?"

"Let's go to your office."

He considered this a moment.

"Uh-uh," he said. "Too risky. We might get caught."

"That's what makes it exciting," she said.

He thought this over.

"No," he said, "anywhere else, but not my office."

She drained her glass and put it down.

"Your office or nothing," she said.

He watched her for a clue, then realized she wasn't bluffing. It was a deal-breaker. He began to perspire heavily.

This is amazing, she thought. Why can't I ever do this when it matters? Why do I only have power over people when I no longer want them?

"I just can't do it, Judy," he said. "I really want to make love to you, but I just can't jeopardize my job by doing it in my office. Do you understand that?"

"Perfectly," she said, signaling for the check.

"So we'll go to a hotel?" he said hopefully, already trying to figure out what excuse he'd tell his wife on the phone.

"No," she said. "I don't think you heard me. I said it was your office or nothing."

He let her pay the check. When she stood up to go he grabbed her arm. *Grabbed her arm.*

"O.K., you win," he said hoarsely.

The security guard in the lobby of the Hancock Building had them sign in. She signed Valerie Solanas, the name of the woman who'd stabbed Andy Warhol. They went up in the elevator, which was too brightly lit and made him look even less attractive than he had in the bar. God, she thought, what did I ever see in this creep?

They alighted at his floor, walked down the corridor, and he unlocked the suite of offices occupied by the accounting firm of Gordon & Graubart and let them in.

He ushered her into his own office, which was smaller than they both had hoped, and locked the door from the inside. He took a step forward and put his arms around her, but she pushed him away.

"No," she said. "You undress first."

He nodded, and clumsily removed his shoes, suit jacket, trousers, tie, shirt, and socks.

"Now you," he said.

She pointed to his undershorts. After a moment, he lowered them and dropped them to the floor.

"My, my," she said ambiguously.

Then she slowly stepped out of her shoes, and removed her jacket, skirt, blouse, slip, pantyhose, bra, and underpants. He drank in her body, amazed at his good fortune. When he again stepped forward to embrace her, she held him at arm's length.

"You know," she said, "as much as I want you, Ted, I'm still pretty upset with you for the way you treated me back in college. You can only have sex with me if you apologize."

"Jesus, Judy," he responded, "what can I say? I was an asshole. I'm sorry I hurt you, I really am. I really want you now."

"That's not good enough," she said, taking his hand, passing it lightly over her nipples, and removing it. "Get on your knees, Ted. Beg me. Tell me how you hunger for me."

He gave her a crooked smile, dropped to only one knee, as if this compromise might preserve his dignity, then realized that preservation of dignity was not going to get him much, and he went down on both knees. He was staring straight at her muff.

"I want you very, very badly, Judy," he said. "I'm so damned horny for you I'm about to explode. I'll do anything in the world to have sex with you now, anything."

"Walk toward me on your knees," she said. "Tell my vagina what a creep you are, what a lowlife. Tell it that you don't deserve me, that you didn't then and you don't now. Speak directly into it but don't actually touch it till I give you permission."

He gave her a sickly smile. He walked toward her on his knees, stopping an inch from her pubic mound. My God, she thought, it really is true — scratch a sadist and find a masochist.

"Go ahead," she said.

"I'm a creep," he said. "A lowlife. I didn't deserve you then and I don't deserve you now. But I want you more than anything I've ever wanted in this world."

"Good," she said, "now tell it without words."

He did. He was as good as she remembered. When she'd had enough she reached into her purse, handed him a condom, and made him put it on. When he did, she allowed him to enter her. He climaxed in about thirty seconds and then collapsed on top of her.

With her pulse pounding in her throat and temples she put one arm around his hairy back and with the other reached once more into her purse.

When he was dead she opened his door and walked out into the office corridor. She was exhilarated and naked and splattered with blood. She was enjoying the risk now, was actually getting aroused by it. She found the women's room and cleaned herself up with soap and water and paper towels.

She returned to Greco's office and went around wiping it clean of her prints. When she was through she got dressed and left, pulling the door shut behind her.

It took forever for the elevator to come, which was odd, because she didn't think anyone else was in the building. She realized the security guard was going to be getting a second good look at her, but she didn't care. Let him take her goddam picture. When she reached the lobby she went to the book and signed out.

"Mr. Greco still up there?" asked the guard.

"Yes," said Judy.

"He be up there much longer?" he said.

"I should think so," she said.

It was nearly ten P.M. when Judy returned to the Ritz-Carlton. Although she hadn't eaten dinner, she had no appetite. Suddenly overcome by weariness, she lay down and fell soundly asleep.

She awoke an hour later, refreshed. She telephoned Le Manoir and confirmed her lunch reservation for the following day. Then she called room service and ordered the swordfish steak, an arugula salad, a bottle of Chardonnay, a Perrier with lime, and a decaf espresso.

After dinner she had a bubble bath, watched half of *Casablanca* on TV, and went to sleep.

Theodore Greco's body was discovered at eight-forty-five A.M. by Milton Graubart, elderly senior partner of Gordon & Graubart, who had his secretary telephone the police and then took a Valium and lay down on the couch in his office.

By nine-fifteen the Chicago police had arrived and sealed both Greco's office and the women's restroom as crime scenes, and by nine-thirty homicide detectives Watzlawick and Zagorski arrived and began interviewing employees of the firm.

By one-twenty all employees who were in attendance had been questioned, as well as the Hancock Building's chief of security. He provided the sign-in book, which showed that Greco and someone named Valerie Solanas had entered the building at approximately eight-ten P.M. Thursday night, and that Miss Solanas had exited the building alone at nine-forty-five.

Stanislaus Zlatkoff, the security guard who had been on duty Thursday night, was awakened at his home, and Detectives Zagorski and Watzlawick went out to interview him.

Zlatkoff described the woman accompanying Greco as blond, blue-eyed, and about thirty years of age. She was, he said, quite attractive and well dressed. He'd gotten a good look at her both on her way in and on her way out of the building and felt that he would recognize her if he saw her again. He recalled that when she left he asked her if Greco was still upstairs, and she had replied in the affirmative. When he asked her if she thought he'd be up there a long time, he said she'd once more replied in the affirmative.

Both Zagorski and Watzlawick felt that, were any suspects to be found, Zlatkoff would be useful in picking the woman who called herself Valerie Solanas out of a line-up, but the chances of locating her so that she could be put into a line-up were at this point not impressive.

Friday morning at nine A.M. Judy appeared in the waiting room of Stuart Sherman's office. Two middle-aged matrons with short gray hair and perfect posture were reading *National Geographic*. An elderly man with a wheeze who hadn't done a good job of shaving thumbed apathetically through several back issues of *People*. A frail and serious boy of perhaps twelve exchanged earnest whispers with his buxom mom about whatever he'd come to see the doctor about.

After filling out the form for new patients on a clipboard that the nurse had given her, Judy waited for well over an hour to be called, getting angrier and angrier. It was inconceivable that he could already be so far behind this early in the morning. Now, she thought to herself, I have *two* reasons to kill you, Dr. Sherman.

At ten-fifteen the nurse ushered her into an office with a desk and showed her to a chrome-and-Naugahyde chair opposite it. There were many framed diplomas on the wall — too many for just one doctor, unless he'd also put up certificates from high school and grammar school — and photographs of his wife and teenaged children on a sailboat, everyone looking very nautical and wind-blown. It took Sherman another fifteen minutes to appear, holding the clipboard with the form she'd filled out.

At his appearance her heart had begun to race, her hard exterior to slip. Please, God, let me be strong, she prayed, please just let me pull this off. She wondered if it was proper to ask God's help in setting people up to kill them. She closed her eyes briefly and tried to remember that this was a role and not real life, that it was not she who was doing this but someone she'd created, that the someone she'd created had no history with Stuart Sherman, had never been hurt by him, and was therefore not vulnerable to him.

When she opened her eyes she had almost convinced herself that she was not Judy Wells but Monty Black.

"Good morning, Miss Black."

"Good morning, Dr. Sherman."

"Sorry to have kept you," he said.

"My time is your time," she said pleasantly.

He looked to see if she were being sarcastic, decided he couldn't tell, and allowed himself something between a chuckle and a throat-clearing to cover both possibilities.

He took her medical history, which she offered truthfully, then asked what her complaint was. She said she just wanted a routine physical since she hadn't had one in a couple of years.

The nurse escorted her into an examination room and told her to undress and be seated on the leather table covered with a continuous roll of white wrapping paper. Fifteen minutes after she undressed Sherman reappeared with the nurse, having examined God knows how many other patients in the interim.

He began tapping her chest and listening to her breathe. At one point during the examination the nurse left the room for a moment.

"What do you think," said Judy when the nurse had gone, "am I in better shape than the last time you saw me?"

Sherman looked startled. He glanced at his clipboard and then at her.

"Have you been here before?" he asked.

"Oh, no, not here," she said. "The last time you examined me was in a Chevy."

Sherman regarded her quizzically.

"And," she said, "I *wasn't* in as good shape as I am now, although it was several years ago. Do you remember a girl named Judy Wells?"

It took seven seconds for Sherman's mental retrieval system to come up with something for Judy Wells.

"*You're* Judy Wells?" he said.

She smiled. His face grew pink with embarrassment.

He looked again at his clipboard.

"It says here your name is Monty Black."

"A lot has changed," she said.

The nurse returned. Sherman was somehow able to continue the examination, but Judy noted with pleasure that his hands now shook. When the examination was finished he bade her farewell and left the room. She got dressed and returned to his office. Sherman was seated behind the desk. He had clearly not expected to see her again.

"Ah," he said. "Well, Judy, I must say it was an unexpected pleasure seeing you again."

"Yes," she said, "for me as well. I thought perhaps we could catch up a bit over lunch."

"Um, well, sure, that might be nice sometime," he said, although from his tone it was clear he was pretty well booked for the next twelve years.

"I don't mean sometime, I mean *today*," she said.

"Today? Oh, no," he said, "that's very kind, but I'm afraid I can't. Some other time would be great, though. Just give my receptionist a call and we'll try to work something out."

She looked at her watch.

"It's eleven-forty," she said. "I have a twelve-twenty reservation at Le Manoir. I'm buying."

Ambivalence flooded his face, briefly giving him a tic.

"Boy," he said, "Le Manoir. I must admit I've always been curious about that place."

"Then satisfy your curiosity," she said.

"I can't," he said. "I can't break an appointment with the person I'm meeting on such short notice."

"If they had an invitation to Le Manoir," she said, "they'd do it to *you*."

He wrestled visibly with his conscience.

"If I *did* come with you," he said, "I couldn't let you pay."

"Of course you could," she said brightly.

His smile was slow in coming, but when it did it was pretty appealing. She could see how he had broken her heart.

"I'll change my other engagement," he said. "This will be quite a departure from my usual routine."

"I can absolutely guarantee that," she said.

60

"Bonjour, Madame Black," said the obsequious maître d'. He seated them side by side at the requested table in the back and took their drink orders, an unusual honor. Her preparation had obviously paid off.

"They appear to *know* you here," said Sherman, impressed.

"It seems so," she said.

The drinks appeared and they began to chat about their lives since last they'd seen each other. He was married, he said, to the same Chi Omega from Northwestern he'd been seeing when he dated her — this was offered with no apology, for which she was thankful. He had three kids, all of them athletes as well as scholars. They lived in Highland Park.

She felt very connected to him, having been to his home, met his wife, peed in his toilet, looked in his medicine cabinet, and left her underwear in his pocket. Sherman was open and pleasant and it took frequent efforts of will to remind herself what a prick he had been when he'd dumped her. It was possible he'd be able to resist her advances. If so, she would probably let him live.

She half-seriously asked him if he'd like to have an affair. He blushed and, addressing that part of her suggestion he thought might be serious, emphasized that he had a pretty happy marriage and believed in monogamy. She congratulated him on his fidelity and mentally rehearsed her next move.

When the wine list came she looked at it and suggested he order a Batard-Montrachet. He checked the price and paled. She reminded him who was paying. He ordered it.

When the sommelier returned with the wine and asked him to taste it, Judy reached under the tablecloth and unzipped Sherman's fly. He paused in the act of reaching for the wine, but otherwise betrayed nothing.

As he began to sip the wine, Judy reached into his undershorts and, watching his face intently, got a good grip on his penis and squeezed it gently. Sherman almost choked.

"Monsieur?" said the sommelier nervously.

Sherman grew stiff in her grasp and shook his head.

"No, no," he said, "the wine is quite good, monsieur, quite good."

"Merci, monsieur," said the sommelier, and began to pour.

By the time the sommelier departed, Sherman had arrived at full extension. His face was beaded with perspiration and extremely red. He stared straight ahead, unable to meet her gaze.

"I . . . cannot go along with this," he said in a strained, stuffy voice that belied the fullness in her hand.

"I understand," she said, slowly relaxing her grip, then tightening it.

"It's just not . . . something I choose to do at this point in time," he said.

"I don't blame you one bit," she said. Relaxing and tightening.

"You know, this really isn't fair," he said. "I want you to stop what you're doing . . . immediately."

"O.K.," she said, recalling similar discussions in a Chevy, but with the roles reversed. "I will. Very soon."

By the time they reached her room at the Ritz-Carlton it was nearly three-thirty. They had consumed two bottles of the Batard-Montrachet and several cognacs. They were both giggling and maintained an upright posture only with difficulty. She locked the door behind them and chained it, then advanced on him. She took off all his clothes and threw them on the floor. He offered no resistance. When he was naked he undressed her.

She picked up her purse, took him by the hand, and led him into the large and opulent bathroom. He looked questioningly at her. She placed her purse on the sink, turned on the tub tap, then seated him in the bath and poured in bubble bath. He smiled and pulled her in with him.

She reached into her purse, took out a condom, and had him put it on. Then she lowered herself upon him and rode him, but the water caused technical problems and he was forced to withdraw. She rose in the tub and, without a word, positioned his head between her legs and gently pushed his face into her.

He began eagerly licking her, cupping her buttocks with both hands. She tilted her head and tried to glimpse his neck. Her view was obscured by his busy head. With the fingertips of her left hand she lightly brushed her reference points — the adam's apple, the ear, the thick muscle of the neck — and located the carotid artery.

He's failed the test, she thought, but I could still spare him, I could let him live. And then she thought, but why? What's in it for *me?* An affair with a married man who lives in another city? With a man who cheats on his wife? He had told her he was happily married and monogamous. Now he had his happily married monogamous tongue in her vagina. The man was a liar, a betrayer, like all men.

Standing in the tub with him continuing to lick her, she shifted her position slightly and let her left hand stray to the sink. She located her purse and withdrew the small utility knife.

But he really did seem so nice now, she thought. Yes, but he wasn't *then*, when they'd known each other before — and this wasn't about now, this was about then. She replayed the scene in the Chevy. With her vulnerably telling him of her love. With his cavalier announcement that he wasn't available to her, that he was going with the Chi Omega from Northwestern, that he was practically *engaged*. With her incredulous tears. With the days, weeks, months, *years* of pain and hurt and feelings of worthlessness that followed their breakup.

The pulse in her head was now throbbing so strongly she could barely see. With her right hand she grabbed him roughly by the hair and pushed his face hard against her pubic mound. With her left she stroked his neck, extended the blade with her thumb, and then plunged it deep into his carotid artery.

Before he died he had thrashed around a lot, turning the bathwater red, and she had finally cracked his head hard against the bathtub faucet to make him stop. Just before he lost consciousness she told him why, but she wasn't positive he'd heard her. A pity.

It took her a while to clean up the bathroom, drain the tub, haul the body out of it, and roll it into the closet, then to bathe and clean up and dress. She packed leisurely. Then she phoned the hotel cashier to prepare her bill, phoned the garage to have her car brought around, phoned for a bellboy to help with her bags. She left a sizable tip for the maid.

The bellboy was about twenty and looked like he played varsity football. He was very cute and muscular and he seemed to find her attractive. There was a time, she thought, when I would have given anything to get this kind of reaction from a varsity football player.

He put her two bags on his cart and asked if there was anything else.

"I don't think so," she said. "Unless I forgot something in the closet."

"Shall I check?" he said.

"Please," she said.

His moving toward the closet where Sherman's body lay produced the tingle between her legs that she'd known it would.

"No, never mind," she said as his hand closed over the closet doorknob. "Everything is here."

"You're not staying with us tonight, Miss Black?" inquired the Japanese clerk behind the desk.

"No, I'm afraid not," she said. "My plans have changed."

The clerk looked at his black rubber diver's watch.

"It's nearly five o'clock," he said. "Even if you'd had a late checkout, I'd have to charge you for tonight."

"I know that," she said. "I don't mind."

"I hope you've enjoyed your stay with us."

"I have indeed," she said.

She let the cute bellboy take her bags down to the garage and put them in the trunk of the Mustang; she gave him a large tip and a flirtatious smile.

"Come back and visit us again real soon," he said.

"I plan to," she said.

61

When the maid was able to speak coherently the manager went into the room and looked at what was lying on the floor of the walk-in closet. Then he trotted quickly out of the room, locked the door behind him, and phoned the police from the desk in his office. He requested that they handle the investigation and the removal of the body as discreetly as possible.

Within ten minutes two unmarked police cars pulled up outside the hotel and four plainclothes homicide detectives went up in the elevator to the reception floor. They conferred briefly with the manager in the reception area and with the young bellboy. A woman with long black hair pressed forward to hear them.

". . . left early, knowing she'd be charged . . ." was a fragment of one of the sentences she was able to make out from the manager.

". . . good-looking older woman, a blonde . . ." was one from the bellboy.

"Judy? Judy is that you?"

The voice penetrated to her spine. She spun around. A woman her mother's age was peering intently into her face.

"Judy Wells, as I live and *breathe!*" said the woman, throwing her arms around her, kissing her on the face. "You look *fabulous,* dear, simply *fabulous!*"

"Mrs. Konig," said Judy, looking past the foolish woman to the cops, trying to see if they had noticed anything, cursing herself for having come back and lingered in the lobby. "How delightful to see you again."

"What are you doing in Chicago, dear? Your mother said you were in New York, writing for some magazine. The *New Yorker,* wasn't it?"

"*New York* magazine, yes. Well, I'm actually here on assignment," she said, seeing one of the cops glance in her direction. "In fact, I'm here for *such* a short time I didn't even tell the folks I was coming."

"Didn't tell mom and *dad?*" said Mrs. Konig, shocked. "Oh, but you really *must* tell them! You really *must!* It would *kill* them to hear that you'd been in the Windy City and hadn't even popped up to Lake Forest to say hello."

"Well, they won't know I was here unless you tell them," said Judy with a conspiratorial wink.

Mrs. Konig grinned, titillated at the chance to help perpetrate a deception on her friend.

"Shall it be our little secret, then?" said Mrs. Konig, an instant recruit to the covert intelligence community.

"I'd really appreciate that," said Judy.

"All right, dear," said the woman, squeezing Judy's hand and peering deeply into her eyes through the new bond of shared secrecy. "It was lovely to see you again. Lovely."

"It was lovely to see you too, Mrs. Konig," said Judy.

"Hedy," insisted Mrs. Konig.

"Hedy," said Judy.

When Hedy Konig released her hand, Judy walked quickly toward the elevators. The detectives and the bellboy were disappearing into the manager's office.

Well, *that* was certainly stupid, Judy, she chided herself. Maybe you want to get caught.

Detectives Watzlawick and Zagorski spent three hours at the Ritz-Carlton hotel. After sealing the crime scene they interviewed several hotel employees.

Andy Yastrzemski, the young bellboy who'd taken the blond woman's bags down to her car, described her as very slender, medium height, attractive, and about forty years of age. He said she was driving a black or dark blue Mustang convertible. He thought it had Illinois plates, although he didn't remember any numbers or letters. He said she was flirtatious and a good tipper for a woman. He was surprised to hear that she was a suspect in a grisly homicide.

Peter Yamamoto, the desk clerk who'd pointed out to the blond woman that she'd be charged for the extra night, described her as taller than average, strawberry blond, tan, cheerful, about thirty-two years of age, and a good sport. He too was surprised to hear the crime she was suspected of committing.

Raoul Santiago, the wiry room service waiter with acne scars who'd brought her dinner the previous night, described the woman as voluptuous, with large breasts visible through the dressing gown in which she'd answered the door. He had wondered at the time whether she was coming on to him, and made the decision not to try and find out. He couldn't recall the color of her hair nor how old she was, but thought she might have been somewhere in her late forties.

The blond woman had signed the register as Monty Black. She'd given an address on Benedict Canyon in Beverly Hills. They called Beverly Hills and found the address did not exist. She had paid her bill in cash.

Watzlawick and Zagorski had found little of interest in the sealed hotel room, except for the body on the floor of the walk-in closet and the clothing of the victim, which had been thrown in the corner of the closet. The credit cards, driver's license, and business cards in the victim's wallet and jacket pockets identified him as Stuart Sherman, M.D., a doctor of internal medicine and a resident of Highland Park.

Sherman's body had a deep cut in the neck and had suffered a blow to the rear of the skull. The victim's face had been worked over. Aside from the fact that Sherman had apparently been killed in the bathtub and then placed in the closet, the m.o. was strikingly similar to that of the Greco case they'd investigated earlier in the day. And the attractive blond woman whom the security guard in the Hancock Building described accompanying Greco to his office was so similar to the one described by employees of the Ritz-Carlton there was little doubt in the minds of Detectives Watzlawick and Zagorski that they were dealing with the same perpetrator.

Friday night. Natale was out at a movie with Cheryl. Max was alone in the apartment, lying on the Castro convertible, thinking about his wife and son and about how they were no longer a family, feeling the distance between himself and everyone he knew. They were like stars in a constellation, which appear from a distance to be in closely related groups, but which are in reality light years apart.

He had never felt lonely before Sam and before Babette. Before becoming a husband and father he had always lived alone and loved it. Now, despite how unpleasant his marriage had been lately, being on his own felt uncomfortably incomplete, as if he were no longer an independent organism but a specialized organ cut off from the rest of its system.

He needed to talk to someone. Natale had once been good for that, B.C. — Before Cheryl. Joanie Jarvis might have been good for that if he'd been able to trust her, but there was no longer any point to couples therapy since he and Babette were no longer a couple.

There was Susan, of course. She had seemed genuinely sympathetic and genuinely able to understand the nature of his concerns, and she had so graciously invited him to call her whenever the need arose, day or night.

He took out the crumpled cocktail napkin with her number on it, went to the phone, and dialed. It rang three times and then Susan's voice said: "Hi, I can't come to the phone right now, but if you leave your name and number and the time you called after the beep, I'll get right back to you."

I can't come to the phone right now. The universal euphemism for I'm not home. As if potential robbers, hearing this, were duped into believing that you're in the shower or on the toilet and not out of the apartment.

Beep.

"Hi, it's Max. Segal. And it's, let me see, eight-fifteen on Friday night, and I was just wondering if you might be free to go and maybe grab a bite to eat and, uh, talk and . . . stuff like that. I'm at Tony Natale's. The number here is . . . 555–7378. Hope to hear from you. Bye."

Max hung up, feeling stupid. Why did those machines always make you feel so damned vulnerable? Because they forced you to put your needs on record with no provision for a response. The more he thought about it, the notion that a woman as attractive as Susan Simon would be free for dinner on Friday night on a moment's notice was absurd. As if she had nothing else to do. As if she were just sitting by the phone, waiting for his call. He hoped she wouldn't find his suggestion presumptuous.

He could just imagine her now, out with some glamorous fellow journalist at a posh restaurant in Midtown, drinking champagne and eating whatever the hell it was they ate in posh Midtown restaurants in Manhattan. In a few hours she would come home and check her machine and hear his stupid, vulnerable message and know what a needy, socially inept asshole he really was.

At the moment that Max's message was being recorded in New York, the owner of the answering machine was dining alone in Wolfie's Tavern, a blue-collar bar on the outskirts of Champaign, Illinois, on two shrimp cocktails and a double vodka on the rocks.

She had driven into the university town about forty minutes before and registered at the Best Western motel. Then she drove to Wolfie's in order to get something to eat without having to suffer noisy crowds of students drinking beer by the pitcher. When she completed her dinner she would drive over to Austin Richards's house at the edge of campus, park across the street, try to catch glimpses of the professor through his lighted windows, and remember just what it was he had meant to her and what he had done to her so many years before.

64

It was Saturday morning, May 14. Detectives Watzlawick and Zagorski phoned Dr. Sherman's nurse, Lucy Gonzales, at her home and arranged to meet at his office. The plump, middle-aged woman had clearly been devoted to the young internist, for she was so shattered by
his death that she could barely communicate with them.

An examination of Sherman's appointment schedule on the day
he'd been killed produced unexpectedly good results. A patient named
Monty Black had a nine A.M. appointment. They asked Nurse Gonzales
to describe Monty Black and were gratified to hear her say the patient
was blond, expensively dressed, mid-forties, only moderately attractive, and skinny to the point of malnutrition.

They were extremely encouraged to find the notes that Sherman had
taken on the patient's medical history and the form she herself had
filled out. They were even more encouraged to learn that she'd left
samples of urine and blood, and immediately sent both over to the
crime lab. They sealed the office and phoned for a forensic unit.

They thanked Nurse Gonzales for her time and asked her to meet
with a police artist. They hoped her input, along with that of the security man from the Hancock Building and the employees of the Ritz-
Carlton, would be sufficient to put together a composite drawing that
bore some resemblance to the suspect.

Zagorski and Watzlawick then phoned for a computer print-out on
all black or dark blue Mustang convertibles registered to or recently
rented by anyone named either Monty Black or Valerie Solanas.

65

On Saturday morning she dressed in a white silk blouse, beige slacks, and a brown cardigan. After a fast breakfast of plain yogurt with honey, cranberry juice, and herbal tea, she resumed the stakeout in her car across from Austin Richards's house.

Her appointment in his office was at ten-thirty. At ten-ten Richards emerged from his house and walked to his car, carrying an old leather briefcase. When he backed his Saab out of the driveway, she let him get a block ahead of her before she turned on her ignition and pulled out into the street.

At ten-forty the building containing his office appeared to be deserted. She stood in the corridor, trying to muster her courage. She reached into her purse, withdrew the flask of vodka with a shaking hand, and took several searing swallows before she felt the warmth and confidence spread upward from her belly to her head. Then she replaced the flask, checked her reflection in an office window, and knocked on his door. If he'd changed—if his crotch was no longer running his life—she might let him live.

"Come in," he called.

She took a deep breath and entered.

Seeing him up close for the first time in so many years was almost overwhelming. She felt unsteady on her feet and for a moment was certain she was going to faint. Then she remembered who she was — or, more precisely, who she wasn't—and pulled herself up with the hands of her alter ego.

"Professor Richards?" said a much more assured voice than she thought she possessed.

"Ms. Black?" said Richards, swiftly sizing her up and congratulating himself on his decision to grant her the interview.

She hung a smile on her face like a *Do Not Disturb* sign on a motel doorknob and shook his hand. He motioned for her to sit down.

"Well," he said, "I hope you didn't have any trouble finding it."

"Oh, no," she said, "your directions were impeccable."

"Excellent," he said. "So tell me, how long do you plan to be in town?"

That would be the if-I-get-lucky-how-long-do-I-have-to-entertain-you-after-I-screw-you question, she decided.

"I'm driving back to Chicago this afternoon," she replied.

"Pity," he said. "I'd hoped you'd at least have time to let me show you around the campus, maybe even grab a bite to eat."

Or grab anything else within reach, she thought.

"That would have been nice," she said, taking a spiral-bound steno pad and a pencil out of her purse.

She began the interview with harmless questions about the effect of charismatic professors on their students, particularly females. Richards, warming his hands on the glow from his acknowledged charisma, rambled on at some length about the professor-student relationship and the responsibilities of the mentor.

"One thing our readers would be particularly interested to know," she said, "is approximately what percentage of your students you succeed in having relations with."

She was at first embarrassed to have ended her sentence with a preposition, but then realized he'd probably never notice it in the minefield.

He was at first certain he'd heard her incorrectly, but then realized she'd said precisely what he'd feared. His face began to darken.

"I'm not sure I understand your question," he said.

"I'm sure you do," she said, "but I'll be glad to rephrase it for you: What percentage of your students do you succeed in fucking?"

His face grew darker.

"I neither have *relations* with my students," he said evenly, "nor do I *fuck* them. And now this interview, Miss Black, is terminated."

Interesting how they switch from Ms. to Miss when pissed, she noted.

He arose behind his desk. She remained seated.

"As a matter of fact, Professor, I have proof to the contrary."

"*Do* you?" he said, his voice acidic.

"Yes," she said. "I was a student of yours, Professor, and you fucked me in this very room. On that very desk."

If his face got any darker it was conceivable a racial change might occur. It was conceivable he'd become an American Indian.

"Get out of here," he said.

"You have a port-wine stain the size of a half dollar on your right buttock," she said. "And a brown mole on the underside of your penis."

The anger and the dark hue began to leach out of his face.

"Who are you?" he asked after a few moments.

"When I was a student here," she said, "I was a brunette and my name was Judy Wells."

He studied her face, then shook his head.

"The name doesn't ring a bell," he said.

"The name doesn't ring a bell," she said. "You always did have a refreshing way with words. So, I remember your birthmarks and your warts, Professor, and you don't even remember my name. What a pity. Well, perhaps you'd remember *these*."

She stood up and unbuttoned her blouse, exposing her breasts. He looked at them automatically, then realized it was a mistake. She saw the ambivalence in his enlarged pupils.

"Look familiar, Professor?"

"Listen," he said, in a rapid, flustered voice, "I don't know what it is you intended to accomplish by coming here, but I really must insist that you leave immediately, or else I shall have to call campus security and they will remove you forcibly."

"Oh, I wouldn't want you to do that," she said, beginning to button up her blouse.

"Good," he said, marveling at how easily he had regained control of the situation. "Now then, if you simply leave quietly and without a fuss, there won't be any need for this to go any further. Your superiors at *Mademoiselle,* if indeed you work there, need never hear of this."

"Good," she said. "Just tell me one thing."

"All right," he said, secure enough now to be magnanimous.

"Didn't my breasts look at all familiar to you?"

His sense of mastery began to slip a little.

"Frankly, no," he said.

242

"That's odd," she said, swiftly unzipping her slacks, dropping them to the floor, and stepping out of them. "What about my legs?"

"All right," he said, reaching for the phone, realizing he had never been in control at all, "that's it, that's quite enough."

He checked a number on his phone and dialed.

"Actually," she said, "it isn't *nearly* enough. Who was it who said 'Too much isn't nearly enough'?"

She unbuttoned her blouse again and dropped it on the floor as well. A pair of translucent beige nylon panties was all that remained.

"Hello, security?" said Richards into the phone, his voice a little shaky.

She climbed up on his desk, inserted her thumbs into the waistband of her panties, and slowly urged them downward.

"This is Professor, uh . . ." His voice trailed off.

She pulled the panties below her pubic thatch. His vocal cords had ceased to function. Sweat beaded his forehead and upper lip. She took the phone from his hand and replaced it in its cradle.

He didn't resist. His eyes were welded to her crotch. Droplets of sweat slid off his eyelids. His breathing sounded labored. Perhaps I won't have to kill him, she thought. Perhaps he'll have a coronary right here. She began to chuckle throatily. She stepped out of her panties and tossed them over her shoulder. A slight, involuntary shudder of pleasure passed over him.

"You *do* remember," she said, beginning to feel the excitement in her throat and in her belly. "How nice."

"But I don't *want* to go to church," said Sam.

"It isn't church," said Max, "it's synagogue."

"I don't *want* to go to synagogue."

"If you like you can bring your cars and play with them on the floor there."

"I don't *want* to play with my cars on the floor there. I want to play with my cars on the floor *here*."

Max looked at the carpet, hating himself for what he was about to say.

"If you come with me to synagogue," he said, "maybe afterwards we can go to FAO Schwarz and buy another car."

Sam looked up, delighted, totally open to bribery and totally unselfconscious about his openness.

"Can I have *two* cars?" he said.

It didn't matter, finally, that Sam was playing with his cars on the floor of the synagogue. As far as Sam was concerned, he was in his own home. After the service they had lunch at the Oracle, where the waiters fussed over the boy as though they didn't have to swab down the floor underneath his table every time he ate there.

"Max, when are you coming home?" said Sam unexpectedly in the middle of lunch.

"I don't know," said Max. "Why do you ask?"

"Because I don't like you to live with Tony Natale."

Max was astounded that the three-year-old remembered Tony's name. If he'd picked that up, what else had he gotten?

"Why don't you like it?" said Max.

244

"Because I don't like it," said Sam. "Tony Natale is a bad man."

"No, he isn't," said Max. "Why do you think Tony is a bad man?"

"Because he makes you stay with him and not with me."

"Honey, Tony Natale isn't *making* me stay with him. I'm staying with him because I want to."

"Why do you want to?"

"Because. . . ." Max tried to think of how to explain this to a three-year-old. "Because Mama and I are very angry at each other right now. And sometimes when people are very angry with each other it's not good for them to live together."

Sam looked at his food, thinking God knew what.

"Are you angry with *me?*" asked Sam.

Oh, Jesus.

"No, sweetheart, I'm not angry with you," said Max. "I'm only angry with Mama."

"Then why don't you just come home and live with *me?*" said Sam.

When they got to FAO Schwarz for his payoff, Sam forgot all about where Max lived and threw himself at the Brio train setup, where he remained, totally transfixed, for nearly two hours, pushing the tiny wooden trains along the double- and triple-tiered tracks through the maze of tunnels, bridges, roundhouse turntables, and classification yards.

Max stood the requisite parental distance from his son in the noisy and crowded store, not too close to make him feel over-supervised, not too far to make him feel abandoned. He surveyed the now-familiar wares: unreasonably authentically detailed subminiature electric trains so small that a complete track layout with station and mountains and tunnels fit into an attaché case; gasoline engine–powered models of Mercedes and Lamborghinis large enough for a child to sit in and drive; stuffed grizzly bears and camels and lions and elephants the approximate size and cost of the living beasts upon which they'd been modeled.

Imagining the sort of parents who could afford to buy such toys for their children and what possessing such hideously expensive playthings must do to a child's sense of reality never failed to produce a shudder in Max.

When it was time for the store to close Sam would not diminish the intensity of his play. Max pointed out to him that it was time to go, but Sam refused to listen. Max explained that the salespeople had to go home and eat their dinners. Sam was unimpressed.

Max picked the child up and tried to carry him out of the store and Sam began to shriek. Customers and salespeople stared, certain a child was being abused or abducted. Max figured Sam was reacting to their unsatisfying discussion at lunch about living arrangements and opted to let him continue playing for a while longer.

Customers left, salespeople left, and Sam continued to play with the Brio trains. A large Black security guard strode over, clearly irritated.

"The store is *closed*," he said to Max as to an errant child.

"Don't tell *me*," said Max, inclining his head in Sam's direction, "tell *him*."

The guard regarded Sam with no expression, then hunkered down beside him.

"The store is *closed*," said the guard to Sam in the same voice he'd used with Max.

Sam continued to play, completely unaffected.

"O.K., Sam," said Max. "You heard the guard. We have to leave right now, this minute."

"Why?"

"Because if we don't he might arrest us."

This caught Sam's attention.

"If he arrests us, Max," said Sam helpfully, "you can shoot him with your gun."

The security guard looked appropriately wary.

Oh my God, thought Max. I have never *ever* talked of guns or shooting to my child, I have been so careful, and yet he has such thoughts —his father has a gun and can shoot people with it. How have I already damaged him in ways I haven't even suspected?

67

According to the FBI there are now about six thousand unsolved murders in the United States, and thirty to one hundred serial murderers currently at large.

Unlike interstate transportation of stolen artwork, murder isn't a federal crime. But since 1972 the FBI has been quite interested in violent crime, especially serial murders with a sexual element.

The FBI distinguishes between mass murder, in which many people are killed at a single time, and serial murder, in which a series of four or more people are killed over a period of time. Serial murders usually have a sexual element — rape and/or sexual mutilation — and are often so bizarre and vicious that local police aren't equipped to deal with them. Serial murderers often travel from state to state, so local police aren't even aware of related cases.

The FBI's National Center for the Analysis of Violent Crime (NCAVC) at the FBI Academy in Quantico, Virginia, computer-analyzes every unsolved murder reported to it by local police departments. Agents of the NCAVC's Behavioral Science Unit (BSU) have conducted in-depth interviews of thirty-six sex murderers and serial killers in prison and analyzed their crimes. By comparing data on known crimes with those of unsolved crimes, the BSU can project profiles of unknown killers with startling accuracy.

The FBI field office that has jurisdiction over Champaign, Illinois, is located in Springfield. When Special Agent Ralph Collins in Springfield heard about the homicide of the English professor at the University of Illinois he realized the case was probably linked to the two homicides the day before in Chicago and possibly even to a couple in New York several weeks before.

Collins phoned his counterpart in the Chicago field office, then placed a call to the chief of detectives' office in New York.

Captain Ed Grimes took the call from Collins in New York. Grimes had been in the job for thirty-seven years and was not a huge fan of the federal agency. Like most city cops, he felt that the FBI acted in a superior and patronizing manner, and often claimed credit in the media for solving cases they'd been involved with only peripherally.

The FBI was aware of its poor image and had taken steps to change its interaction with local police in recent years, but old biases die hard. Grimes was still leery of the feds, and when Collins requested that New York send autopsy reports and crime scene evidence to the BSU at Quantico, Grimes was somewhat evasive.

After talking to Collins, however, Grimes called Lieutenant Ron McIlheny at Manhattan North Homicide. McIlheny had a more benign attitude toward the feds. When Grimes relayed Collins's request for autopsy reports and crime scene data, McIlheny was more than happy to comply.

68

"Two-Five squad, Segal."

"Max, it's Susan. Susan Simon."

"Susan! How are you?"

Caruso looked up at the mention of Susan's name and gave a loud Bronx cheer.

"I'm good," said Susan. "I'm really sorry I wasn't home Friday night to take you up on your kind dinner invitation. If I was I'd love to have gone."

"Oh, hey, listen, *I'm* sorry for calling you on such short notice," said Max.

"Oh, hey, *listen*, *I'm* sorry for *cal*ling you on *such* short *no*tice," mimicked Caruso in falsetto.

Max glared at him and made a threatening gesture with his fist.

"Not at all," said Susan. "I'd have been home eating a TV Dinner, but a girlfriend from my gym took me out to a new place in Tribeca."

"Ah," said Max, wondering whether she was just sparing his feelings and, if not, why she hadn't returned his call until now. He never understood why people didn't return his calls immediately.

"I'd really love a rain check," said Susan. "Are you by any chance free tonight?"

"Tonight?" said Max delightedly. "Yeah, tonight would be great. I'll pick you up around eight, O.K.?"

"Eight would be perfect, Max. I look forward to it."

Max hung up the phone with a huge grin on his face.

"You look like you fuckin' ate the canary," said Caruso.

Max tried to turn off the grin but couldn't.

"So you're taking her to dinner, eh?" said Caruso.

Max shrugged.

"I sure hope she's buyin'," said Caruso.

"Why?" said Max.

"Why?" said Caruso. "Because she's fuckin' *using* you, man, can't you see that? She's fuckin' picking your brain about these cases for her fuckin' story in *New York* magazine, and *you* act like she's suckin' up to you because you're God's gift to women."

"She's not using me, she's not picking my brain, and she's not sucking up to me," said Max irritably. "She's a classy lady who likes me and, if it's any of your business, she happens to have genuine sympathy for my marital situation."

"Your marital situation, eh?" said Caruso, shaking his head in pity. "You poor asshole. She's a fuckin' *phony*, Max. I seen it the minute I laid eyes on her. Why can't *you* see it?"

"Why isn't it possible that she just likes me and enjoys my company?" said Max.

"Get real," said Caruso. "She's a hot lookin' *rich* bitch. The fuck you think she needs with some poor fuckin' detective third grade with a wife and kid?"

"Segal, Caruso, Haggerty, Ruiz, listen up," called McIlheny, striding into the squad room.

"Yeah, boss?" said Haggerty.

"Yes, Lieutenant?" said Max.

"They've had two homicides in Chicago and one in Champaign, Illinois, over the weekend. Same m.o. as the Smiley and Petlin cases."

"No shit," said Caruso.

"The FBI has requested we send autopsy reports and crime scene evidence down to their unit at Quantico," said McIlheny. "I told them we'd comply. I'd like you guys to make that your top priority."

"Did they say anything about a blond woman in connection with any of the three cases in Illinois?" asked Max.

"I don't have any of the particulars, gentlemen," replied McIlheny. "That's why I got *you*."

Max got on the phone to Chernin at the morgue and arranged to pick up the Smiley and Petlin autopsy reports and all crime scene evidence, including photographs. Then he called the Champaign police and got the particulars of the Austin Richards homicide from a sergeant named Striker.

Max then called Chicago. The homicide cops who had caught both the Greco and Sherman cases in Chicago, Watzlawick and Zagorski, were in the field. Their lieutenant said they'd call back as soon as they could be located, but by four o'clock, when Max and Caruso were ready to end their day tour, they hadn't been found.

Max went back to Natale's and got ready for his date with Susan Simon.

69

She was wearing the same damned cologne again. One whiff of it made Max a little goofy. She looked so sensational when he met her in the lobby of her building that he spontaneously leaned over and kissed her on the cheek. Inhaling her cologne at such close range was like downing a shot of gin. He wondered if women had the same olfactory response to men's shaving lotions.

She was more dressed up than he, which made him slightly uncomfortable. He regretted not wearing a tie and toyed briefly with the idea of taking her someplace really swell — maybe Toscana, where Natale had proposed to Cheryl. But he decided he couldn't afford the tab and, more importantly, he couldn't bear the humiliation of having the maître d' give him one of the house ties and insist he wear it.

He asked if she liked Greek, and when she said yes he flagged a cab and took her down to Nineteenth Street to the Oracle. The minute they walked in Max realized he'd made a colossal mistake. The waiters all asked about Sam, and stared at Susan as if she were a homewrecker responsible for ruining the child's life.

They sat down in a booth next to a window facing Second Avenue and, to dissipate memories of his son's shenanigans there, which threatened to plunge him into suicidal depression, Max ordered a bottle of retsina. Susan ordered Absolut on ice but had to settle for the house brand of vodka.

After each of them had had three drinks Max began to babble about his son. He showed her Sam's picture. He repeated Sam's latest witticisms. He told her about Sam's sticking hamburger in his ear and about his trying to eat saltines from between his toes — feats which at the time had made Max livid but which tonight, especially with alcohol in his system, made him maudlin with nostalgia. Susan smiled at the anecdotes and appeared oddly moved.

"It's obvious how much you love your son," she said.

"I'm sorry to be babbling about him this way," he said sheepishly. "It must be terribly boring, especially for someone who doesn't have children herself."

She shook her head, gazing into his eyes so seriously he wondered if he'd inadvertently said something profound and been too drunk to notice.

"On the contrary," she said, "I can't tell you how appealing it makes you."

They had spinach pie and moussaka and Max got Susan to switch to retsina. She said she didn't really like the taste, but after a while she didn't seem to mind it. Max ordered a second bottle, not particularly because he liked the taste himself, but because he could afford it.

He told her about the Hyena killings, about meeting Babette, about tracking the killer with her. About Babette being unable to stay with her mother and her lecherous stepfather any longer and about how she'd moved in with Max purely as a temporary convenience. About falling in love and not touching her because she was a virgin and a Catholic and she thought premarital sex was a mortal sin. About coming back home one night after work to find the apartment in darkness and Babette unconscious on the floor and then being attacked from the shadows by the knife-wielding killer. About nearly dying in the ensuing struggle. About Babette regaining consciousness, picking up the Hyena's gun, and shooting him in the face at point-blank range, saving Max's life. About Max's recovery in the hospital and about marrying Babette and about having a baby and about love going into the toilet.

By the time they had finished their baklava and their second bottle of retsina and Max had paid the check, they were half in the bag. Max flagged a cab and when it almost ran him down he deftly sidestepped it like a toreador sidestepping a charging bull, which sent Susan into gales of laughter.

They got in and Max gave Susan's address. When the cab took a hard turn it threw Susan off balance into Max's lap. Instead of helping her regain her balance he held her there, and when she looked up at him he kissed her. She melted. So did he.

When the cab pulled up in front of her building Max paid and followed her into the lobby and didn't even ask for an invitation upstairs. In the elevator they slid into each other's arms and missed her floor and had to push the button again to get there on the way back down.

Once inside her door they tore at each other's clothing in a fever and sank to the living room carpet, devouring each other with animal noises. Both were starved for affection. Both sensed the other's tremendous need. Their love-making had an intensity that was new to both of them.

"My God," he said, lying in her arms after they had climaxed simultaneously, "is *this* what it's supposed to be like?"

"I wouldn't know," she said. "I've never even come close before."

She traced the pattern of the Hyena-inflicted knife wounds on his back, his left shoulder, his right forearm, and she kissed the scars. He tenderly kissed her lips, her cheeks, her hair, her eyes. He caressed her thighs and belly and buttocks. Caress a wife and you caress years of stored hurts, angers, fears, and memories. Caress a stranger and you caress someone without a past, without a personality, someone who just sprang to life by spontaneous generation, who's an empty canvas upon which to paint your fondest or darkest fantasies.

"I think I'm falling in love," he whispered.

She put a finger to his lips and shook her head.

254

70

When Max got back to Natale's place it was four A.M. and the apartment was dark. Natale's snoring in the adjacent bedroom had the regularity, if not the aesthetic appeal, of ocean waves cresting and crashing on the beach. Max got undressed and made up the Castro convertible as quietly as possible, suspecting he could have performed extensive structural demolition with a jackhammer and not seriously risked waking his roommate.

Susan's scent lingered on Max. All he had to do was raise his wrist to his nostrils to get a fresh fix of it and re-experience the ecstasy of their love-making.

He wondered what was happening to him. When he'd blurted the unthinking suspicion that he was falling in love with her she'd put a finger over his lips and shaken her head. Why? Was she saying it was too soon to speak of love, or was she telling him such love could never be reciprocated?

He wondered if he truly could be falling in love with her. He wondered whether it were possible to fall in love after knowing her for so short a time. He wondered whether such a thing were possible while he was still married to Babette, the mother of his child. It seemed terribly wrong.

It seemed terribly right. The smell of her cologne was on his flesh, the taste of her flesh was on his tongue. He wondered how he was going to wait until their next date.

She lay in bed, hugging her pillow, pretending it was Max. She had never been loved the way Max had loved her tonight, never with that intensity, that sensitivity, that gentleness, that vulnerability. Yes, vulnerability. That's the thing that was most appealing to her about Max, more than all his other appealing qualities: his emotional vulnerability. Nobody that vulnerable could possibly hurt you.

None of the others had had that. They'd been guarded, defended, closed off, and she'd chosen to ignore it, to pretend that they were accessible because she had needed to delude herself. With Max it would be necessary to delude herself no more. With Max all things were possible. It might just be that Max was the one good man left in all the world.

Tomorrow she would call up Dr. Glass and inform him that her therapy was completed. There was no longer any need for therapists when you had found total happiness.

71

"The way we figure it happened," said Max Segal, thirty-two, a plainclothes detective based at Manhattan North Homicide, *"the killer, who was known to Smiley, had some kind of S and M sex with him, then severed his carotid artery. The killer watched him die, then bludgeoned his*

No.

"The way we assume it happened," said Max Segal, thirty-two, who, were he not a plainclothes detective at Manhattan North Homicide, could easily have had a successful career as a film star in Hollywood, *"the killer*

Yes.

72

A gun. A big silver gun, pointed straight at a man, pointed straight at . . . Max! The gun was pointed at Max, and a woman with long yellow hair was holding it. The woman was sitting cross-legged on the end of a huge bed, a bed the size of a football field, and she was holding this enormous silver gun with both hands and pointing it at Max. The woman was stark naked, but at the tips of her breasts instead of nipples she had bullets, silver bullets.

And then the woman with the yellow hair was leaning forward and pulling the trigger of the big silver gun and in slow motion you could see the bullet leave the barrel and fly straight at Max, straight at his face, and then it hit, the impact shattering his face into a million fragments, like fragments of a mirror, only these fragments were not glass but blood and bone and tissue, and they were splattered all over the room.

Babette began to scream and the scream awakened her. She was soaking wet. She looked over at Max's side of the bed to make sure he was all right and then she remembered that he was gone. The bastard had left her, just as she had always known he would.

There had been a time in her life, before she had become a mother, when such dreams bore some resemblance to events as yet unspooled. Now they were in all likelihood nothing more than the Play-Doh of eager therapists. From her readings in psychology books, she had a fairly good notion of what a therapist might make of that dream.

At the most basic level, though, it could simply have been a true memory of a real event — a reliving of the traumatic moment seven years before when she'd saved Max's life by shooting the monster who called himself the Hyena point-blank in the face. But then the therapist

258

would want to talk about guns as penises and the fact that the woman was naked on a bed and the fact that Babette was angry at Max and very horny and afraid that he was going to bed with other women and all the rest of that garbage.

She hated that she was dreaming about Max. She hated that Max had left her. She didn't know if she wanted him back, but she was absolutely positive that she didn't want him going to bed with other women.

Detective Zagorski reached Max at Manhattan North Homicide the following morning at ten o'clock. He verified the facts that Max had been given about the Greco and Sherman cases and added the descriptions of the blond woman given by nurse Lucy Gonzales, bellboy Andy Yastrzemski, desk clerk Peter Yamamoto, room service waiter Raoul Santiago, and security guard Stanislaus Zlatkoff.

Zagorski said that a computer search of all Illinois-registered and rental agency–leased black and dark blue Mustangs had failed to turn up anyone named either Monty Black or Valerie Solanas. Since the first homicides had occurred in New York there was a good possibility that the killer lived there and was only visiting Chicago and Champaign, in which case the Mustang had most likely been rented at either O'Hare or Midway airport. Zagorski said they would canvass the employees at all the rental desks of all the car rental agencies at the two airports.

Sherman's autopsy had turned up a couple of interesting things, said Zagorski. For one thing, gourmet food and wine were found in his stomach. There were many restaurants in the vicinity of Sherman's office where such food and wine could have been consumed, but Zagorski felt a canvass of the area would eventually turn up restaurant employees who might provide valuable information about the killer.

Second, the suspect had left a blood sample at Dr. Sherman's office, which they'd sent to the crime lab for typing. Due to the current case overload at the lab, the blood sample had been temporarily misplaced, but Zagorski felt confident that it would soon be located and analyzed. If and when the suspect was found, this would be a valuable means of identification.

If and when. Max had the sinking feeling that the more they learned about the elusive blond woman, the further beyond their reach she danced. Manhattan. Chicago. Champaign. Would she return to Manhattan or would she continue westward, butchering men in a pattern that had meaning to her alone, a pattern that could never even be imagined by sane minds?

If Smiley, Petlin, Barmack, Greco, Sherman, and Richards had all been killed by the same person, it looked as though she was taking greater and greater chances of being caught. The first two homicides had been in the victims' own apartments, where only a doorman might possibly remember her. The third — assuming Barmack's death was indeed the work of the same perpetrator — had been outside on the terrace of an empty apartment, where the doorman would have remembered her going up to look at it with the victim. The fourth had been in an empty office, where she'd had to sign in and out with a security man. The fifth had been in her own hotel room, where she had willingly exposed herself to the scrutiny of several hotel employees.

The killer was either getting more and more confident, or else she wanted to get caught and was beginning to despair that the authorities would never accomplish this feat without her direct intervention.

74

"This fucking form is fuckin' bullshit," said Caruso.

"*Tell* me about it," said Max, reading over his shoulder.

To Max and Caruso the Violent Criminal Apprehension Program (VICAP) report was just one of the many forms whose preparation kept them from active investigation of the cases they were employed to solve. They sweated and cursed over it like jocks with football scholarships struggling over final exams. But they were impressed in spite of themselves at the depth and detail of the information requested.

"Look at this fucking thing," said Caruso. "Fifteen pages, a hundred and eighty-nine questions. Listen to this: 'Did the victim have outstanding physical features (crossed eyes, noticeable limp, physical deformity, etc.)? . . . Offender was in possession of property of others (check all that apply): body parts, clothing, credit cards. . . . If the offender initiated contact with the victim by means of deception, indicate the type of deception below: posed as authority figure, posed as businessperson, asked victim to model or pose for photos, offered job, money, treats, or toys, implied family emergency or illness, asked for or offered assistance, caused or staged traffic accident, phony police traffic stop, solicitation for sex, offered ride or transportation, other deception. . . .'"

"I know," said Max.

"'Instrument used to write or carve on body: knife or other sharp instrument, blood, lipstick, writing instrument. . . . Was there evidence to suggest a deliberate or unusual ritual/act/thing had been performed on, with, or near the victim (such as an orderly formation of rocks, burnt candles, dead animals, defecation, etc.). . . .'"

"Hey, Sal, I can read it myself, huh?" said Max.

"'Location of bite marks: face, neck, abdomen, breasts, buttocks, groin, genitalia. . . . Elements of unusual or additional assault upon victim: victim whipped, burns on victim, victim run over by vehicle, evidence of cannibalism/vampirism. . . .'"

"Gimme a break, would ya?" said Max.

"'Dismemberment method: bitten off, cut — skilled/surgical, cut — unskilled/rough-cut, hacked/chopped off, sawed off, other (specify). . . .' I mean, if we knew the answers to half these fuckin' questions," said Caruso, "we'd have that bitch already collared."

"We *know* the answers to half of these questions," said Max, "and we don't know what *city* she's in."

When Max entered the apartment to pick up Sam for dinner at the Oracle Babette looked at him oddly.

"Are you involved with somebody?" she said.

"What?" he said. "What?" is what three-year-olds say when they need to stall for time, he thought.

"Have you recently become involved with a woman?" said Babette. "A blonde?"

"What makes you say that?" said Max.

"You have, haven't you?" she said.

Max shrugged. "What's the difference?" he said.

Babette searched his face for signs of how to react to this apparent admission that he had another woman to love, and found nothing helpful. Her eyes itched and smarted. Although she willed them not to, they began to fill with water. She had a sudden overwhelming feeling of suffocating dread.

"Please," she said, trying to hone her meaning so that he wouldn't misunderstand, "don't see her anymore."

"Why not?" said Max dully.

Babette stared at him a moment longer.

"I had . . . a dream about you and a woman," said Babette. "She shot you to death."

Max felt a chill pass over his scalp, back, and shoulders.

"What is this supposed to be," he said, "some sort of hot psychic flash?"

"Forget it," said Babette and went to get Sam.

She hadn't had a psychic dream, Max reassured himself. Babette was just an understandably jealous wife trying to get rid of the competition. Susan wasn't someone to fear; Susan was the best thing in his life now.

76

Stroke . . . stroke . . . stroke . . . stroke . . . stroke.

"So what did you think of him, precious?"

Stroke . . . stroke . . . stroke . . . stroke . . . stroke.

"Wasn't he *nice,* darling?"

Stroke . . . stroke . . . stroke . . . stroke . . . stroke.

"How would you like to have him as a *daddy?*"

Maybe she was getting a little ahead of herself, talking to the cat about daddies. But Max was such a wonderful man, and he had made such beautiful love to her. None of her other lovers had ever cared about her pleasure. With her other lovers sex had been little short of rape.

Not with Max. Max had even told her he loved her! No man had ever told her that before, except her father, of course — whatever *that* was worth. It had frightened her a little when Max said it; she hadn't known why. Perhaps because she was afraid to start hoping again. To start trusting somebody again. To open herself up to that kind of vulnerability again.

But Max was someone she could trust. She had known it the minute she'd met him. The way he'd taken care of her and protected her feelings from his insensitive partner, Caruso. The way he talked about his son. No, Max would never violate her trust. She was safe with him.

A remarkable thing was happening to her as a result of loving Max and being loved by him. The hard, brittle, ancient shell of anger that had insulated her from men for so many years was cracking, peeling, breaking up into small fragments and falling away from her, leaving something fresh, tender, and very new exposed to the warmth of the sun.

There were still men alive in Chicago who had hurt her, oh, yes. She had written their names on a sheet of paper. Roger Newfield. Dave Eckerd. Alan Bonner. Frank Weston. Donald Price. Boys who had broken her heart in high school and grammar school. They didn't matter any longer. They had no further power to torment her. She was loved. She was safe now. She forgave them.

She took the list over to her wood burning fireplace, struck a match, and set it afire. If only those men knew how close they'd come to death. They'd been saved by one good man, by Max Segal. They would never know it, but they owed him their lives.

And then there were the men she'd killed. Irv Smiley. Freddy Petlin. Walter Barmack. Teddy Greco. Stu Sherman. Austin Richards. It was sad, really, that they'd had to go. Sad, but unavoidable. Now, too late to help them, but in time to help herself, she forgave them as well.

77

The FBI Academy at Quantico is located on seventy-nine acres of evergreen woods in the state of Virginia, forty miles south of Washington, D.C. The Marine Corps shares Quantico with the FBI and the Drug Enforcement Agency.

The FBI Academy is a twenty-five-million-dollar complex of attractive modern buildings connected by a series of glass-enclosed corridors to make passage comfortable during bad weather. The buildings contain classrooms, dorms, a cafeteria, a PX, a gym, and a huge indoor pool in which trainees learn to swim with loaded weapons.

Along the edge of the complex are a series of beautifully landscaped shooting ranges on which trainees learn to kill. The wholesome-looking young men and women wear black fatigue pants, black combat boots, gray T-shirts, dark blue shooting caps with huge white letters on them reading FBI or DEA, and mouse-ears to muffle the explosions of their matte black plastic seventeen-shot nine-millimeter Glock automatic pistols.

Beneath the buildings is a basement that looks like a ship's engine room. Below that, in a windowless, airless sub-basement, are the offices of the BSU.

Data from the VICAP forms is computer-analyzed, but ninety-eight percent of the BSU's work is think tank — four or five agents sitting around for hours, studying photos and other evidence from crime scenes, autopsy reports, pathologists' opinions, and then brainstorming. Who are the victims' known associates? What made the victim attractive to the killer? What can be deduced about the killer from his behavior at the crime scene? Was the killer organized or disorganized? Did he use a weapon found at the scene or bring his own?

Was the body moved? The face covered? Battered? Mutilated? Every detail meant something.

Then the team constructed a profile of the killer. The agent in charge of the case wrote a report and phoned it to the local police. The process could take six weeks. A priority one case could be processed within a week.

Sometimes the agent in charge of a case flew to the crime scenes and spent several days in the field. If the killer was found within that time the agent might watch local police take him down, but wouldn't participate.

Special Agent Jim Cody of the BSU had caught the Richards case from Champaign, the two linked cases from Chicago, and the three from New York. The cases had been designated priority one. After an hour of looking over the VICAP forms, the crime scene photos, and the autopsy reports, the BSU decided to send Cody into the field while the trail was fresh.

78

Their second night of love-making was, if possible, even better than the first. If there was slightly less passion there was considerably more tenderness, and it went on and on and on until she thought it would never stop. And then it stopped and that was good too.

She lay in Max's arms and he caressed her with a touch so light it felt like the fluttering of tiny butterfly wings.

"You're an exquisite lover," she said.

"Thank you," he said.

"If you're this good with your wife," she said, "I don't know how she ever let you go."

"I *used* to be this good with my wife," he said. "I haven't been for many years."

"No?"

"No. You know, I'd forgotten I was good. I'm grateful to you for helping me remember."

She smiled up at him.

"Last night you said you loved me," she said. "I tried to silence you. I don't know why. I think I was frightened."

"Of what?" he said.

"It was too soon, I think. But now, even though it's only twenty-four hours later, I'm no longer frightened."

"I'm glad," he said, continuing to caress her.

"I love you too," she said.

He wrapped his arms around her and covered her face with kisses.

"I think I just died and went to heaven," he said.

"I do love you," she said. "I haven't been able to think about anything since last night but how much I love you."

He grew hard and soon began making love to her again. This time it went on almost as long as before. When it was over they were wet with perspiration and slightly chafed. He licked the salty moisture from her face. She giggled.

"Tell me," she said casually, "what about the future?"

"What?" he said. The three-year-old's response to the unexpected question. He was hoping he hadn't heard her correctly.

"What does the future hold for us?" she said.

"What do you mean?" he said, realizing he'd heard her correctly.

"I know you love me, Max, but what are your plans for us? Ah *mean*," she said, switching to a parody Southern accent to soften the query, "whut are yore in-*ten*-shuns, suh?"

He didn't laugh as she thought he might.

"My intentions?" he said. He had stopped caressing her.

"Yes," she said, somewhat taken aback by his sudden coolness. "I don't mean right now, Max, I mean down the road a bit. I mean is marriage a possibility for us after your divorce? Because if it is I'd like to know. And if it isn't, well, I guess I'd like to know that, too."

He was hardly even touching her now. Warning lights were snapping on all over her system. She was trying not to panic.

"Listen, babe," he said, trying to get a caress going again and losing his formerly light touch, "I told you I love you and I meant it. But give me a break, I'm not even officially *separated* yet, so how can I possibly know about plans after a divorce?"

He'd said "babe." That was bad, she sensed, worse than "give me a break." Babe wasn't at all the correct word of endearment from him in this situation. But he did say he meant it when he'd told her he loved her. *Meant* it. Past tense of *mean*. But he'd said it *now*. Even after the terrible blunder of asking about the future. He said *now* he'd meant it when he'd told her he loved her. That had to be an indication that things were still all right between them, that she hadn't completely blown it with her unthinkingly horrible request for reassurance about the future.

"O.K., I can understand that," she said, not understanding, or, what was worse, beginning to understand only too well. "I'm sorry I asked that. It was stupid of me. The last thing I want to do is pressure you, Max."

No, don't apologize, she thought, you're only going to make it worse. They hate apologies. And don't say you were stupid, and don't

270

call attention to the fact that you were pressuring him. If he didn't think you were pressuring him before, he'll surely think so now.

"O.K., babe, I know that," he said.

Babe again. Oh, shit. I'm blowing it, I'm blowing it again. Please let me stop before it's too late. Please don't let me make it worse than it is already and then maybe it can still be saved somehow, sometime, on some other day when I'm not out of control, because now I'm out of control and I can't stop myself and I don't know what the hell to do about it.

"To tell you the truth, I don't really care that much about the future," she said. "I mostly care about now, and now is perfect."

Bullshit, bullshit, *bullshit,* she thought. How can he read that as anything but panicked bullshit from a woman who is even more insecure and desperate than he feared ten seconds ago? Verbal diarrhea, that's what I've got, and I can't stop because I'm totally out of control. She felt herself getting nauseated.

"Listen, Max," she said, lurching into a sitting position, "I don't feel so well. Maybe you'd better go."

"What's wrong?" he said, instantly concerned.

Better, she thought. Concern is better than what I saw there a moment ago.

"I don't know," she said. "I think I had too much retsina. I'm a little sick to my stomach."

Yes, that's it, blame it on the drinking. That they understand. They get drunk and say things they regret under the influence of alcohol all the time.

"Oh, baby, I'm sorry," he said. "Here, lie down and I'll get you a cold washcloth for your forehead."

Baby. Baby is eighty times better than *babe.* And he really looks concerned. I can't believe it. Telling him I drank too much and want to puke my guts out may be saving the day!

"A cold washcloth would be nice, Max," she said, watching him intently. "And then you really must go."

He went to the bathroom, ran the tap, came back with a dripping washcloth that he briefly spun around in the air to cool, and then draped it over her forehead. He seemed attentive, caring, concerned, loving. *Loving.*

"Thanks, Max," she said. "And now get out of here."

Yes, that's it, *get out of here.* The perfect tone.

"Are you sure?" he said. "Because if you like I could sleep over and take care of you."

Sleep over and take *care* of you! She'd saved it, she really had!

"No, Max, really, I'm fine," she said. "I just need to be alone now and sleep this off."

"O.K.," he said. "I hope you'll be O.K. I'll call you tomorrow morning, O.K.?"

Three O.K.s, she noted. Now *he's* the one who's nervous.

"You do that," she said. You bastard.

79

Special Agent James Cody was fifty years old and had, in ascending order of importance, gray eyes, gray hair, high cheekbones, a bachelor's degree from Fordham, a law degree from Yale, a four-year hitch in the Marine Corps, a divorce from a twenty-year hitch in a failed marriage, and a throbbing headache from having consumed four Gibsons before going to bed the previous night.

Cody spent an hour alone in the sealed office of Professor Austin Richards. Then he went back to the Champaign police department and looked over what they had.

What they had was not very satisfying. The Cook County coroner's report, based on a substandard autopsy performed by a Champaign physician, photos from the crime scene which showed few of the things he was looking for, and woefully inadequate notes made by the local law enforcement personnel whom he was careful not to disparage because of the new image the Bureau was trying to foster.

Striker told Cody that his men had already talked to Richards's widow, his graduate assistant, the janitor, and several secretaries employed in his office building during the week. Nobody had seen Richards or anyone else enter his office on the day he was killed, and nobody had seen anyone leave. If Richards had an appointment to meet someone there was no record of it anywhere.

When Cody asked if his men had canvassed the local hotels and motels Striker admitted they hadn't had a chance. Cody politely refrained from asking what they'd been doing instead, then made the calls himself. There weren't that many places to canvass. The desk clerk at the Best Western checked the register and verified that a woman named Monty Black had arrived there late Friday night, May Thirteenth, and checked out at noon on Saturday, the Fourteenth.

Striker grabbed a camera and a fingerprint kit and went with Cody over to the motel. The room had probably been rented out several times since Monty Black stayed there, so dusting for prints was pointless, but Striker wanted to do something to offset his growing humiliation at his men's lack of thoroughness.

The register was indeed signed "Monty Black" in blue ballpoint ink and a tiny hand. Cody asked to borrow the signed page and phoned in the license number that she'd written next to her name, requesting an immediate computer check. Then they went to look at the room.

The room was small, depressing, and nondescript. A cheap color TV was bolted to the dresser. A cheap clock-radio was bolted to the bedside table. A hugely unappealing painting of the Chicago lake front was bolted to the wall, in case someone with horrid taste was tempted to take it home.

Cody told Striker not to bother dusting for prints. When they returned to the police station Special Agent Ralph Collins from the Springfield office had arrived.

Collins was an athletic-looking man of perhaps forty with thinning red hair and a moustache. Like Cody and most FBI agents, he was intelligent, articulate, and fairly laid back. Cody called again about the license number and was told it was a phony. And the names Monty Black and Valerie Solanas had coughed up nothing either.

Cody phoned detectives Zagorski and Watzlawick in Chicago, who reported that they'd recovered the Mustang by canvassing the airport rental agencies. The vehicle had been thoroughly examined, with special attention paid to the rearview mirror, a classic repository of latent prints. They'd found nothing.

The rental contract was signed "Caroline Busey." They'd run a check on the driver's license number and found that it was a real Illinois license. It had been issued in the name of Caroline Busey, but the signature resembled that of Monty Black and the given address was a Laundromat in Mattoon, Illinois.

The bill had originally been put on a credit card, then paid in cash. The credit card data had been thrown out.

"Mrs. Richards, I'm Special Agent Cody of the FBI, and this is Special Agent Collins. We're terribly sorry about your loss, and we're sorry to have to be talking to you now. I'm sure you'd rather be alone,

274

doing anything in the world but talking to us, but it could prove enormously helpful in apprehending your husband's killer if you could spend a few minutes chatting now."

The widow nodded, opened the screen door, and ushered the two men into a living room that could have profited from a good vacuuming and the burning of ninety percent of its furniture. Her eyes were red, but she was through crying. Cody caught a whiff of bourbon from her direction, so she apparently wasn't through drinking. She had stringy blond hair, sensual lips, perfect teeth, a face that looked like it had once been quite pretty, and a body that she had really let go to hell.

"How can I help you gentlemen?"

Cody and Collins sat down on a sofa whose cushions sagged forward precariously, threatening to spill them off onto the floor. The widow seated herself in a wicker rocker that some child had made it his personal mission in life to unweave.

"Mrs. Richards," said Cody, "would you have any idea whom your husband was seeing Saturday morning in his office?"

She looked at them and did not reply.

"Mrs. Richards?" said Collins.

"What do you want me to say?"

"Excuse me?" said Collins.

"What do you want me to say? He didn't tell me he was going to see anybody, he said he was going to grade some papers. The coroner said he'd probably been fucking shortly before he died. I can promise you it wasn't with *me*."

Cody and Collins nodded, uncomfortable with grieving widows who knew their husbands were philanderers and who used words like "fucking."

"And you don't know who she might have been?" said Cody.

Again she didn't reply.

"You don't know who she might have been, Mrs. Richards?" said Collins.

"No," she said. "Austin made it a point never to acquaint me with the women he intended to fuck. The man had an extraordinary amount of class."

80

"Sam, I have a surprise for you," said Max above the grinding screech of brakes of the Lexington Avenue subway.

"What, Max?"

"I said I have a surprise for you," Max repeated, shouting. "And by the way, I'd really like it if you'd start calling me Dada again."

"What's the surprise, Max?"

Max acknowledged his son's independence with a fixed smile. It was healthy that Sam didn't automatically give in to every suggestion his father offered him. It showed the boy had spunk, strength of character, and a mind of his own. It showed the boy would not be a wimp. It was also a royal pain in the butt.

"You know, Sam, *anybody* can call me Max, but you are the only person in the entire world who's entitled to call me Dada. Did you know that?"

"What does *entitled* mean?"

"Able to. Allowed to. It means nobody else can do it but you. So when you call me Dada instead of Max, that makes you very special."

The train ground to a shuddering stop. The doors opened.

"What's my surprise?"

"Your surprise is that, after we're done with the zoo, we're going to go to a friend of mine's house for dinner."

"When? *This* day?"

"Tonight, yes."

"What friend, Tony Natale? I don't like Tony Natale."

"No, it's not Tony Natale. Why do you say you don't like Tony Natale? You haven't even *met* Tony Natale."

"But I don't like him."

276

"Well, this isn't Tony Natale, this is a friend named Susan Simon."

He had the sudden uncomfortable suspicion that taking his young son to meet his new lover was at best parentally inappropriate and at worst psychologically damaging, but he opted to suppress it.

"Is Susan Simon a girl?"

"Yes."

"Does she have a vagina?"

"Uh, yes."

"Do I like her?"

"You haven't *met* her yet, but I think you'll like her."

"Why *do* you?"

"Why do I think you'll like her? Because. Because *she's* a nice person and *you're* a nice person and nice people tend to like each other."

The doors closed. The train lurched forward again, throwing him against the child.

"Does she have lots of toys?"

"No, but she has a cat."

"Oh. Do I like cats?"

"Yes."

They arrived at the Bronx Zoo to find that half the children in the city and their parents or teachers had had the same idea. They waited in line for nearly forty minutes to get into the zoo, and when they finally did Sam seemed more interested in transportation than animals. He wanted to ride on both the Skyfari cable car and the Bengali Express train, both of which necessitated additional forty-minute waits. The zoo was intelligently laid out, with most animals displayed in natural-looking settings indigenous to their native lands, and moats rather than bars protecting the inmates from the visitors. Max was surprised at how much everything cost.

All they could see from the impressively high-riding and potentially vertigo-inducing Skyfari cable car were hawk-eye views of zoo facilities under construction and one lone ostrich. All they could see from the earthbound Bengali Express was more construction, two Thompson's gazelles, and a yellow bulldozer.

For lunch they waited in line for forty minutes at the Flamingo Pub to get two Zoo Keeper's Specials. Zoo Keeper's Specials were cheeseburgers in cardboard boxes shaped like raccoons, with plastic masks shaped like wart hogs' snouts in each box. The lunch, which they ate at an outdoor picnic table overlooking a pond full of graceful pink flamingos, was quite expensive too.

After lunch Sam said he wanted to ride on the Skyfari and the Bengali Express again, but Max, wary of further expense and further waits on line, convinced him to go take a look at the lions. When they got to the lion house, however, they found a sign on the cages which said "We've moved." The lion house was under construction.

In three hours they'd managed to see only eleven animals. Between tickets for admission, rides, and lunch, Max had already spent thirty-three dollars. That was three dollars a head for each animal they'd seen. If he'd known it would cost three bucks a head to look at animals he might have chosen a different activity.

Passing a souvenir stand, Sam decided he had to have an expensive and unattractive inflatable plastic pig. Max told him the pig was out of the question. Sam threw a tantrum. Shocked parents and children stared, transfixed, as though three-year-olds throwing tantrums were an exotic phenomenon. Max clung to the thrashing child, trying to remember this was not about inflatable pigs but about fathers leaving home, trying to reassure Sam in enlightened parentese that it was O.K. to be angry and that Max still loved him, when one of Sam's flailing feet caught Max squarely in the testicles.

Max doubled over in pain and shouted Sam into silence, as bystanders slipped off discreetly to phone the hotline for abused children.

81

Detectives Watzlawick and Zagorski picked Special Agent Cody up at Midway Airport on Chicago's South Side and began briefing him as soon as he got into their car. The excitement of recovering the black Mustang had faded with the revelation that the car was clean and the rental agreement data falsified. If the suspect had left any latent prints on the vehicle, they'd been destroyed by subsequent renters and diligent maintenance crews.

Like Cody, Watzlawick and Zagorski had had fruitless sessions with Greco's and Sherman's widows. Greco's had not been surprised at her husband's infidelity, Sherman's swore he'd never been unfaithful to her. Neither wife was able to come up with any leads.

A session with the police artist, including bellboy Yastrzemski, desk clerk Yamamoto, room service waiter Santiago, security man Zlatkoff, and nurse Gonzales, had produced a composite that detectives were currently using in a canvass of all Near North Side restaurants capable of serving the quality of food found in Dr. Sherman's stomach.

Greco's personal office and his firm's women's room, as well as Sherman's examination and consultation rooms, had yielded nothing in the way of leads, but Monty Black's hotel room was not quite so disappointing.

From the carpet they'd recovered brown, black, and blond hairs, and fibers characteristic of wool, cotton, and synthetic blends from guests' clothing. In the shower trap they'd found hairs from several guests, including, presumably, Monty Black. The hairs — scalp, axillary, and pubic — were all brunette. A few of them had intact root sheaths.

All mirrors, doorknobs, and other shiny surfaces had been wiped clean of prints. There was unfortunately nothing in the bathroom wastebasket because the maid had cleaned the room not long before the suspect checked out.

The fact that the scalp hairs in the shower trap were only brunette appeared curious to Cody. Since most people lose up to one hundred twenty-five hairs a day, and since the suspect was blond and had presumably taken at least one or two baths or showers in the room during her stay, he wondered why no blond hairs had shown up in the trap.

It was possible, though unlikely, that they had all slid down the drain. If not, that suggested the blond woman was a blonde everywhere but in the shower.

A wig? Perhaps. Human hair has scales — flattened cells thinner than a molecule of DNA, all pointing toward the tip. If you run your finger along the shaft of a normal human hair it feels smooth in one direction, rough in the other. Wig hair, if not synthetic, is human hair that has been scaled to reduce tangling. If scaled, it is smooth in both directions. If unscaled, a hair from a human-hair wig, without a root sheath, would look like any other human hair under a microscope.

Of course, human-hair wigs were now a comparative rarity. Since the blond hairs recovered from the carpet appeared to be human rather than synthetic, Cody felt there was little likelihood they'd come from a wig. Still, you had to play all the angles.

82

The idea of inviting Max and his son over to her apartment for dinner was probably ill-conceived to begin with. She didn't know anything about kids and should have picked someone less important in her life on whom to practice.

But Max had been so solicitous of her feigned illness on their next meeting that she'd blurted out the dinner invitation. She'd also made a mental note to use illness as a stratagem with him in the future.

She got out her good silver, china, and crystal and set the table with her best linen. This was not so much for Sam's benefit as Max's. She cooked what she thought a kid might like: tiny filet mignons with ketchup and pommes frites, German chocolate cake, Häagen-Dazs chocolate ice cream, and Coke. She decorated the apartment with crepe paper streamers and helium-filled balloons. Maybe it was overkill, but she really wanted the kid to like her. Maybe someday, if things worked out . . . well, who knew? Maybe someday the kid would be half hers.

The doorbell rang promptly at six. She checked her face in the mirror, flashed a rehearsal smile, then rushed to the door. Max and a very subdued Sam entered the apartment.

"Sam," said Max, "this is my friend Susan. Susan, this is Sam."

"Glad to meet you, Sam," said Susan, stooping and extending her hand.

"Do you have toys?" said Sam, ignoring her hand.

Susan looked up at Max with an anxious smile on her face.

"I told you she didn't have toys," said Max. "I told you she had a cat."

"Well, where *is* it?" said Sam irritably.

"I'll get her," said Susan, disappearing into the bedroom.

Max flashed Sam a warning look that Sam pretended to ignore. Susan reappeared, carrying a fat gray tiger cat who was as anxious to be elsewhere as was Sam himself.

"Sam," she said, "this is Sheena. Do you want to pet her?"

The cat measured Sam with flat yellow eyes.

"No," said Sam.

"*Pet* her," said Max between clenched teeth.

Sam petted the cat's massive head. The cat emitted a faint, high growl of distant menace.

"What was *that*?" said Sam.

"Nothing," said Max.

"Is she going to *bite* me?" said Sam.

"Oh, no," said Susan, "she never bites."

"O.K.," said Sam, faintly reassured.

Sam patted the cat's head again. The cat opened a mouth full of frightening-looking teeth and hissed like a reptile. Sam burst into tears. Susan spirited the cat into the bedroom and locked it inside.

That was the high point of the evening.

Sam hated the cat, hated the apartment, hated the balloons and the other decorations, and when it was time to sit down and eat he hated the food.

"I *hate* this," he said. "I *hate* it here. I want to go *home*."

With a painful, face-stretching smile, Max rapidly explained to Susan what an exhausting day they'd had at the zoo and that the way Sam was behaving had to do with exhaustion and not with the wonderful dinner she had prepared. Then he turned to Sam and, without a pause for breath, explained what a wonderful dinner Susan had prepared and how nice she was to have done it and what a pity it would be to leave before they at the very least had their *dessert,* their chocolate *cake* and chocolate *ice* cream.

"I *hate* it here," said Sam. "I want to go *home*."

Babbling apologies, Max scooped up Sam and headed for the door, vowing to return within the hour, and then they were gone.

Susan sank into her chair. The dinner had been an unqualified disaster. She could not have envisioned a worse scenario if she'd tried. Her lover's son hated her. Perhaps the son's hatred would poison the father's love as well.

She couldn't afford to let that happen. She had to neutralize the son's hatred. But how? She didn't know. Perhaps the son would have to die. Yes, and she could exploit the father's grief at his son's death. Clasp him to her bosom. Comfort him. Make him dependent on her strength.

Max did return, but it took more than an hour. They nibbled the cold filets together and Max helped her clean up. They put romantic tapes on the stereo, made hefty cocktails and took them into the bedroom, but were unable to build a believably romantic mood. Rather than accept this and reschedule they pretended the mood was there and faked it.

Their love-making was like flat champagne. Their expressions of affection sounded awkward and heavy. She felt she was beginning to lose him.

"So," she said, knowing this was very likely the worst possible time to bring it up but feeling powerless to stop, "have you given any more thought to our future?"

Max sighed and shook his head.

"I need time, babe," he said. "I'm not even separated yet."

Babe again. The warning word.

"There was a comedienne about a year ago," she said, "who had a wonderful routine. She said she'd spent years trying to find a way to let guys down easily. She told them, 'Let's just be friends,' she tried all these additional Dear John techniques, and the guys just hung around and hung around and wouldn't leave. And then, she said, she hit on the perfect way to get rid of them. She told them, 'I want to marry you and have your child.' The guys disappeared so fast, she said, they left skid marks."

She waited for the laugh. Max only smiled. Something tightened in her chest. This man is capable of hurting you, she thought. He is not your ally, he is your adversary. You are going to have to stop trusting him.

When school wasn't in session the block between First and Second on Nineteenth Street was fairly quiet. Wearing her wig and mirrored sunglasses, she strolled up and down the block, waiting for Babette and Sam.

Chances were they'd be together. Except when Babette left the boy with the neighbor, Mrs. Rensvold, they were inseparable. She looked at her watch. According to her calculations they'd be coming outside any minute now, assuming they were coming out at all. It was a nice day, though, so it was hard to imagine she'd keep him in. Unless he were ill. She hoped he wasn't ill. Not with anything minor, anyway.

There they were. Good. Babette maneuvering Sam in the stroller out of the vestibule, onto the sidewalk. She'd never gotten a good look at Babette before. The woman was attractive, certainly, but had clearly let herself go. The hair piled haphazardly atop her head, the lack of makeup, the awful clothes. Max could do better.

Babette wheeled the stroller toward Second Avenue. Monty gave them half a block, then began to follow.

84

On Sunday Max went over to the apartment to pick Sam up and Babette said the boy wasn't feeling well. Nothing serious, just a low-grade something or other. It might not be wise to take him anywhere. Babette seemed softer somehow, and Max elected to stay in the apartment and play with his son there.

After lunch Sam actually asked to take a nap, a first in Max's memory. Max put him to bed, something he hadn't done in a long time, and was then reluctant to leave. Babette invited him to stay through the nap and he did.

They opened a bottle of soave and talked in a leisurely low-key fashion. Babette asked tactfully about Max's new girlfriend and, wondering whether he was being indiscreet, Max related the events of the disastrous dinner at Susan's.

Babette was at first upset at Max for taking Sam to see the woman, but by the time he got to the part about the cat hissing and Sam screaming and saying how much he hated it there they were both laughing so hard they nearly wet their pants.

They stopped laughing and looked at each other.

"Whew," said Max.

"I know," said Babette.

"How long has it been since we laughed like that?" he said.

"Pretty long," she said. "As long as we've had Sam. Maybe longer."

"Yeah," he said. "Jesus. We had a few good laughs in the old days, though, didn't we?"

"Yeah," she said. "Getting knifed by psychopathic killers was a hoot."

He chuckled and studied her face, then looked at her body and saw the outline of her breasts through her loose blouse.

"Why do you look so damned sexy today?" he said.

"You think I look sexy?" she said, color seeping into her cheeks.

He nodded. She poured herself another glass of soave and held his gaze. It was the first sustained eye contact they'd had in a very long time.

"You know something?" he said.

"What?"

"Sometimes I miss the hell out of you," he said.

"Sometimes I miss the hell out of *you*," she said.

She lowered her eyes. Tears slid swiftly and silently down her cheeks. He reached across the table, touched her face gently, and kissed her tears. She raised her lips to his. With a whimper they reached for each other across the table and held on tight, upsetting the bottle of wine and not caring.

After a while he led her downstairs to their basement bedroom and they lay down on the bed that they'd shared for seven years and made love with more passion and pleasure than they had at any time since the birth of their son.

When Sam awoke from his nap they put on their clothes, walked back upstairs, and played with him until dinner. After dinner Max gave Sam his bath, put him to bed, and went through all the boy's bedtime rituals as though they were part of a religious ceremony. It was like old times.

"I love you, Sam," Max whispered as he kissed his son's cool face and inhaled the fragrance of his hair.

"I love you, Max," the boy whispered sleepily in reply.

Max chuckled silently at his son's obstinance, wound up the music box that played incessant choruses of Brahms's Lullaby, and tiptoed out of the room. He and Babette sat down at the dining table, drank more wine, held hands, and didn't speak. When there was no more wine in the bottle he pulled her gently out of her chair and guided her back down to their bedroom.

They undressed and caressed each other in silence, drifting in memory eddies from the time before things had gotten so tense and unpleasant between them. Like a filmed montage, brief scenes of their lost love drifted through their mutual consciousness, silent slow-motion scenes of ease, gentleness, vulnerability, trust, and mutual adoration.

At what point had their relationship lost its suppleness and elasticity, at what point had it begun to grow dry and brittle and no longer able to stretch, to irreparably snap over so ludicrous an issue as a mocha éclair?

Their silent caresses grew directional and urgent. He entered her again and the languorous montage gave way to lustier images.

"Oh, Max," she said when they had finished, "I love you."

"I love you too," he said.

She lay in his arms and he stroked her hair and became gradually aware of a vague feeling of discomfort and dread. There was, he sensed, an understandable reluctance to return to a tense and angry relationship whose problems were still unresolved, but there was also something else. There was, he realized, inexplicable guilt for cheating on his mistress with his wife.

"Max," said Babette tentatively, "do you think you might possibly like to maybe . . . move back in with us?"

He sighed.

"I *would* like to," he said. "But it's not that simple anymore, I'm afraid."

"What do you mean it's not that simple anymore?"

"I mean, it's just not that simple anymore."

June became January.

"Surely you don't mean because of *her?*" she said, growing rigid in his arms.

"I just mean that I have some things to resolve."

"Swell," she said, getting out of bed, hastily wrapping a sheet about her naked flesh, trying to clothe her vulnerability much too late. "Go and resolve them."

85

"The fuck's wrong with *you?*" said Caruso.

"Nothing," said Max.

"The fuck it ain't," said Caruso.

"It's not important," said Max.

"Well, you can tell me or not," said Caruso, "but I'm sure as shit not letting you *drive* in that condition. Slide over."

Max slid over and let Caruso drive. They headed up the FDR to the Triboro and the Grand Central Parkway. They were going to JFK to pick up Special Agent Cody. Unlike most other places in the country, people in New York didn't pick people up at airports, but Manhattan North Homicide was up in Harlem so they figured what the hell.

"So," said Caruso, "you gonna tell me or what?"

"It's nothing," said Max. "It's boring."

"So bore me."

"O.K., said Max. "Yesterday I spent the night with my wife, and now I don't know what to do about Susan, O.K.?"

"*I* know," said Caruso.

"What?"

"*Dump* the bitch," said Caruso. "She's poison."

Special Agent Cody was older than Max had figured, judging from his voice on the phone, and he was trying so hard not to step on their toes that Max got over his initial defensiveness quickly. Caruso was another matter, however. Caruso took every question that Cody asked as a criticism and it made things sticky, to say the least.

At Cody's request they took him to both Smiley's and Petlin's apartments. They hadn't filled out a VICAP report on Barmack, but when they briefed Cody on the case he asked to see the building at Central Park West and Ninety-second as well. Then they went back to Manhattan North Homicide to meet with McIlheny and to look over the case folders.

After examining the medical examiner's report on Barmack and enlargements of the autopsy photographs, Cody said that in his opinion the small cut on Barmack's nose looked as if it had been made with the same blade that was used on Smiley's and Petlin's necks.

"So that means Monty Black or Caroline Busey or whatever the fuck she calls herself has homicided eight people so far," said Caruso.

"Eight?" said Cody warily, wondering how he'd miscounted.

"Yeah," said Caruso. "Richards, Sherman, Greco, Smiley, Petlin, Barmack, plus the female and the juvenile Barmack hit when he fell. Eight."

"Eight," said Cody, relieved, "right."

"So what can you tell us about her that we don't already know?" said Max.

"Well," said Cody, "I have to go back down to Quantico and brainstorm this with the rest of the BSU team for a couple of days."

"I know," said Max, "but before you do that, what can you give us?"

"Not to put me on the spot or anything," said Cody, smiling.

"Not to put you on the spot or anything," said Max.

"Well," said Cody, "these homicides are all up-close-and-personal kinds of deaths. The offender appears to be someone all the victims knew. She's female, and only fourteen percent of known serial killers are female. She's probably blond, blue-eyed, in her mid-to-late thirties, nicely dressed. She has enough money to indulge herself in luxury rental cars and hotels, and she's probably a southpaw."

"What makes you say she's a southpaw?" said McIlheny.

"Take a look at the autopsy photos," said Cody. "Check the close-ups of the neck wounds. See this? At the end of each cut is what we call a trailer, a little tail. It break the skin but it doesn't penetrate the surface. Now in these photos the trailers indicate that the incisions were made from the victim's right to his left. Cuts like that are typically made by a left-handed person."

Max and Caruso exchanged covert glances.

"Oh, right," said Caruso. "We don't call them trailers is what threw me."

"What makes you say she's *probably* blond?" asked Max.

"Well," said Cody, "I'm not saying this means anything, but none of the head hairs recovered from the shower trap at the Ritz-Carlton crime scene were blond, and it's my impression there were no blond hairs recovered from either the Smiley or Petlin traps either."

"They recovered blond head hairs from Petlin's *carpet,* though, and from the one in the Ritz-Carlton," said Max.

"Right," said Cody, "so we know she's a blonde most of the time, but maybe not in the shower. She could be wearing a wig. It's not out of the question."

"Oh, Jesus," said Max, "don't take away her being a blonde. I mean, Christ, that's one of the few things we've got. That and her AB blood type. Maybe you don't think she's got blue eyes either."

"You mean she could be wearing blue contacts?" said Cody.

"Why not?" said Max. "And maybe it's not even a woman. Maybe it's a fuckin' *transvestite.* Why not take *everything* away from us? Why narrow down our search at all? Why not make *everyone* a suspect?"

"Calm down, Max," said McIlheny. "Nobody's saying she's not a blonde. Jim just said we shouldn't confine our thinking to blondes, that's all. Right, Jim?"

Jim, thought Max. Suddenly McIlheny and Cody were very tight.

"Right," said Cody. "So. What else do we know about her? We know she seduces her victims, probably has sex with them, cuts their throats, works their faces over, and, in the last case at least, that of Professor Richards, she urinates on them."

"She's a pisser," said Caruso. Nobody laughed.

"The whole thing is probably a revenge scenario of some kind," said Cody. "Urination is a common gesture of contempt in subcultures such as motorcycle gangs, but here the urinator has given us an inadvertent clue. Urine contains the ABO blood-grouping substances, and the urinator in this case has proven to be a secretor, which means she's among the eighty percent of the population from whose bodily fluids it's possible to identify a blood type. She's AB, which is a type found in only three percent of the population."

McIlheny nodded with satisfaction, as if this information made the killer more accessible to them.

"The Chicago police said the killer left a blood sample and a urine specimen when Dr. Sherman examined her," said Max. "The blood sample was apparently lost, but I wonder if anyone has thought of comparing the urine found on Professor Richards with the specimen she gave Sherman."

"They thought of it," said Cody with a wry smile. "Unfortunately, now they've also lost the urine specimen."

Hoots of bitter laughter from the men.

"Right," said Cody. "Well, then. What else can we project about her? Chances are she's not psychotic. The incidence of psychosis among murderers is no greater than in the general population. That is, she's probably able to distinguish between reality and fantasy at any given moment. It's safe to assume she's a psychopath, however, which means she's self-centered, narcissistic, amoral, and a master manipulator. She's incapable of feeling remorse or guilt, and she's equally incapable of feeling love, except perhaps for a pet dog or cat."

"If she's a psychopath," said Max, "doesn't that mean she's incapable of learning?"

"Well," said Cody, "that's one of the places where we part company with the therapeutic community — their idea is that psychopaths are incapable of learning, and therefore they constantly get into trouble. But we're talking about a higher level of sophistication in a psychopath here. This gal learns from her experience and gets better and better at what she does as she goes along. She doesn't learn in terms of emotional development, she just refines and modifies her behavior."

"But we've seen her take greater and greater risks as the crimes progress," said Max. "She starts off with two homicides in victims' apartments, but then she goes for one in a vacant apartment, a couple in offices after hours, and even one in her own hotel room where the chances of being apprehended were considerable. How do you figure that?"

"The risk of getting caught probably intensifies her pleasure," said Cody. "The bellboy told us when he picked up her bags she suggested he check the closet, the place she'd stashed the body. His hand was on the doorknob before she called him back. The greater the risk, the more intense the pleasure. That's a part of the pattern too."

"Christ," said Caruso.

"Chances are she replays the homicides in her mind after she does them," said Cody, "kind of like replaying a golf game in your mind. You miss a five-foot putt and your mind won't let you forget it. You replay it till you get it just right and then your mind allows you to let it go."

Nobody he was talking to had ever played golf, but they got the general drift.

"You say that she's capable of learning from her experience and modifying her behavior," said Max. "So how come she stays with the same m.o., which links her crimes together?"

"She's probably getting too much satisfaction out of the m.o. to change it at this point," said Cody.

"You think she might ultimately change it if she does more homicides?" said Max.

"She might very well modify her *conscious* m.o.," said Cody, "but not her subconscious one. And she'll never change the parts that continue to give her satisfaction. For example, I'd be very surprised if she ever changed from a knife to a gun. Most serial killers use personal weapons like knives, rather than distancing weapons like guns, out of a warped desire for intimacy. The blade gives her more contact with her victims. It increases her feelings of power and control."

"What are the chances of catching this bitch?" said Caruso.

Cody turned his palms upward.

"She might make a critical mistake—fear she's about to be caught and get into a psychopathic panic that will cause her to make a series of mistakes," said Cody. "Outside of that, gentlemen, she's pretty much free to keep killing people until she gets tired of it. The way our system or any other democratic society is set up, we have absolutely no defense against a smart and resourceful murderer."

"'Once a man has enjoyed a woman's favors, nothing is surer than that he will no longer desire them, for one does not desire what one possesses.' You know who said that, Max?"

"No, who?"

"Casanova."

"Is that right?" said Max, yawning. "What's the point, Susan? You're saying I don't desire you anymore because I've enjoyed your favors?"

That did it. The yawn as much as the hideous, bored question he'd just asked. She had a flash of terrifying clarity: his rapidly waning interest, the withdrawal of his love, the letting her down easy, the absolute suffocating wordless scream of being totally abandoned. It was too late to save him, but not too late to save herself.

"Oh, no," she said, "quite the contrary."

"Pardon me?"

"Quite the contrary," she said. "It's *I* who don't desire *you* anymore."

Max got up on one elbow.

"You want to run that past me again?"

"With pleasure," she said. "You're an amusing young man, Max, and we've had some enjoyable evenings together, but now they're beginning to pall. I don't wish to be your lover anymore."

"I think I know what's happening here," said Max. "You figured I was getting tired of you, so you decided to dump me first. That it?"

"Dear boy," she said, cupping his face. "Sometimes you seem so young. It's *over*, Max. How did Dorothy Parker put it? 'By the time you swear you're his / Shivering and sighing / And he vows his passion is / Infinite, undying . . . / One of you is lying.' *I* was lying the other night when I said I was feeling ill and wanted you to leave. I wasn't ill, dear, I just wanted you to leave."

Perfect. The "dear boy" and the cupping his face and the blatant patronization were absolutely dead perfect. Keep it going, she thought.

"You wanted me to leave because you asked me about our future and I was evasive," he said, beginning to wonder if there were something seriously off in his perceptions then or now.

"Do you remember my telling you about the comedienne who said she'd found the perfect way of letting a man down easily by saying, 'I want to marry you and have your child'?"

"Yeah."

"That's what I was doing with *you*, love," she said. "Why do you think I had you bring your child to dinner? Why do you think I asked you about our future? Because I want to get married? *Please*." She laughed richly. "J.B. Priestley said, 'Marriage is like paying an endless visit in your worst clothes.' If I had wanted to get married, Max, I would have, I assure you."

"I'm not sure I'm getting this," said Max. "You're saying you asked me about our future and had me bring my child to dinner because you wanted to scare me away?"

"Exactly," she said, a pitying smile on her face.

Max stared at her. It was too ironic. Tonight was the night he had planned to start scaling down, tell her they'd been going at it a little too intensely and he just wanted a little time to cool off, to cut down from every night to maybe twice a week. Now it was *she* who was giving *him* the old heave-ho. He did not feel relief. He felt that somebody had stepped on his chest and crushed it.

"Listen," he said, "I can understand it if you want to cool off a little. Maybe that's not such a bad idea. Maybe we need time to think. Why don't we cut down from every night to, say, twice a week?"

She frowned and laughed and shook her head.

"Max, Max, Max, you're not listening to me, darling. I don't want to cut *down*, I want to cut *off*. I don't want us to see each other anymore."

"You're serious?" he said. "You're absolutely serious?"

"Absolutely."

"All right," he said, getting out of bed, scrambling into his clothes, feeling suddenly awkward and foolish to be naked in the sight of a woman who no longer found him attractive. "I'm going."

*   *   *

294

When Max left she pressed her ear to the cold metal door, listening for the elevator that would take him down the shaft and away from her bed forever. Then she wept so loudly she frightened the cat.

It had been a brilliant performance. Sarah Bernhardt herself couldn't have done it more convincingly. The Parker and Priestley quotes offset the hideous blunder of the one from Casanova. And telling him she'd asked about their future and invited Sam to dinner to scare him away was nothing short of genius.

She went to the liquor cabinet and took out the bottle of Absolut. If she could just manage to get through the next twenty-four hours without dying of heartbreak, she'd survive.

87

He was still in a state of disbelief when he emerged from Susan's building and hit the street. By the time he got back to Natale's apartment it finally sank in. Susan and he had broken up. Susan had actually dumped him. *She* had dumped *him*. He had been so certain she was in love with him, it was difficult to register that he'd been dumped.

He still thought it possible that she'd suspected he was losing interest in her, which was true, and had dumped him before he could do it to her. If that were the case then she still loved him and, at least theoretically, it should be possible to get her back.

Assuming he *wanted* her back. Why in fucking hell didn't he just thank his lucky stars she'd relieved him of the burden and the guilt of gently getting rid of her? Why didn't he just go back to Babette and Sam and forget her?

Because she was exotic, for one thing. She wasn't much older than he was, but she was infinitely more sophisticated. She knew about fancy restaurants and gourmet food and wine and had money and access to a life he would never experience without her. Maybe that was part of it —the unfulfilled fantasy of having her show him the good life, the easy life that city cops only glimpsed from the edges.

Then there was the sex. Sex with Susan, especially that first night, had been the most exciting of his life. She was wilder, more aggressive, more responsive, more perverse than Babette or anyone else he'd ever slept with. Even if the last couple of times they'd made love left something to be desired, he knew that the other was there to be tapped.

And there was also his ego. He couldn't accept the idea that she had dumped him. It was an outrage. How *dare* she do that to him? If anybody was going to break off their relationship it should have been

Max. Standing there in her bedroom, putting on his clothes, and being looked at naked and without love by a woman who had just rejected him made him feel like some pitiful loser shmuck.

He hated the feeling. He hated her for making him feel that way. If she had truly gotten tired of him and truly wanted to break it off, surely there were kinder ways than pressuring him to get serious and then inviting his *son* to her house for dinner. If only for what she had put Sam through at that detestable dinner, he hated her guts. What was worse, he still wanted her back.

Max came in and slammed the door so hard the dishes in the kitchen cabinet clattered.

"Had a good time tonight, I see," said Natale dryly.

"She fucking *dumped* me," said Max, "can you fucking believe that?"

Natale squinted.

"Who dumped you?" he said. "Susan?"

"No, Michelle fucking Pfeiffer. Who the fuck you think I've been out with?"

"How could she dump you?" said Natale. "I thought she was *insane* about you. I thought she was pressuring you to *marry* her."

"That's what I'm saying, Tony — she was insane about me, she was pressuring me to *marry* her. How the fuck could she have dumped me?"

"Maybe you misunderstood her."

"Oh, right," said Max, "I misunderstood her. I happen to have total recall for personally demeaning remarks. Here are some direct quotes, Tony, I've got them memorized. Quote number one: 'I don't wish to be your lover anymore.' Quote number two: 'I don't want to cut *down,* I want to cut *off.*' Quote number three: 'It's *over,* Max.' And then I got to hear a couple of swell quotes about love and marriage from Dorothy Parker and J.D. Priestley. Who the fuck is J.D. Priestley?"

"J.B. Some British playwright," said Natale. "Jesus, I can't believe it. You poor sonofabitch. You must feel like a real piece of shit. I'm really sorry, man."

"Yeah," said Max, "thanks, Tony. I wish I could say that helped."

"Christ, you look even worse today," said Caruso. "What happened now?"

"We broke up," said Max. "She dumped me. It's finished."

"You and Babette?" said Caruso. "Jeez, I'm real sorry to hear that."

"Not me and Babette, asshole, me and *Susan*."

"You and *Susan?* You broke up with fucking Susan and you're not jumping for fucking joy? Give me a fucking *break*. You don't know what lucky is. Getting rid of that phony piece of shit is as good as winning the Lotto. *Better*."

"Thanks for being so sensitive to a colleague's pain," said Max.

Every time she did two-handed pull-downs, the chain attached to the bar that she held raised a stack of weights in front of her. Every time she released the bar upward it lowered the stack of weights in front of her. Each time the weights were lowered, a long, pointed steel spike descended through a tunnel of round holes in all the weights that weren't being raised. It gave her pleasure to imagine that the spike was descending each time through the neck of Max Segal.

"Wow, you're really *cookin'* today, Judy," said Ronnie, the trainer with the man's build and the woman's breasts. "You have a good time last night or what?"

"Not exactly," said Judy. "I broke up with my boyfriend."

"Whoa," said Ronnie. "What happened? You catch him with his hand in your best friend's pants?"

"No," said Judy, "I just realized he was a snake like all men, so I decided to get rid of him before he tried to hurt me."

"Smart move!" said Ronnie. "The last thing you need is some scumbag dickhead asshole shitting all over you."

"Right," said Judy.

"Men are good for one thing, and one thing only," said Ronnie. "It just so happens a zucchini is better at it, though, and it don't go to sleep on ya right afterwards or forget to callya the next day either."

"Right," said Judy.

"So tell me," said Ronnie, leaning forward eagerly, "how'd ya do it to him?"

Judy smiled.

"I just told him I was tired of him and didn't want to see him again," she said.

"Yeah?" said Ronnie, wanting more.

"At first he didn't believe me," said Judy. "He thought maybe we ought to cut down to twice a week. Twice a week, right?"

"Right," said Ronnie, anticipating the punchline.

"I said, 'Read my *lips,* dickhead, I don't want to *see* you again.'"

"You actually used those words?" cried Ronnie delightedly.

"As God is my witness," said Judy.

Ronnie emitted a shriek of animal joy and gave Judy a high-five that almost shattered her hand.

Caruso wouldn't have admitted it to anybody, least of all to Cody, but he'd been impressed with how the FBI man was conducting his investigation.

At various times Caruso himself had considered applying to the Bureau, but he'd somehow never quite gotten around to it. He secretly doubted he had the academic ability, and after a while he realized he was probably too old, and then he'd forgotten about it altogether.

He was intrigued by what Cody seemed to know about profiling. Although it was based on a lot of psychological bullshit that he didn't believe on principle, some things Cody had said about psychopaths certainly rang true.

He'd been impressed by what Cody called trailers and how Cody felt they indicated the killer was left-handed. Not that left-handed people were so unusual. He was left-handed himself. So was his kid brother. So was his father. So were two of the detectives in the squad, Hicks and Rafferty. So was that twat reporter from *New York* magazine, Susan Simon.

Susan Simon. What a phony. He had taken an instant dislike to her that was as intense as Max's hots for her. Thank Christ she'd dumped Max, although he couldn't think why. It was his impression her hots for Max were even greater than Max's were for her.

Caruso wasn't impressed by *everything* Cody had said, though. Like the stuff about the perp maybe wearing a wig and not being a blonde. He didn't blame Max for jumping all over him on that one. Although, to be fair about it, if they really hadn't recovered a single blond hair from the traps where she'd showered, it wasn't impossible the perp was wearing a wig the rest of the time.

Christ, that would really fuck them up, if they had to start all over again, looking for a woman with dark hair. Brown or black hair was what most women had, not red, certainly. So dark hair and—O.K., why not go the whole route that Max half-seriously suggested—brown eyes.

A well-dressed woman in her mid-to-late thirties, with long, dark hair and brown eyes, who was left-handed. What did that look like? It looked like Susan Simon, that's what.

Susan Simon. Wouldn't *that* be a pisser! Oh, if only it were possible. How he'd love to nail her ass to the wall. There was about as much chance of the killer being Susan Simon as there was of Caruso's being invited to the Pope's wedding.

On the other hand, maybe it wasn't so far-fetched after all. The fact that CSU found a latent print in Petlin's apartment that proved to be Susan's didn't mean dick by itself—they'd also found Max's and Caruso's—but put that together with other things, like her being left-handed and her knowing about the S and M equipment in Petlin's drawer, and maybe it meant something after all.

How he was going to put her together with Smiley, Petlin, and Barmack, much less the three in Illinois, he didn't know. It might not be a red-hot lead, but if it was even lukewarm it was better than anything they had going at the moment.

"Hey, Max, Susan ever happen to mention where she grew up?"

"What?"

"Susan ever mention growing up in Chicago or going to college at the University of Illinois, anything like that?"

A massive sigh.

"What're you getting at, Sal? You think Susan is the blond woman? You think Susan Simon is our fucking killer?"

"Max, why don't you open your eyes and see that twat for what she is?"

"Sal, why don't you take a flying fuck at a rolling doughnut?"

90

Desperate times called for desperate measures and Max was getting desperate. It was unthinkable to him that Susan had cut him off. Just when they were beginning to build something together, just when they were beginning to find out if they could have a future together. He had to get her back at any cost.

He knew it was probably irrational, but he felt as though he couldn't survive without her. He needed her warmth, her understanding, her affection, her sophistication, her erudition, her . . . body. He felt that what he'd had with her that first delirious night could never be recaptured with any body but hers.

He had to get her back at any cost. When he got her back, then he would decide whether he wanted to keep her. He would make her an offer she couldn't refuse. Desperate times called for desperate measures.

91

"Murder is the easiest crime to get away with," said Max Segal, a detective from Manhattan North Homicide investigating the still-unsolved tragic slayings of Irving Smiley and Frederick Petlin which occurred early last month. "That's because it's so hard to make a homicide arrest that'll stand up in court. We're in a numbers game — cops have to maintain a high clearance rate on murder cases, but the D.A. has to maintain a high rate of convictions. We're all more interested in our batting averages than in justice."

The abrasive young detective, who punctuated his phrases by trying to suck particles of pizza from between his crooked teeth, explained the system of justice to a reporter whom he'd taken on an illegal joyride up to Harlem to investigate what he termed a grounder — cops' baseball-oriented slang for an easily-solved murder case.

The system works differently up in Harlem, of course. It's a fact that if a defendant asks to see an attorney you can no longer interrogate him or you are violating his civil rights, yet this reporter overheard three young Black men, accused of a shooting on 110th Street, repeatedly request an attorney and repeatedly be ignored. The cops' cynical attitude, Segal confided to me, was that in court their defense attorney would assume their civil rights had been violated anyway, so there was nothing to be gained by not violating them. . . .

Joan Didion had been right — a reporter's presence always did run counter to people's best interests, a reporter was always selling somebody out.

She took a long swallow of vodka from the glass on the desk and looked over her manuscript. The phone rang. She wondered whether

304

to answer it or let the machine pick it up. She decided to let the machine pick it up. At the beep the caller began speaking:

"Uh, hi, Susan, it's Max. I've been thinking a lot about—"

Heart pounding, she picked up the receiver.

"This is Susan," she said. Flat voice. Give the bastard nothing.

"*Susan.* Oh, hi. It's Max. As I started telling your machine, I've been thinking a lot about our discussion last night, and, well, I've come to certain realizations about our situation."

"Yes?" Still the flat voice. Good.

"Well," he said, "assuming I was right in thinking, you know, that the reason you wanted us to stop seeing each other was that you felt I wasn't serious about you. . . ."

He had paused to get corroboration that his assumption was correct. To give him that corroboration would cost her too dearly. She said nothing.

"Well," he continued, uncorroborated, "I can certainly understand how, if you were serious about me, how you'd want some indication that your feelings were being, you know, reciprocated and everything. I mean, I think that's only fair . . ."

He sounded tortured, desperate. She couldn't believe it. Sooner or later, she thought, they all come round. All you have to do is treat them badly.

"So, uh, what I've decided," he continued, "after a lot of soul-searching, is the following. I am prepared to—"

"Max, I'm sorry but I've got another call waiting. Is this going to take very long?"

"Uh, no, not . . . no," he said, obviously a little ticked, although not enough to tell her to go fuck herself. "O.K., I'll be brief. Here it is, Susan. I'm not even officially separated yet, but to let you know I'm serious about you, I am prepared—provided you're willing to resume seeing me again, that is—I'm prepared to set up a tentative schedule under which I will, uh, cause certain significant things to occur—"

"What sort of significant things are you talking about, Max?"

Her heart was thundering so loudly in her ears she couldn't hear. Her skin had started to prickle all over, and a definite tingling had begun to take place between her legs. She took another swallow of vodka.

"Uh, well, things like, uh, making the separation formal," he said, "and, uh, actually going out and getting a lawyer involved and starting the whole divorce thing rolling, and then, uh, ultimately, you know, announcing our, uh . . . our engagement."

Announcing our engagement! She felt weak. She placed one hand against the top of her desk to brace herself. She didn't know whether she was going to have an orgasm or fall to the floor in a faint. She took another swallow.

"Susan? Are you still there?"

Speak. Say something. You must be able to form words and utter them aloud.

"I think that you . . . merely want what you can no longer have," was what she was finally able to put together.

"No," he said, "that's not it. That's not it at all. I know it might look that way, but that's not what I feel for you at all."

"What," she asked, "*do* you feel for me?"

"Love," he said, his voice breaking slightly. "I love you, Susan. I want to marry you. I want you to be my wife."

She began to throb and pulsate between her legs. It was entirely possible that she *would* be able to achieve orgasm during this conversation. The man was clearly insane. Were he a stranger, she might pity him.

"And do you want me physically too?" she said.

"Yes," he said, "I want you physically too. I want you so much I can taste it."

"Really?" she said, taking another swallow, her hand beginning to shake, her body buzzing with electricity. "What can you taste?"

"Your pussy," he said a little breathlessly. "I can almost taste your pussy."

"Can you?" she said, her voice strange and choked. "Please listen to me, Max . . ."

"Yes?"

"I do not want you. I do not love you. I do not want to be your wife. I feel nothing whatsoever for you anymore, and I wish you not to . . . call me or write me or attempt to see me or . . . contact me in any way."

"Susan, please, just *listen* to me —"

She slammed down the receiver just as the shuddering waves of orgasm began to overwhelm her.

"So," said Natale, "any fast-breaking news on the Susan Simon story?"

"Uh, no, nothing much," said Max, hoping he wouldn't pursue it.

"Nothing *much?*" said Natale. "Is that 'nothing much,' as in 'something happened, but you're gonna have to pull it out of me'?"

"I, uh, did talk to her on the phone today," said Max casually, "but it was, you know, not very conclusive."

"You called her or she called *you?*"

"Oh, no, I called her," said Max.

Natale winced and shook his head.

"And?" he said.

"Oh, you know," said Max, "we talked about it pretty thoroughly, and what we decided, we pretty much decided to give it a rest for a while. I mean, she's sort of broken up about the whole thing and she kind of needs to get her head together."

"In other words," said Natale, "you called up, demeaned yourself by begging for her to come back, and she refused."

Max nodded sheepishly, his face getting terribly flushed.

"Did you offer to marry her?" Natale inquired quietly.

"What do you do, tap the fucking phone?" said Max, so humiliated he couldn't look his friend directly in the eye.

"No," said Natale, "but I've been there myself, plus which I treat a lot of sick puppies in my profession. And you're a very sick puppy, my friend."

"You don't know how much it helps for you to tell me that," said Max.

"So what are you planning to do, Max, keep pursuing her, keep begging her to come back, keep demeaning yourself till you have no self-respect left at all?"

"No, of course not. I hope not. I don't know," he said miserably. "I don't even know why I want her back at this point."

"Because you can't have her. Because she's finally gotten smart enough to treat you as badly as you think you deserve to be treated. And the more you pursue her, the worse she's gonna treat you."

"You're probably right."

"There's no probably about it. Forget her, Max. Go back to Babette. Or find somebody else. You want to have Cheryl fix you up with one of her hot young friends?"

"No."

"Why not?"

"Because. I'm not looking for sex."

"What are you looking for, love?"

"Maybe."

"'Love is the delusion that one woman differs from another'—H.L. Mencken. 'Many a man has fallen in love with a girl in a light so dim he would not have chosen a suit by it'—Maurice Chevalier."

"Now *you're* giving me quotes?"

"Yeah, and here's one from Freud, who said being in love 'at times takes the form of a mild psychosis.' I want you to promise me you'll give up this obsession with Susan, because that's what it is, Max, an obsession."

"I know."

"Will you promise me that?"

"Sure."

"Don't say 'sure,' say, 'As God is my witness, Tony, I promise I will give up my obsession with Susan.'"

"As God is my witness, Tony, I promise I will give up my obsession with Susan."

"You're full of shit."

"I know it."

93

"Boss, you got a minute?"

"Sure, Sal, what's up?"

"I been thinkin' about something relative to the Smiley and Petlin cases," said Caruso, "and I just wanted to bounce it off you."

"Go ahead."

"O.K., well, what I been thinkin' is, here we are bustin' our hump lookin' for blonde broads with blue eyes for I don't know how long, right? And I got to thinkin', what if Cody's idea about the blonde not being a blonde isn't as fulla shit as we thought. I mean, what if I got a long shot of an idea of a brunette who I like for a suspect, only I got nothin' to back it up yet?"

"Go get something to back it up. Go interview her."

"Yeah, I know, only what if she hates me and wouldn't consent to the interview?"

"Go get Segal."

"What if she hates Segal even worse than me?"

"Go get Haggerty or Hicks or Rafferty or Ruiz. Who's your suspect?"

"It's a real long shot, boss."

"Who is your suspect, Sal?"

"Susan Simon."

"The reporter?"

"Yeah."

"What the hell makes her a suspect?"

Caruso shrugged.

"A hunch."

"A *hunch?*"

"Yeah. Plus she knew about the S and M equipment in Petlin's apartment and nobody told her. Plus she's a southpaw. Plus I read her as wrong the first time I met her."

McIlheny stared at Caruso for a moment as if he hadn't heard him.

"Are you out of your mind?" said McIlheny in a terrible calm voice. "Are you seriously suggesting we tell a member of the press that she's a suspect in a murder case just because she's a southpaw and you have a *hunch?* A member of the press who is, by the way, neither blonde nor blue-eyed? Do you have any idea of the can of worms you're thinking of opening up there? Do you? Get *real,* Caruso."

It was a mistake to go to McIlheny. He should never have done it. Susan Simon knew he hated her and would never talk to him. And now that she and Max were busted up she wouldn't talk to him either. One of the other guys in the squad could do it under the pretense that they were helping her with her research, but it would be very tricky. If she thought she was a suspect she'd get rid of anything incriminating that might be in her apartment.

If she really was the killer, Caruso might be able to find something in her apartment to incriminate her. But if they started snooping around, she'd destroy it before they ever got a search warrant.

Sometimes you could claim justification for a warrantless search — if there was an emergency, if lives were in danger, if it was night and no judge could be found to issue a warrant. Certainly none of those was true here.

He could watch her and learn when she was out, slip into the building, and jimmy the lock to her apartment, but that would taint the case, of course. Even if he found absolute fucking proof in her apartment that she was the killer, an illegal search would make it impossible to ever get an indictment against her, and no D.A. in the world would ever touch it. She'd go scot free.

The thing was to dig around a little and get something that linked her to the homicides without either tainting the case or causing her to become suspicious.

"Doc, lemme askya something. A purely hypothetical question, O.K.?" said Caruso.

"O.K.," said Aram Kaprilian.

"Let's say I'm looking to link somebody to a case and they don't fit the description of the suspect, but I just got a wild hair up my ass they might be who we're lookin' for. What could I do?"

"Are there fingerprints you could match? Blood, hair, fibers? Anything like that?"

"No fingerprints," said Caruso, "but there's a few hairs, and let's say there's also ABO blood grouping from a urine specimen. Oh, and let's also say there's a blood sample that a lab in Chicago lost and then found again. What could I do with that? Hypothetically?"

"Hypothetically?" said Kaprilian, pushing against the bridge of his glasses with his forefinger and sliding the skin of his nose out from underneath it with his thumb and third finger.

"Yeah."

"Well," said Kaprilian, "if you could manage to get any cellular material from the suspect to match against the blood sample from Chicago — like at least ten hairs with intact root sheaths, or a dried blood stain at least the size of a quarter, or even dried saliva on a cigarette butt — you could do DNA fingerprinting."

"What the hell's that?"

"DNA fingerprinting?" said Kaprilian. "Only the hottest new thing in forensic science, Sal. It's going to revolutionize forensic science the way that fingerprinting did at the beginning of this century. It's about a thousand times more accurate in identifying suspects than the most precise blood-typing tests."

"No kidding," said Caruso. "So if I got you hair or blood from a suspect, could you do DNA fingerprinting in the lab here?"

"No," said Kaprilian. "No public agency is equipped to do it yet. The FBI is spending a fortune to develop its own system and they could eventually take over the field, but for now only three private companies in this country do DNA fingerprinting — Cellmark Diagnostics in Maryland a company called Cetus somewhere in California, and Lifecodes right here in Valhalla, New York, on the Sawmill River Parkway. These companies hold patents on three different probes — there's no no standardization yet. They've been doing lots of business in paternity suits, and now they're starting to work on rape and homicide cases too."

"If I got you a sample," said Caruso, "could you get it to the company on the Sawmill River Parkway?"

"It's an expensive procedure, Sal — it costs anywhere from eight hundred to a thousand bucks," said Kaprilian. "An assistant D.A.

would have to authorize it. You'd have to show him enough to convince him to authorize it."

"If I had enough to convince an assistant D.A. to authorize it," said Caruso, "why the fuck would I need to do DNA fingerprinting?"

"Good point," said Kaprilian.

"O.K.," said Caruso, "let's say I can get him to authorize it. How the hell does it work?"

"Well," said Kaprilian, "DNA is a three-foot-long double-stranded microscopically thin chemical strip, tightly wound inside every cell of our bodies. It's the famous double helix discovered by Watson and Crick in 1953, O.K.?"

"O.K.," said Caruso.

"The three billion bits of DNA in the double helix are the genetic blueprint that produces a human body," said Kaprilian. "DNA is made up of forty-six chromosomes — twenty-three of them contributed by the mother's egg, twenty-three by the father's sperm. Every cell derived from that fertilized egg is going to have the identical DNA. You with me so far?"

"Absolutely," said Caruso.

"Good," said Kaprilian. "O.K., so the DNA in each cell holds a lot of information, a staggering amount of information. Some sequences of it tell the body how to make a nose, a lung, a toe, a gall bladder, and so on, and those sections are the same for everybody, O.K.?"

"O.K.," said Caruso.

"But some sequences in the DNA chain," said Kaprilian, "whose function isn't clearly understood yet, repeat themselves incessantly in a kind of genetic stutter. These sections are called polymorphisms, or junk DNA, and they vary so widely from person to person that there's virtually no possibility that any two people in the world — except identical twins — will have the same pattern."

"Who thought all this up?" said Caruso.

"A British geneticist at the University of Leicester named Dr. Alec Jeffrys," said Kaprilian. "In 1985 he discovered a way to isolate enough bands of this junk DNA to produce a DNA fingerprint. His discovery enabled Scotland Yard to solve the rape-murders of two fifteen-year-old girls in the Leicestershire countryside. Do you remember reading about that?"

"Uh . . . yeah," said Caruso. "They ever use it in this country?"

Kaprilian nodded.

312

"In November of 1987," said Kaprilian, "DNA fingerprinting was instrumental in convicting a serial rapist in Orlando, Florida. You read anything about that?"

Caruso shook his head.

"If I read at all anymore," he said, "it's about homicides, not rapes. I don't have time to read for pleasure."

Kaprilian looked at him to see if he were kidding. Caruso's face betrayed nothing and he wasn't known to have a sense of humor, so Kaprilian didn't laugh.

"O.K.," he said, "let me see if I can explain DNA fingerprinting in layman's terms. First, DNA is extracted from cells of blood or semen left at a crime scene, right?"

"Right."

"Next, special restriction enzymes — molecular scissors, if you will — snip the DNA into different sized fragments. Next, these fragments are placed on a glass slide in an agarose gel and exposed to an electric field. The gel acts as a sieve, separating the fragments according to length. The shorter fragments move farther across the slide than the longer ones, forming a pattern of invisible bands. The invisible band pattern is transferred to a nylon membrane by a process known as Southern blotting. The nylon membrane with the DNA material is then put into a solution containing radioactive DNA probes — short sequences of lab-made DNA that stick wherever they find complementary sequences on the DNA strands. You with me so far?"

"No problem," said Caruso.

"Good," said Kaprilian. "Then X-ray film is exposed to the now-radioactive DNA. On the film appears a pattern of black bands which is finally visible to the eye. The band pattern — which looks like the bar code on boxes of detergent in the supermarket — is called a DNA fingerprint, and it can be compared to other DNA fingerprints made from the blood of a criminal suspect. And that's really about all there is to it."

"How about that," said Caruso. "And this stuff is really foolproof, huh, Doc?"

Kaprilian smiled.

"If you leave DNA material at the scene of a crime," he said, "it will soon be like leaving your name, address, and social security number."

94

The human body, Caruso mused, ingests food and processes it into shit. The human home ingests purchases from drugstores and super-markets and processes them into bags of garbage. Garbage contains the most intimate and revealing artifacts of people's lives — artifacts that, if illegally seized while in the home, taint cases and set guilty perps free. But once those artifacts have been put in garbage bags and placed on the street, the courts have ruled they belong to anybody who wants them.

Caruso knew she was home. He'd seen her enter almost three hours be-fore, carrying a bag of groceries. How long did it take to cook dinner, eat it, clean up, and put out the garbage? There was definitely a sanita-tion pick-up on this block tomorrow morning, he'd made sure of that, so waiting across the street from her apartment building was a decent gamble. Unless, of course, she didn't put out her garbage every night.

Caruso slumped down lower in the driver's seat of his old Chevy station wagon. It was after ten P.M. He had already worked a day tour and was technically off duty. Staking out Susan Simon's apartment on a half-baked hunch, waiting for her to throw out her garbage, wasn't going to earn him a cent in overtime. He preferred to think of it as a hobby. If he couldn't think of it as a hobby, he would have to think of it as an obsession.

Max was taking an after-dinner stroll, nothing more than that. The fact that it was a balmy spring night and that he was sorely in need of exercise was somewhat offset by the fact that where he'd chosen to take his after-dinner stroll was roughly sixty blocks uptown of where he'd had dinner.

He moseyed up First Avenue to Fifty-second and turned east. Say, this block looks familiar. Isn't this . . . why, mercy me, what a coincidence. Here I am, just taking a stroll after dinner and where should I find myself but on the very block where a former lover of mine happens to reside. Well, as long as I'm here, I might as well meander on down the block past her apartment. Maybe I'll catch sight of her going in or coming out, and if she's alone, maybe somebody will suggest having a drink or a cup of coffee or something, you never know.

If she's alone. What would he do if she were with some guy? What if the guy was attractive and they were holding hands or something to indicate she was intimate with him? Would he go berserk and do something really stupid? Of course not. He would never do anything stupid. He was a New York City homicide cop. And the fact that he was required to carry a loaded weapon at all times, on duty or off, made him even more reluctant to do stupid things than he would be ordinarily.

Now he was at mid-block. Now he was passing in front of her building. Now he was peering up at her windows, trying to catch a glimpse of her. He counted floors from the street to make sure the windows he was peering up at were the right ones. They were.

She was home, she was definitely home. The windows were lit. It was, let's see, eleven-forty. She'd be done with dinner by now, finished watching the eleven o'clock news, maybe tuned to Carson. Maybe getting ready for bed. Maybe wearing only revealing underthings as she padded about her apartment, maybe only a pair of panties. Maybe totally naked. It was, after all, a warm night. He could visualize that. God, could he ever.

The guy walking up the street had stopped outside her building. Now he was looking up at the building, maybe trying to see something in the windows. The guy was awfully familiar looking. The guy was his fucking partner, Max! Fucking Max was standing outside her fucking building, waiting to catch a peek at the woman who had fucking dumped him. The poor sick fuck!

Caruso slid down so low in his seat he couldn't be seen. The last thing he needed now was to be made by his lovesick partner and have to explain what he was doing there. Fucking Max wouldn't be too thrilled about being caught there himself. What if fucking Susan came down with her fucking garbage while fucking Max was standing there gawking up at the fucking windows? What then?

Fucking Max moved on. Caruso shifted his position on the station wagon seat enough to track Max to the end of the block. Max looked about, turned around, and came back. Shit!

When he passed in front of her building again Max stopped. For a moment Caruso feared his demented partner was going to go right up the walk, enter the building, and ring her bell, but if that was what Max was thinking he resisted it. Max continued walking back toward First, then finally hung a turn downtown and disappeared. Whew!

Twenty-three minutes later Susan Simon left her building carrying a brown bag of garbage. She set it carefully down on the curb beside three others, went back inside, and closed the door.

Six minutes later Caruso cautiously got out of the station wagon, looked both ways to make sure the coast was clear, then ambled across the street. He picked up the bag of garbage and hot-footed it back to his car.

He was extremely pleased with himself and with his bag of garbage. So far his gamble was paying off.

Two soft black bananas clinging to a common stem. The box, safety seal, and cotton from a bottle of Extra-Strength Tylenol. Shards from a shattered sixty-watt lightbulb. The carcass of a grapefruit. Two empty cans of Fancy Feast catfood. A flesh-colored Band-Aid, the sticky ends pressed together.

The carcass of a small roasted chicken. A crumpled grocery list. A wilted head of Boston lettuce. An empty container of coffee-flavored Dannon yogurt. An empty bottle of Perrier. A dried tube of G. Sen Mat Satin makeup by Stendhal.

Solicitations from six charities, one of them marked "Final Notice!" Three printed inserts from utility and credit card bills, explaining their newest and most convenient computerized formats yet. Four letters of congratulations from companies notifying her that she had won a Lincoln Continental, a week in Honolulu, ten million dollars in cash, and a wallet-sized personal calculator. A used tampon rolled up in a thick wad of toilet paper.

"Paydirt!" said Kaprilian, pointing to the tampon with the forefinger of his surgically gloved hand, then using his thumb and third finger to push the bows of his glasses back to his nose.

"You'll send the tampon out for DNA fingerprinting?" said Caruso hopefully.

"And the Band-Aid," said Kaprilian. "But first we'll type the blood here."

"How soon will it be before we know something?"

"The process takes anywhere from two to four weeks," said Kaprilian.

"Two to four *weeks,*" said Caruso. "I need it one helluva lot sooner than that."

"I'll see if I can lean on them a little," said Kaprilian. "Have you gotten an assistant D.A. to authorize this yet?"

"Um, yeah," said Caruso. "Definitely. Well, more or less."

96

It was lovely. She'd rejected him and he'd come crawling back to her and she'd been able to devastate him with the lie that she no longer wanted him. It was lovely but it was not enough.

She could think of nothing but the way in which she'd miraculously seized power in a relationship gone rotten and of what she could do with it now that she had it. She ached for him, despite knowing his obsession with her was based on sickness.

She spent all day and all night, in dreams and in prewakeful states, fantasizing things to do with him. She didn't want him back. She couldn't let him go. She was tied to him in a bond more intimate than marriage. For the first time, and for probably not very long — she knew men better than to kid herself about that — Max Segal was *hers*. For this magical period during which he was under her spell she could do anything she wanted with him. She didn't know what she wanted. She had known what to do with her other exes, but with Max she was ambivalent.

What might decide it for her was to have some time alone with him, away from the stresses of the city. A weekend perhaps, where she could scrutinize him at close range and try to determine exactly how damaged he was and what, if anything, could be salvaged. A weekend in a potentially romantic setting, where whichever way she decided to go would work.

She started doing research.

97

"Degraded yourself with Susan lately?" said Natale, entering the apartment.

"No," said Max, giving him the finger.

"Sure?" said Natale. "No more humiliating phone calls begging her to take you back? No tortured, supplicating letters hand delivered to her mailbox? No bouquets of long-stemmed red roses with melodramatically worded cards? No furtive strolls past her apartment at odd hours of the night, peeking into her windows, hoping for chance encounters on the street?"

"Fuck you," said Max.

"Aha!"

"Fuck you," said Max.

"I only ask because I love you," said Natale.

"Take your love and shove it up your ass."

"Isn't that a country and western song title? Listen, if you were spending half the energy on the Petlin and Smiley cases that you spend on your obsession with Susan you'd have collared the blond woman by now single-handedly."

"Nobody's *ever* going to collar the blond woman," said Max. "The blond woman is going to keep slicing the throats of middle-class professional men in New York and Illinois till she's too old to wield a knife. The blond woman will take her place in the serial murderers hall of fame along with Jack the Ripper, the Boston Strangler, the Hillside Strangler, Son of Sam, Wayne Williams, John Wayne Gacy, Henry Lee Lucas, Ted Bundy . . ."

"Dennis Nilsen . . ." said Natale.

"Dennis Nilsen?"

320

"*You* remember Dennis Nilsen," said Natale. "The guy that propped up the stiffs he'd killed at his dining table so he'd have company at dinner?"

"Oh, *that* Dennis Nilsen," said Max.

"And let's not forget Jerry Brudos," said Natale, "who used his victims' breasts as paperweights. Or Ed Gein, who liked to lounge around the house in his victims' skins. But my favorite is still Ed Kemper."

"The guy from Santa Cruz?" said Max.

"Ed Kemper is my all-time hero," said Natale.

"Get out of here," said Max. "Not more than Gacy?"

"Don't get me wrong," said Natale, "I *love* Gacy. Gacy could not only sodomize and kill three dozen boys and bury them under his house, he was also a man big enough to dress up like a clown and go to hospitals to entertain sick kids. I do love that."

"And I *hope* you're not forgetting what Gacy said when they collared him," said Max.

"He never thought they'd get him for murder, he thought they'd get him for operating a funeral home without a license. I do love a sense of humor in a serial killer, but Kemper is still my hero."

"What's so great about Kemper?"

"Well," said Natale, "Kemper picked up coeds in his car, killed them, fucked them, dismembered them, and then he —"

"Wait," said Max, "he fucked them, then he killed them? Or he killed them, *then* he fucked them?"

"He killed them, *then* he fucked them."

"Oh, *that* makes sense," said Max.

"After that he killed his mom," said Natale. "Beheaded her, fucked her head, cut out her larynx, and put it down the disposal because he was sick of her yammering at him."

"So it was justifiable homicide."

"I've seen the interview tapes," said Natale. "The man's a prince. Brilliant, articulate, psychologically savvy, *and* he has a sense of humor."

"You can see that from what he did with his mom's larynx."

"Two psychiatrists examined him in-depth after his release from Atascadero — after he'd killed his grandparents when he was a teen? At the time of the examinations he had a coupla gals' heads hidden in his apartment. Both shrinks gave him a clean bill of health. One said Kemper was less of a threat to society than his motorcycle."

"Yeah, those motorcycles can be dangerous as shit."

"The thing about Kemper, though, is how *nice* he was. He's the kinda guy you wouldn't mind knockin' back a few beers with periodically. Liked cops, too. Drank with the Santa Cruz cops at the cop bar practically every night the year he was doing the coeds. Cops didn't even believe him the first coupla times he tried to give himself up to them. He was too nice. The D.A. who prosecuted him said, 'Ed Kemper is the nicest mass murderer I've ever met.'"

"O.K., O.K.," said Max, "you've convinced me. Kemper's nicer than Gacy. And he is definitely in the serial killers hall of fame. Now what's it gonna take to get the blond woman in there with the guys?"

"I dunno," said Natale. "Maybe killing somebody really interesting."

"Like who?"

"Like you."

Outside on the sidewalk, across the street, looking up at the windows, she could easily make out the two men as they passed back and forth in front of the living room windows.

One of the men was Max, of course, the other was the man he was staying with, Anthony Natale. Natale, she had learned from her research, was a police psychologist. He was divorced from his wife of twenty years and was sleeping with a succession of women half his age. A fitting companion for Max. It was not likely the world would miss either one of them were they to die.

98

The body of Max Segal, thirty-two, one of the detectives from the Manhattan North Homicide squad currently investigating the Smiley and Petlin murders, was found on the morning of Saturday, May 28, in a motel on Suffolk County's fashionable South Fork. Like Smiley and Petlin, Segal's carotid artery had been severed and his face disfigured.

"It is not apparent at the present time," said Lieutenant Ronald R. McIlheny, commander of the elite Manhattan North Homicide task force, "whether the person who killed Max Segal was the same perpetrator as in the Smiley and Petlin cases or whether it was a copycat killing. Needless to say, we are not going to let the death of a brother officer go unpunished."

Late Friday afternoon the phone rang at Manhattan North Homicide, but when Detective Haggerty picked up and identified himself the caller disconnected.

The phone rang at Natale's, but when Natale's machine picked up and identified itself the caller disconnected.

The phone rang at Max and Babette's apartment, but when Babette picked up and identified herself the caller disconnected.

The phone rang again at Manhattan North Homicide, and when Max answered it the caller said:

"Don't speak my name aloud or I'll hang up."

"O.K.," said Max, barely able to breathe at the sound of her voice.

"I've been thinking about our last conversation quite a bit," she said, "and I now feel that I may have been a bit too harsh with you."

"Good," said Max.

"I'd like to see you again and attempt to determine my true feelings."

"O.K.," said Max.

"You're off at four this afternoon?"

"Yes," said Max.

"Can you meet me at five?"

"Where?"

"First Avenue and Fifty-second Street — *don't* repeat that aloud. Meet me on the northeast corner at five sharp. Don't get your hopes up and don't mention this to anybody either, because I doubt that anything is going to come of it."

"O.K."

The line disconnected.

Caruso turned to Max.

"Who the hell was *that?*" he said.

"Nobody," said Max.

At five sharp, feeling excited and unsteady, Max waited on the northeast corner of First Avenue and Fifty-second Street. Northbound weekend rush hour traffic on First was quite heavy. Max looked east on Fifty-second but didn't see Susan scurrying up the block as he thought he might. He felt something unfamiliar. Fear. Why the fuck was he afraid of her? It wasn't her, it was the power they'd discovered she had over him.

A car honked on First Avenue. He ignored it. It honked a second time. He looked. It was a flashy black car, a late model Trans Am. The driver was beckoning to him. It was Susan.

He got into the Trans Am. The car took off up First Avenue. He looked at her and found it hard to breathe.

"Hi," he said.

"Hi," she said.

He hadn't expected to see her in a car. He'd thought she wanted to meet him on the corner and go back to her place and talk. He was surprised when she turned onto the FDR going north.

"Where are we going?" he said.

"Someplace we can talk."

"Let's start now," he said.

"O.K.," she said. The FDR was slow. She changed lanes twice, jockeying for an opening.

"When I picked you up on First Avenue just now," she said, "I got a severe emotional jolt. I didn't like that."

"Me either," he said.

"What?"

"I felt the same jolt when I saw *you,*" he said. "I didn't like it either."

She reached for something in her purse, a flask, and took a slug from it.

"What's that?" he said.

"Vodka."

"Can I have some?"

She handed it to him. He took a gulp and felt the liquid fire flow down his esophagus. She reached for the flask and took another swallow.

"The thing that I don't understand," she said, "is that it's not unpleasant to see you again. I shouldn't be telling you this, but I've missed you."

"I've missed you terribly," he said.

Traffic had ground to a halt. They looked at each other like boxers, trying to size each other up. He leaned over and gave her a tentative kiss. She melted. They held each other very tightly. Both longed to blurt out vulnerable things that they were certain to regret.

The light changed. The driver of the van behind them leaned on his horn, homicidally enraged to be losing the seven inches of progress the line of traffic would gain before the light turned red again.

100

Caruso was on his way home, driving south on the FDR when his beeper went off. He took the Fifty-third Street exit and stopped at a gas station to use the pay phone.

The message said to call Aram Kaprilian. It was urgent. Caruso dialed the number. Kaprilian picked up on the first ring.

"Crime lab, Kaprilian."

"Doc, its Sal Caruso. The message said urgent."

"Hello, Sal. I think I have what you were looking for."

"What's that?" said Caruso, holding his hand over his other ear to deaden traffic noise.

"We've typed the blood on the Band-Aid and the tampon. It's AB."

"Holy shit," said Caruso.

"More importantly, I just called Lifecodes. They've compared the DNA on the Band-Aid and the tampon to the blood sample from Chicago."

"And?" said Caruso, not daring to hope.

"And it looks like we've got a match," said Kaprilian.

Caruso let out a war whoop.

Caruso dialed Max at Natale's. It was going to give him extraordinary pleasure to inform his partner that Susan Simon, the bitch who was dumping on him, the twat who Caruso had spotted for a phony the minute he met her, was their serial killer.

The fact that Caruso was at this moment no more than two blocks from Susan Simon's apartment made it particularly convenient. He could just go over there now himself and pull her in, but he assumed that Max would get some satisfaction out of being in on the collar.

"Hello?"

It was Tony Natale. Not one of Caruso's favorite people.

"Tony, it's Sal Caruso. Max there?"

"No, Sal, he's not."

"You happen to know where he is?"

"As a matter of fact, I caught him leaving just as I was coming in. I think he had a date with Susan."

"Oh, no," said Caruso. "Oh, *fuck* no."

"What is it?"

"What is it?" said Caruso. "I just learned Susan is the blond woman is what."

"Excuse me?"

"Susan Simon is our serial *killer*," said Caruso. "They just did a DNA fingerprinting on stuff I swiped from her garbage — a Band-Aid and a fucking tampon."

"Holy shit," said Natale, truly impressed.

"You think he went to her apartment?" said Caruso.

"I don't know," said Natale. "It's possible. Holy shit, Susan's the *killer*. Holy fucking *shit!* What are you going to do?"

"Call for a little back-up, then go over there and take her," said Caruso.

"I'll meet you over there," said Natale.

"Stay the fuck away," said Caruso. "I don't need no fucking head-shrinkers over there, I need guys with guns."

"You fucking faggot, the day I can't outshoot you I'll put a fucking bullet in my mouth," said Natale, hanging up and racing to get his service revolver.

101

Traffic on the Grand Central Parkway was worse than on the FDR, but not half so bad as that on the Long Island Expressway. Construction crews, in their infinite wisdom, had chosen to block off two eastbound lanes with road cones for the Friday evening rush hour, although neither construction crews nor road building equipment were anywhere in sight.

He asked where they were going. She said it was a surprise. He told her he hadn't brought any clothes along with him. She said that with any luck they wouldn't *need* clothes where they were going. She drank more from the flask and he worried that it might impair her driving. He offered to exchange places with her and she said O.K.

It was seven P.M. Shortly after they exchanged places the traffic passed the coned-off lanes and started moving faster. She drank more from the flask and got into a frisky mood.

"It's cold in here," she said, "don't you think?"

"Not at all," he said.

"I'm cold," she said and turned the heater way up.

"I hope you're warm now," he said after a few moments, "because I'm boiling."

"Aww," she said and helped him out of his sportcoat and threw it on the back seat. Then she unfastened his shoulder holster and untied his tie and threw those in the back as well. Then she unbuttoned his shirt.

"What are you doing?" he said.

"Just trying to make you more comfortable," she replied, smiling mischievously, helping him out of his shirt, arm by arm.

She unbuttoned her blouse so he could see her breasts but she didn't take it off. Instead she got down on the floor and, replacing his foot on the accelerator briefly with her own, removed his shoes and socks.

The traffic speed was up to sixty by now and the heat in the car close to ninety.

"Susan, I can hardly breathe in here," he said.

"Then let me give you a little more air," she said, unbuckling his belt, unzipping his fly, and tugging his trousers down below his hips.

"I don't think this is what the DMV considers safe highway driving," he said growing stiff.

"*You're* not drinking, *I* am," she said.

More substitutions of her foot on the accelerator for his as she tugged off his trousers. Once he nearly lost control of the wheel, hit the shoulder, and swerved back into the fast lane. A horn blared angrily at them. He was now driving in his underpants.

"*I* know what," he said. "Let's pull off the road and fuck."

"Don't even think about it," she said.

"Why not?"

"We have a motel reservation and we're late as it is," she said. "It's not guaranteed, so I don't know how long they'll hold it."

She shrugged off her blouse and put her arms around him, allowing her erect nipples to graze his chest.

"I'm pulling off the road," he said, turning on his blinker.

"If you do," she said, turning off the blinker, "we're going straight back to New York."

"You're not serious," he said.

"Completely serious," she said.

She took her arms from around his neck, but only to remove her skirt. Now they were both wearing only underpants. Hers were so transparent he could see the dark blur of bush through the nylon.

"Why can't we pull off the road?" he said.

"Because," she said, "those are my rules. If you don't like them you don't have to play."

He started to say something but his terrible fear of losing her flashed briefly and he thought better of it. He continued to drive in the fast lane, hating his fear and trying to pretend it wasn't there. She lay down on the seat with her head in his lap and very slowly teased his cock out through the fly of his underpants and put it into her mouth.

330

102

At the moment that Caruso was speaking to Natale at his apartment the night tour at Manhattan North Homicide was catching a "triple." Two Rastafarian Jamaicans with dreadlocks had bought some "heavy weight" — two kilos of coke — from three Dominican dealers and left the apartment with their purchase. A short time after the transaction the Jamaicans returned to the apartment with Uzis, literally blew the three Dominicans out of their shoes, took the Dominicans' money and their entire stash of coke. A "misdemeanor homicide," but still a triple. Triples were big deals.

When Caruso called the squad the line rang and rang and nobody answered. Finally he hung up. You weren't supposed to make a collar alone if you could avoid it.

Susan's apartment was in the Seventeenth Precinct. Caruso consulted his pocket directory of NYPD telephone numbers, then called the Seventeenth PDU and asked for back-up. O'Rourke and Moreno were working the night tour and said they'd meet him at the building forthwith.

Susan's building was a brownstone. Getting through the lobby door wouldn't be a problem. Lobby locks were easily picked. If she had the standard three Medeco locks on her apartment door, though, a pick wouldn't be much use.

Cops knew many ways of getting into apartments. You could go down into the basement and shut off all the electricity — anybody but a highly experienced criminal would come out of his apartment if the power went off. You could blow smoke under the door and yell "Fire!" You could pour water under the door and yell "Flood!" You could have a uniform knock on the door and say that a relative had had a serious accident. If there was a fire escape you could come through the window — most windows were much easier than most doors. If there was a super on the premises he could give you the keys. If all else failed, you could get Emergency Service to drill out the locks.

Shortly after Caruso arrived at Susan's building, O'Rourke and Moreno pulled up in a Plymouth Fury. As they stood outside the door, deciding which method of entry they preferred, Natale pulled up in a cab.

"I thought I told ya I don't need no fuckin' head-shrinkers," said Caruso.

But Natale was Max's friend, and he *was* a cop, so Caruso figured what the hell. They went in the front door and looked at the names on the bells. One was marked "Simon/Wells." Caruso rang the one marked "Super."

After a moment an irritated female voice asked who it was. Caruso said, "Police," but the woman wasn't buying it. She came out of her ground-floor apartment carrying a baseball bat, a woman of maybe sixty with orange hair and jugs that hung to her waist and a Louisville Slugger. She stared through the glass of the lobby door at the detectives' gold shields for several minutes before she finally decided to let them in.

"What you want?" she said.

"One of your tenants is a suspect in a homicide," said Caruso. "We need the keys to her apartment."

The woman's eyes widened.

"Which tenant?" she asked.

"Susan Simon."

"I knew it," said the woman.

"Who's Wells, her roommate?" said O'Rourke.

The woman shook her head.

"No, that's *her* — Miss Simon. That's her other name."

"Why does she have two names?" said O'Rourke.

"She's got more than that," said Caruso.

All four men drew their service revolvers and stood to either side of the door, out of any possible line of fire. Caruso banged loudly on the door. There was no response. He carefully unlocked all three locks and swung the door inward. All four men entered the apartment commando style.

The apartment was empty. Caruso realized that if he had phoned ahead from the service station, prepared to use an unidentifiable accent if Susan answered, he could have ascertained that she wasn't home and not needed to call for back-up.

"See if you guys can find anything that indicates where she mighta gone," said Caruso, beginning to make his own search.

It wasn't likely they'd find anything. They didn't truly know what they were looking for. Perhaps a scrap of paper with the name and number of a restaurant. Possibly a movie timetable torn from that day's newspaper. All four men systematically searched the apartment.

"There's a cat litter pan in the john, but no cat," said Natale. "I'll bet she dropped off her cat with a neighbor because she's taking Max away for the weekend."

Sitting on top of a magazine rack next to the john was a yellow pages for Suffolk County. On a hunch Caruso turned to "Hotels and Motels."

"Bingo!" he said, walking into the hall.

The men came over to look. There were penciled notes all over the "Hotels and Motels" pages. One had today's date.

"Son of a bitch," said O'Rourke. "She took him to a motel on fucking Long Island."

"That would be my bet," said Natale. "A final romantic fling before she kills him."

"Son of a bitch," said O'Rourke.

"Question is," said Caruso, "*which* motel?"

"Shit," said Moreno, looking at the section, "there must be three hundred fucking listings there."

"But there can't be more than twelve or fourteen with pencil marks," said Natale.

"She's got a phone in the bedroom and one in the crapper," said Caruso, ripping the pages out of the directory. "Tony, you take one page and I'll take the other. Ask if they have reservations for Simon or Wells. Or Black. Or Busey."

"Or Solanas," said Natale, going into the bathroom.

"Solanas?" said O'Rourke. "Who the fuck's Solanas?"

"It's a name she signed in with at the security desk of the Hancock Building in Chicago," said Natale.

"How the fuck you know *that?*" said Caruso, astounded.

"I know a *lot* of things about this case you don't think I know," said Natale with a self-satisfied smirk.

Natale and Caruso began their calls. They identified themselves as New York police officers and asked if there were any reservations in the names of Simon, Wells, Black, Busey, or Solanas. Caruso struck out completely on all his calls. But on his last attempt, to a motel in Napeague called the Ocean View, Natale hit paydirt.

"Yes," said an elderly gent after consulting the reservation list, "we do show a reservation commencing tonight for one of the names you mentioned."

"Which one?" said Natale.

"Black," said the elderly gent. "It's a Mr. and Mrs. M. Black, a couple from Manhattan."

M. Black. M for Monty. Natale made excited hand signals.

"They got a reservation for Black," he said.

Caruso got on the other phone.

"Was the reservation made by a woman or a man?" asked Caruso.

"A woman, I believe," said the elderly gent.

"They arrived yet?" said Caruso.

"Nope, can't say as they have," said the elderly gent.

"You know what time they're expected?" said Caruso.

"About eight, the lady said."

"Where are you located, sir?" said Caruso.

"Right on the dunes, just south of the highway," said the elderly gent. "Just past the Getty station. You can't miss it."

"What're you thinking," said Natale when they hung up, "a chopper?"

"'Less you want to get there after she's killed him," said Caruso, picking up the phone again and grabbing his NYPD pocket phone directory.

Getting official clearance for an NYPD helicopter in an emergency, Caruso knew, especially for one occurring at night and on a weekend, was a bureaucratic nightmare.

You had to observe the correct night command notifications. First you called your supervisor — your sergeant or lieutenant — and he called Borough Command and told them the situation. Then Borough Command called the commanding officer of detectives, Borough of Manhattan North Operations, and the citywide captain responsible for covering all districts where the regular district commander wasn't on duty. Then the citywide captain called the Chief of Detectives' Office.

The Chief of Detectives' Office called the chief of detectives himself and notified an assistant chief and his executive officer. The chief of detectives would authorize calls to the East Hampton Town Detectives Division to apprise them of the situation, and to the Special Operations Division to authorize a flight from Floyd Bennett Field in Brooklyn, where the Aviation Unit was located.

Caruso had worked briefly in the Aviation Unit and knew it maintained three types of helicopters: the Bell 206, which held four people including crew, the Bell 222, which held seven, and the Bell 412, which held eight or nine and was the chopper most often used by the mayor. Counting the pilot there were five of them, so they'd probably be sending the 222.

There was a prescribed hierarchy of who could board the helicopter. Caruso, as the homicide cop on the case, was of course eligible. Lieutenant McIlheny, his supervisor, was also eligible, as was one PDU detective and the captain who was covering the district from the Detective Bureau. Since O'Rourke had originally caught the Smiley case, he was the eligible PDU detective. Natale wasn't eligible, but he was a police shrink and the perp was a psychopath. Since the covering captain wasn't available, the chief of detectives allowed Natale on board.

Caruso figured the designated landing site closest to Susan Simon's apartment was the Sixtieth Street heliport on the East River. Caruso, Natale, and O'Rourke left to meet McIlheny at the heliport. Moreno remained behind at the phone in Susan's apartment to coordinate the mission from the ground.

"It's seven-thirty," said Caruso, climbing into his station wagon. "Assuming McIlheny and the chopper get to the heliport by eight, we got a fighting chance to make it to Napeague by eight-thirty and save Segal's ass."

335

103

It was eight-fifty when they pulled up in the parking lot of the motel and it was quite dark. This was fortunate, since both Max and Susan were completely naked.

They found their scattered clothes and dressed in the darkened car with much giggling. Then Max climbed out of the car to get Susan's overnight case from the trunk. He could hear the crash of surf just over the dunes and he could smell the ocean. It was a marvelous smell and he inhaled deeply four or five times before they went in to register.

Max thought the man at the desk in the motel office looked at them a little funny when they checked in, but then he decided he was just being paranoid.

They went to look at the room. It had a small double bed with a white chenille bedspread and a chipped Formica desk with a phone, and it smelled strongly of beachy mildew. But it was fairly nice as motel rooms went and there was a pleasant view of the dunes.

"It's nearly nine o'clock and I'm starving," said Max.

"I'm not," said Susan, grinning lasciviously, "I ate in the car."

"You want to see if they have anything edible in the motel dining room?" said Max.

"Sure," said Susan, pulling up her skirt and flashing her bush, "as long as you save some room for dessert back here in the room."

104

Caruso and Natale were jumping out of their skins. The chopper hadn't landed at the Sixtieth Street heliport till eight-forty-five, and it was now nine o'clock and McIlheny still wasn't there.

"Fuck him," said O'Rourke. "let's leave without the bastard."

"All right, fuck him," said Caruso.

But just as Caruso, Natale, and O'Rourke climbed into the Bell 222 and the pilot switched on the rotor, a car skidded to a stop in the parking lot and McIlheny climbed out and began racing toward the chopper, head down to avoid being decapitated by the rotor blades.

"O.K., there's the boss," said Caruso.

McIlheny climbed into the helicopter, puffing. The short run from the parking lot had taxed his lungs.

"Sorry I'm late, gentlemen," said McIlheny, shouting above the rotor as the chopper lifted into the air. "The Verrazano was a fucking parking lot."

"I've been in contact with the Aviation Unit, boss," said Caruso above the noise as they swung out over the East River.

"Not by radio, I hope," said McIlheny. "The last thing we want is press crawling all over the place and screwing up our collar."

"Don't worry, boss, I used the land line," said Caruso, a little ticked that McIlheny had even raised the issue. "Aviation is coordinating with the East Hampton police to find a landing site in Napeague not too close to the Ocean View. Two unmarked cars will meet us in a field about a half mile away. They're providing four plainclothes detectives and one lieutenant, with SWAT on standby. The turret lights should be enough to guide us in."

"SWAT," said McIlheny. "We don't need SWAT. She's not

the Symbionese Liberation Army, she's a fuckin' broad with a razor blade."

Caruso hadn't heard McIlheny use the word "fuck" before. He figured the boss was excited. This would be a very good collar, with national media coverage, and McIlheny's presence on the scene would help him politically.

"What's your e.t.a. for Napeague?" said McIlheny to the pilot.

The pilot shrugged.

"Shouldn't take more'n thirty, forty minutes to get there, sir, if the weather holds," he said.

"Boss, this here's Timmy O'Rourke of the Seventeenth PDU," said Caruso. "Smiley is his case. And this here's Tony Natale. Being as how he's a police shrink and Max's friend, we thought he might prove valuable on the scene."

McIlheny shook hands and looked down at the Atlantic.

"So what's the scenario, Tony?" he said. "What do you think she's up to with our boy?"

"I think she's planning to seduce him and then kill him because she suspected he was going to dump her," said Natale. "She must've killed the others for the same reason."

Natale tried to read his watch in the dark cabin of the chopper.

"It's nine-fifteen," he said. "Assuming they got to the motel around eight — maybe a little after, allowing for weekend traffic — it's probably going to take them at least an hour or so to get around to going to bed. Then they'll probably have sex, and then, when he's nodded off a little, is probably when she'll do it. My guess is we've got till about nine-thirty, nine-forty-five."

The three other men looked at their watches.

"On that schedule," said McIlheny, "Segal is dead meat."

Natale nodded grimly.

338

105

"I'd like a big wedding," she said.

"How big?" he said.

"Ummm . . . oh, about three hundred people."

"I don't even *know* three hundred people," he said.

"Neither do I," she said. "We'll invite strangers."

"Sounds good," he said.

They were just finishing up dinner in the motel's restaurant. Max looked at the chandelier with the flame-shaped bulbs hanging from the fake stucco ceiling, the mirror treated to look like the mercury was decomposing mounted on the fake brick wall, the wrought-iron privacy screens between the butcher-block Formica booths, and thought he recognized the artistry of the interior decorator from the Oracle.

Max had had the steak sandwich and fries, Susan the chef's salad and three vodkas. Max was beginning to worry she might be an alcoholic.

"You think Babette is going to give you any trouble about the divorce?" she said.

"Uh, I don't know," said Max. "She may, she may not."

"What grounds would you file under?" she asked.

"I haven't really thought about it," he said.

"I've got an idea," she said.

"What?"

"Well," she said, "you told me your sex life was practically non-existent in the past few years. I don't know the name for it, but couldn't you sue for divorce on the grounds that she wasn't available for sex? I mean, I think there's some kind of rule where a wife has to be available to a husband for sex, isn't there?"

"I don't know if there is or not," he said, "but in all fairness, I wasn't much more available to her than she was to me."

"That shouldn't matter," she said. "The bottom line is you haven't had sex with her in years. You can claim it was her fault."

"Uh, I don't know about that," said Max.

"How long has it been since you've had sex with her, a year?"

"No, no, much less than a year."

"How long? Six months?"

"No, no, nothing like that."

"A month?"

"Ah, no. No, I think it was more recently than a month."

"It was? How long?"

"What's the difference?"

"How long?"

"I don't know."

"Well, it obviously hasn't been since you left her, and that's been, well, several weeks now. You haven't slept with her since you left her, have you?"

"Mmmm."

"Max?"

"Yeah?"

"Have you slept with her since you left her?"

Pause.

"Uh, I may have . . . slept with her on, uh, one occasion since that time."

Dead silence.

"Since you've been sleeping with *me*, you mean?"

"Yeah."

"I see."

"It was . . . nothing of consequence, it just, uh, happened is all."

Silence.

"It didn't mean anything, Susan. It was just something that happened, O.K.?"

Silence.

"Susan?"

"Yes."

"It didn't mean anything. You're the one I love, O.K.? You're the one I'm going to marry and have three hundred strangers to my wedding with, not her, O.K.? O.K., Susan?"

Pause.

"O.K."

He looked at his watch.

"Ten-*fifteen?*" he said, feigning an exaggerated yawn. "My God, I hadn't realized it was that late. Boy, I'm ready for *bed*, aren't you?"

"I'm ready," she said quietly.

106

At ten P.M. the helicopter pilot was over the rendez-vous point, a field just north of Route 27 in Napeague, a tiny community between Amagansett and Montauk on the Atlantic Ocean. Two unmarked Chevy Chevettes waited in the field, their removable turret lights revolving to guide the chopper in.

The East Hampton Town Police rented the Chevettes from the local Chevy dealer for the detectives. The four plainclothes cops and the lieutenant worked from eight A.M. to four P.M., but were on call at night like volunteer firemen.

The pilot began to lower the helicopter to the ground.

"C'mon, c'mon, c'mon, c'mon," said Caruso under his breath.

McIlheny instructed the chopper pilot to wait for them in the field. Then he, Caruso, Natale, and O'Rourke climbed out of the helicopter and ran toward the cars. McIlheny caught the toe of his shoe in a small hole in the dark field and came down hard on his left knee.

"Shit!" said McIlheny.

Caruso stopped and turned back to help him up, thinking this is why cop bosses hardly ever left their desks, wondering if McIlheny had ever been agile as a younger man, wondering how much longer this comedy of errors was going to go on and what the chances were that his partner was still alive.

"You O.K., boss?" said Caruso, extending his hand.

"I stepped in a fucking gopher hole," said McIlheny, trying to cover his embarrassment with rage at rodents. "What the fuck is a *gopher* hole doing in this fucking field?"

"That's where gophers tend to put them, boss," said Caruso, pulling the huge man painfully to his feet.

McIlheny limped to the first car and spoke to the lieutenant. Then all four New York cops climbed into the cars and bounced off along the field to Route 27 and the Ocean View motel.

107

Just before she took off her clothes and climbed into bed with him she placed her purse on the night stand to her left. He was trying hard now, all boyish charm and mannish sex appeal, attempting to jolly her out of her mood. She was on automatic pilot.

They made love with mechanical flamboyance, he trying to imagine marrying her, she trying to imagine slaughtering him.

She'd made sure to be on top, but it hadn't given her the control she'd sought. The foreplay was brief. Each pretended this was because they were so eager to fuck. The fucking was strenuous and underlubricated and went on interminably. Neither of them seemed close to the threshold of orgasm, so preoccupied were they with their mutual deceptions. Sensing climax was critical to the next step in whatever they did, they grasped at shreds of overused fantasies to implement their goals.

Finally, fearing it might never end, she simulated the first tentative wavelets of orgasm. He gratefully matched her ersatz rhythms, gripped her like a boogie board, and rode her wavelets till they became breakers, body-surfing in on them until they crashed to shore. It was possible, she thought, that he was faking it. Could men fake orgasms too?

They collapsed to the sweaty pillows, released, relieved, and feigning euphoria. They were both exhausted, he because he'd come, she because she hadn't. She'd been taught that sex was a lot of things. Nobody had ever said it was such hard work.

"Jesus," he said, throwing his arm over her shoulders, "that was terrific. You were sensational."

He was lying, and she knew it instantly. She could smell it. He might just as well have called her babe.

344

She stretched lazily and let her left hand graze the night table till it found her purse. Her fingers silently plumbed its depths, searching for the familiar plastic shape. And then she had it. Carefully palming it in her left hand, she drew it back to her.

"I mean it," he said, "you were just sensational. Where did you ever learn to make love like that?"

She caressed his forehead, his cheek, his neck, trying to find her reference points.

"Shhhh," she said. "Don't talk now. Sleep."

108

The East Hampton cops carried shotguns in the Chevettes as standard equipment. The cars skidded to a stop in the parking lot of the Ocean View motel with a shower of small stones. Caruso, Natale, McIlheny, O'Rourke, and the five East Hampton cops grabbed the shotguns, got out, slammed the doors, and ran into the motel office.

A man of perhaps eighty-five, with a shiny pink scalp and the neck and shoulder configuration of a vulture, sat behind the desk watching *Miami Vice* on a small color set with a poor horizontal hold adjustment.

"Police," said Caruso, flashing his shield. "Did our people call you from New York?"

"Yep," said the man, as if it had been a predominantly social call.

"And you evacuated people from both sides of the room the Blacks are in?"

"Yep."

"Good. What room they in?"

"Seventeen. That's just down the walk on the right as you go out."

"Are they in?" said McIlheny.

"Yes, I believe they are," said the man, intent on *Miami Vice*, "although I expect they've retired."

"Is there more than one exit to the room?" asked the East Hampton lieutenant.

"No, there's just the one," said the man.

Caruso stuck out his hand.

"The key."

The man took the key to seventeen off the hook and handed it to Caruso.

346

Caruso led the way out of the motel office and down the walk, with the other cops close behind him and McIlheny limping, favoring his left knee, bringing up the rear. As they neared the room they could see that the lights were out. Caruso glanced back at McIlheny, who was several yards back by now, and motioned the other men forward.

Dropping down below the sills, Caruso, Natale, and O'Rourke crept past the windows of seventeen to the ocean side of the front door. The others stopped just before the windows. Caruso pressed his ear to the door and listened. Then, as quietly as he could, he inserted his key in the doorknob, turned it clockwise, and shoved the door inward.

"Freeze! Police!" shouted Caruso, as he and the others burst into the room commando style.

"Police! Don't move!" shouted Natale, frantically feeling on both sides of the door for the lights and not finding them.

"Somebody get the fucking lights!" yelled someone.

Natale found the switch and the lights snapped on. Sitting upright in bed, staring at the loaded revolvers and shotguns trained on them, literally paralyzed with terror, were a short bald man with an extremely hairy chest and an obese woman in a gauzy see-through black nightie.

109

This is right. This is necessary. This is what needs to be done now. This is the only logical next step. This is what he deserves and he has brought it on himself, she told herself.

With her thumb she slide the blade out of its plastic case and locked it into position.

"You're so wonderful," he sighed, caressing her back, already half asleep. "How did you get to be so wonderful?"

"Shhhh."

He does not think you're wonderful, he thinks you're a good fuck. His interest in you is inversely proportional to your availability.

"I love you," he whispered, almost unconscious now with post-copulatory fatigue.

He does not love you. He does not need you. He is nothing to you. You do not need him. You do not love him. Love is the victim's response to the rapist. All men are rapists and that's all they are.

She rechecked her reference points midway between his adam's apple and his thick neck muscle and found the slight linear bulge of his carotid. With one finger on the gently pulsing artery for guidance, she lowered the blade, millimeter by millimeter, to his flesh.

110

"Who the fuck is *that?*" said Caruso.

"Oh, Christ!" said Natale.

"Who *are* you?" said McIlheny.

"You mean that's not them?" said one of the East Hampton cops.

"No, it's not them," said Caruso, holstering his gun.

"I don't believe this," said Natale, putting his away as well. "I don't fucking *believe* this."

"Who the fuck *is* this?" said McIlheny.

"I'd say it was Mr. and Mrs. Black," said Natale, chewing his cheeks to keep from laughing. "Excuse me, folks, I think we've made a mistake here. Are you Mr. and Mrs. Black?"

The woman had started to sob, her shoulders shaking.

"It's not her fault," said the man, thrusting himself between the weeping woman and the men. "I talked her into it. If anybody has broken the law, officers, it's me. I'm the one who's guilty and who ought to be arrested, not her."

"The fuck's he saying?" said McIlheny as if requesting a translation from a foreign tongue.

"I believe these people are married to parties other than present company," said Natale. "There's been an unfortunate error, folks. We thought you were somebody else."

"I don't understand," said the man, halfway into his trousers.

"Go back to bed, sir," said Natale, beginning to push the other men out of the room. "We made a mistake. We're sorry to have bothered you. Please return to whatever it was you were doing."

Natale switched off the lights, stepped outside, and pulled the door shut behind them before the nine men exploded into laughter.

"O.K., O.K.," said Caruso, sobering up. "So we fucked up. So it wasn't the Ocean View. But in one of these motels along this beach a brother officer's life is in danger, assuming he's even still alive. Tony, you didn't by some fuckin' miracle bring along those listings from the yellow pages, didja?"

Natale reached into his jacket pocket and pulled out two crumpled yellow sheets.

"God loveya, Tony," said Caruso, snatching at the pages. "You were good for something after all."

All eight men crowded around.

"The fuck we lookin' at?" said one of the East Hampton cops.

"A listing of all the motels the perp was considering going to," said O'Rourke. "We called all the ones she had pencil marks next to."

"You checked reservations for Black?"

"Black, Wells, Simon, Busey, and Solanas," said O'Rourke.

"It's got to be one of the other motels," said McIlheny, grabbing at the pages, "one that *doesn't* have pencil marks next to it."

"Or another name," said Natale.

"Yeah," said Caruso, "or another fuckin' name. And I wouldn't know where in fucking hell to start with *that* one."

"Shit," said one of the East Hampton cops, "just standing around here isn't shit. Why the fuck don't we *do* something?"

"What do you suggest?" said his lieutenant irritably.

"I don't know. Something. Like why don't we just start driving along the beach, rousting people out of motels or something? Anything's better than standing around here."

"*Segal*," said Natale suddenly.

They all turned to look at him.

"I bet she reserved the room in the name of Segal," said Natale. "Because they were checking in together and she wanted it to look like he was in charge."

"Well," said McIlheny, "it's certainly worth a shot."

They trooped back into the motel office, commandeered the two phones, divided up the numbers, and began making calls.

111

As she balanced the tip of the blade on the surface of his softly pulsing carotid, waiting to fire the synapses that would cause the muscles in her fingers to contract and thrust the razor blade into his neck, he began to snore. She looked at his sleeping face — lips parted, emitting foolish sounds — and his tragic vulnerability brought tears to her eyes.

She slowly retracted the blade into its case and, her eyes now running over, retreated into the bathroom and shut the door. She gulped for air in the darkness, then felt for the light switch and snapped it on. Two harsh fluorescent tubes, mounted vertically on either side of the chrome-framed medicine cabinet, blinked on. She stared at her face in the cabinet mirror.

It was a delicate face. A sensuous face. A virginal face. A crying face. A vulnerable face. A murderous face. She thought it both beautiful and ugly with equal ferocity.

You cannot hold him, she thought. Even if you can maintain a tough, disciplined exterior for a while, alternately tearing at his fragile male ego till it's in tatters and then giving him periodic bursts of affection to keep him breathing, playing him like a game fish, giving him a little slack and then reeling him in hard, sooner or later you will weaken and lose control of him because you *want* to weaken and lose control, and you'll be vulnerable with him again and he will tire of you.

He will toy with you like a cat with a small furry animal it has mortally wounded. He will do the human male equivalent which is called letting you down easy, and then he will go back to his wife and that will be the end of you. You will dehydrate and die without his juices and he will live. Is that what you want — for him to live and you to die? Because that's the choice: only one of you can live.

Her hair. Everyone had always admired her hair, even before she'd lost the weight and become beautiful. They liked her black hair for its softness, its straightness, and the way it flipped up at the ends. But none of them really liked black hair when they had the choice of blond. Blond was the hair color of choice in our culture. Blondes had more fun. Gentlemen preferred them. And if you were both blond and blue-eyed you were the national ideal.

She found her vodka refill bottle and took a healthy slug. Then she opened her suitcase and located her blond wig. It was made of human hair and it had cost a lot of money. Anything worth having cost a lot of money. Rose Brill had taught her that.

Watching her reflection in the mirror, she carefully put the wig on, then brushed it out with long, sensuous strokes. Then she got out her contact lens case, removed the two tiny blue lenses, put them in, and admired herself in the mirror. Better, much better.

Hello, Monty. How lovely to see you again. I've missed you. In a moment we'll talk, but first there's a little unfinished business in the other room. Something I had a little trouble with because of my weakness, but it shouldn't be a problem for you at all.

"I got it!" yelled Caruso.

The eight policemen and the elderly desk clerk looked at him expectantly.

"There's a Mr. and Mrs. Max Segal registered in the Sea Breeze motel on Further Lane in Amagansett, right by the ocean. They checked in about nine, went for a snack in the motel restaurant, and just returned to the room. How long a drive is it to Amagansett?"

"Five minutes maybe?" said the East Hampton lieutenant.

"Then it doesn't pay to take the chopper," said McIlheny. "O.K., men, let's get out of here."

The nine policemen raced to their cars.

113

At first he thought it was an extension of his dream, a convoluted maze of blurred and speeding colors. Chasing a naked Godivalike woman riding bareback on a horse through towering red canyons and thick black forests onto a dazzling white beach through foamy surf. Sinking into mustard-yellow quicksand and grabbing for vivid green overhead branches that turned into snakes and being sucked slowly into the mire. Rushing into a wedding ceremony in a synagogue that looked like St. Patrick's cathedral with purple stained glass windows and a hundred-foot-high ceiling and three hundred naked pink wedding guests reaching out for his penis.

But then he realized he'd awakened and what he was looking at in the light from the open bathroom door was real. A naked woman with beautiful yellow hair was sitting at the end of the queen-sized motel bed, legs crossed in a modified lotus position, elbows supported on her thighs, her hands gripping a silver gun — *his* gun, his stainless steel Smith & Wesson thirty-eight-caliber New Chief Special.

Susan. Monty Black. Caroline Busey. Susan. Monty Black. Caroline Busey. Susan. Monty Black. Caroline Busey. The names flashed like neon signs in a diner.

It was funny, really. If it hadn't meant he was going to die it would have been quite funny, the fact that he'd been having an affair with the serial killer he'd been pursuing for the past two months. Fucking Caruso had been right about her after all, damn him. Fucking Caruso had been on to her from the moment he'd met her. Why hadn't Max?

He'd faced death before — rescuing the old people from the burning building, which led to his premature gold shield, scuffling in the dark with the knife-wielding madman who called himself the Hyena

354

—and both of those had happened so fast there wasn't time to be afraid, to do anything at all in fact but move, act, react, and let the adrenaline take him.

Now he had the time to be afraid and he was. He was older than the other times, was a husband and a father now, and he had more of a sense of his own mortality, which was great for personal growth and development but maybe not so great for survival. In crises, the more immortal you felt, the safer you were.

If this woman had cold-bloodedly killed six previous victims there was an excellent chance he would be her seventh. Except that the m.o. was different now. It was a gun this time, not a blade. And if she hadn't shot him already perhaps she had some ambivalence that could be exploited.

He wished Natale were here to give him head-shrinker tips on how to talk to her. He thought of a number of ways to begin but figured that nonchalance was as good a start as any.

"I guess I dozed off," he said. "What time is it?"

If she had heard she gave no sign. Perhaps nonchalance wasn't the right approach after all. He felt a tightness in his chest and throat. He had no idea what to do. Scenes from detective movies and TV shows flickered through his mind.

"If you're going to shoot me, go ahead," he said.

No response. The trick, he recalled from a class he'd once taken in hostage negotiation, was to get a dialogue going. They were less apt to kill you if you could open a channel of communication.

"I don't suppose you've ever fired a Smith & Wesson before," he said. "If not, you might be interested to know that you have to release the safety or it won't shoot."

That was a trick—the Smith & Wesson didn't have a safety.

"The safety is that little gizmo just behind the cylinder on the left-hand side of the weapon," he said.

The little gizmo just behind the cylinder on the left-hand side of the weapon was for popping out the cylinder to reload. If she looked down at the gun for even the briefest moment to figure out how to work it, he'd have time to make a move on her. She acted as if she hadn't heard him.

"The disadvantage of a gun," he said, "is they'll hear the shot. Of course you could muffle it with a pillow, but that would spoil your aim. You'd have been much better off with your knife. Why didn't you use your knife?"

355

She did not respond.

"In a little while," he said, "I'm going to come at you. I won't tell you when, of course. I'm pretty fast, so you'll only have time for one shot. There are a few places you could shoot me that will kill me, but most won't, not for a while anyway, and in the meantime I'll take you down. But if you decide to give me back the weapon I'll do everything I can to help you. You have enough money to hire the best attorneys and they'll probably be able to plea-bargain you down to a reduced sentence. There's no death penalty in New York State, so there's no first degree murder. Second degree will get you twenty-five-to-life, which means you'll be eligible for parole in thirteen years tops. Thirteen years in a rather nice women's facility. You could get a fat book advance and write your memoirs. What do you say?"

She merely stared at him.

"You know," he said, "I'm a stupid guy for you to kill. They'll know it was you and they'll come get you right away."

"Nobody knows you're with me," she said. "I told you not to tell anyone."

"Yeah, but I did, I told Tony Natale."

"I don't believe you," she said, "It's a trick."

"It may sound like a trick," he said, "but it happens to be true. Tony knows I went to meet you. If I'm found dead you're the first person they're gonna come looking for. They don't like cop-killers much in New York."

"Do you know why I'm going to kill you?" she said.

"No, why?"

"Because you're a liar and a deceiver and a betrayer, like all men."

"How have I lied to you?" he said. "How have I deceived and betrayed you?"

"Like all men, you do it so naturally you don't even know you're doing it," she said. "I made you promise not to tell anyone you were going to meet me and you say you told Tony Natale. You either lied when you promised not to tell anyone, or you're lying now about having told him."

"I never *promised* not to—"

"You made love to me and told me that you loved me, and now I learn that at the same time you were making love to me you were betraying me by sleeping with your wife."

"Now wait, sleeping with my wife is hardly—"

356

"*Shut up!*"

"Susan, just let me —"

"*Shut up! Shut up, shut up, shut up!*"

She thrust the pistol forward with both hands, pulling back the hammer into cocked position. He shut up. She calmed down. She took several deep breaths. After a while she continued in a normal voice.

"The irony," she said, "is that I truly fell in love with you."

"You did?"

She nodded.

"I thought you were the only decent man in the entire world," she said. "I truly wanted to spend the rest of my life with you. Isn't that amusing?"

"No," he said, "it's not amusing. I felt that way about you too."

She stared at him.

"I'm just fool enough to want to believe that," she said softly.

"You *can* believe it," he said, "because it's true."

She looked at him in silence for several seconds, then smiled sadly and sighed.

"O.K.," she said. "O.K. Here."

She dropped her right hand, extended the cocked pistol toward him with her left, and tried to untangle her legs from her modified lotus position. She lost her balance slightly, falling forward on one knee, inadvertently tightening the pressure on the trigger.

Uncocked, Max's Smith & Wesson required ten pounds of pressure to pull the trigger. Cocked, it took barely three. In slow motion Max saw her begin to lose her balance and fall forward on her knee. He turned slightly to his right, threw up his arms, and ducked.

The explosion almost burst her eardrums.

114

When the shot rang out Caruso, Natale, McIlheny, O'Rourke, and the five East Hampton detectives had just pulled up in the parking lot of the Sea Breeze motel.

"Oh, no," said Natale.

"Oh, shit," said McIlheny.

"Jesus fucking Christ," said Caruso.

They unholstered their pistols and grabbed their shotguns and propelled themselves out of their cars toward the direction of the shot.

"What room they in?" shouted O'Rourke.

"I don't know!" yelled Caruso.

"The shot came from somewhere over there!" said the East Hampton lieutenant.

"Here?" said Natale, racing ahead of them. "Where?"

"This door here, I think," said O'Rourke.

Caruso banged on the door.

"Open up! Police!" he shouted.

"That's not where it came from," said one of the East Hampton cops, "it came from over here!"

He ran farther up the walk and began pounding on the door.

"Police! Open up!"

The first door opened on a chain and someone peeked out.

"What the hell's going on?" said an angry male voice.

"Segal?" shouted McIlheny.

"That's not Segal," said Caruso. "Oh, Jesus!"

Natale raced back toward the motel office.

"I'll find out what room they're in!" he said. "In the meantime, you guys try to panic as many guests as you can, O.K.?"

115

"Max!" she cried, aghast at the blood, crawling across the bed toward the spot where he'd fallen. "Oh, Max, I'm sorry, I'm sorry, I'm sorry, I'm sorry, I'm sorry."

When a bullet enters a body, if it doesn't tumble or break apart, it may exit cleanly and not cause too much internal damage. The NYPD doesn't want bullets traveling all over the city if they miss or ricochet, so its regulation thirty-eight-caliber ammunition is a low-velocity round that will stop and take down a criminal but will usually neither break apart nor do extensive internal damage.

The bullet fired from Max's revolver entered his upraised left forearm and passed cleanly through it, exited with slightly less momentum, punctured the skin of his chest, fractured his fourth rib, and entered his left lung. No arteries had been penetrated. He was still conscious.

"Call . . . an ambulance," he said as calmly as he could. "Call . . . 911."

"O.K., Max, O.K. Oh my God, oh my God, I'm so, so sorry, oh my God."

She was babbling. She was panicking. She was not moving.

"Immediately, Susan. I need you to do it . . . immediately."

"O.K." she said, "I will. I'll do that, Max, O.K.? I'm calling them right now, O.K.?"

"The phone is . . . on the desk," he said. "Pick it up . . . *now*, Susan."

She got off the bed and, still clutching the revolver in her left hand, went to the phone on the desk. She picked up the receiver and, wedging it between her ear and her shoulder, punched out 911 with her right forefinger. The phone rang and rang and rang, and then she heard someone pick up at the other end.

"I need an ambulance *immediately!*" she said before the person at the other end could even say hello. "The Sea Breeze motel on Further Lane!"

And that was when Caruso kicked in the door and burst into the room, shotgun extended in firing position. In a millisecond Caruso took in Max, lying naked and bloody on the bed, took in Susan, wearing her blond wig, standing naked at the side of the bed, revolver in hand.

"*Don't shoot!*" shouted Max.

Caruso released both barrels and the room exploded.

Police shotguns use two types of loads, either a solid lead slug equivalent to a sixty-four-caliber bullet, which is useful for going through engine blocks and stopping cars, or else a double-O buckshot with nine thirty-two-caliber pellets in each shell. Caruso's load was the double-O buck, which inflicts eighteen wounds and has very little spread at short distances.

The force of the shotgun blast threw Susan up against the back wall of the motel room and spread blood, bone, and tissue out over a wide area.

116

Max lay on his raised bed with chrome bumpers and starched sheets and mercilessly hard pillows in Southampton Hospital, watching *The Tiny Clowns of Happy Town* on the TV set bolted to the ceiling.

The Tiny Clowns of Happy Town was a kiddie cartoon show he had always hated when he'd had to watch it on mornings he got up with Sam. One of the tiny clowns in today's episode was distraught because his mom and dad were getting a divorce. Max didn't think kiddie cartoon shows went in for reality and guessed the show was in ratings trouble and the producers were trying to save it by feigning social relevance.

Max had bandages on his forearm and his chest. Caruso had been able to stop the bleeding in the motel room and then again in the helicopter, and a surgeon at the hospital had sutured up his lung and forearm. This morning Max was resting in relative comfort.

The full impact of what had happened would not hit him for a few more days. His feelings about Susan would take a lot longer than that to sort out.

Had he ever truly loved her as he'd said or had it merely been a sick obsession? It was probably a little of both. The thing in her that he'd responded to initially had nothing to do with sickness or obsession, though. It was fresh and sweet and gentle and oddly innocent. That thing had endured intact within her over the years, despite whatever it was that damaged her in early childhood and bent her into a killer —assuming it was environment rather than heredity that made people psychopathic killers.

With Susan gone he was free to contemplate Babette. Like the quality he'd responded to in Susan, his love for Babette had also endured intact despite the violence done to it by years of marital squabbling. But the prospect of actually going back and living with her filled him with ambivalence. It was likely that the hurt of finding out about his affair with Susan had driven Babette even further away than when he'd left. Even if it hadn't, not much had really changed in their relationship since he'd moved out. It was unreasonable to believe they'd be any more intelligent with each other if he moved back in.

Despite that he missed her. And he missed his son. And he was hurt that they hadn't come to see him. Caruso and Natale and McIlheny and even O'Rourke had already come to see him this morning, but he hadn't even gotten a phone call from Babette. It wasn't possible that she hadn't heard what happened. The *world* had heard what happened.

No press or camera crews had been allowed into his room yet, but the story was on the front pages of all the Long Island and New York newspapers and all over the TV news. The media heard what happened on their scanners and police radios and converged on the Sea Breeze motel as they were trying to get Max out of there. There was footage of bloody Max and bloodier Susan everywhere. PSYCHO-SLASHER KILLED IN HAMPTON LOVE NEST WITH COP WHO HUNTED HER. JOURNALIST COVERED OWN KILLINGS, SLEPT WITH COP ON CASE. The story was a reporter's wet dream.

A heavy-set nurse with black hair and a jutting chest entered the room and gazed at him with an anxious smile.

"How are we feeling today?" she said.

"You we don't know about," he said. "*I'm* much better, however."

"Think you're well enough to receive a few more visitors?"

"Depends on who," he said.

Babette entered the room with Sam.

"Hi, Max," she said shyly.

"Hi, Babette," said Max.

"Hi, Dada," said Sam.

"Hi, buddy," said Max, greatly moved at his son's form of address.

"Are you sick, Dada?" said Sam.

"Nah," said Max. "Just a little tired."

Babette came close to the bed.

"The doctor told me you're going to be fine," she said.

"Funny, that's what he told me too," said Max. "I was thinking of going bowling this evening if I get bored watching TV."

"He said you'll be getting out of here any minute now," she said.

"Yeah," he said. "I have to rest a while, but then I'll be as good as new. Better."

She smiled. He wondered what it was costing her to do that. She chewed her lip, rehearsing something important.

"I'd like you to come back and live with us," she said in a quiet voice that seemed liable to get away from her at any moment. "I'd like to try and make it work this time."

He took a deep breath. He was anxious to hear what his response would be.

"I think I'd like that too," he said finally.

At first she didn't react and he wondered if she'd heard him, but then she bent down and kissed him on his forehead and on his cheeks and on his lips and at that point he felt something in the center of his chest, just to the right of the wound, unclench a little.

"I think I'd like that a lot," he said.

"Are you coming back to live with us, Dada?" said Sam.

"Yes, son, I am," said Max.

"And will Tony Natale let you?"

"Yes," said Max, "I believe he will."

"O.K., Dada," said Sam, "then let's go home right now, O.K.?"